Nehru

Michael Edwardes **Nehru**

A Political Biography

Praeger Publishers
New York and Washington

BOOKS THAT MATTER

Published in the United States of
America in 1972 by Praeger Publishers,
Inc., 111 Fourth Avenue, New York,
N.Y. 10003

Library of Congress Catalog Card
Number: 78–173442

Printed in Great Britain

Contents

Chapter 1
Earthquake in Delhi

A little before midday on Thursday 27 May 1964, New Delhi was shaken by an earthquake. Such seismic disturbances are not unusual in India's capital city, but this one was very appropriately timed and not without a certain obvious symbolism. The day before had died Pandit Jawaharlal Nehru – nationalist leader, heir of Mahatma Gandhi, one of the architects of independent India and its first Prime Minister. A few moments after the tremor, the gates of his residence, where some half a million people had filed past the body on its raised wooden platform, were closed. Some of the crowd tried to climb over the gates for a last look at the man who had led them, lectured them, sometimes even bullied them, and had received from them in return reverence and affection. As they were driven away by the guards, three people were trampled to death and others were injured.

Inside the vast grounds of what before independence had been the mansion of the British commander-in-chief, the body was lifted on to a gun-carriage, the head slightly raised and the rest covered by an Indian flag. The day was very hot and the flowers spread over the bier began to wilt. In the oppressive and sickly air were the sounds of Sanskrit *mantras*, chanted by a group of Hindu priests, and the rather banal English words of *Abide with Me*, sung by a number of Christians for the only apparent reason that it had been one of Gandhi's favourite hymns.

At 1.20 P.M. the cortège was ready to move. In front was a jeep carrying the general commanding the Delhi area. Then the gun-carriage, drawn by men of the services, with others, arms reversed, marching in slow time on either side. Behind followed a number of motor cars. In the first, in a white sari Nehru's daughter, Indira Gandhi, with her younger son, Sanjay. As Nehru had no son, it would be Sanjay who lit the funeral pyre that waited six miles away on the banks of the sacred River Jumna, near the place where sixteen years before the body of Gandhi had been cremated. Behind the first car were others, with Nehru's sisters and more members of his family, political leaders, and the representatives of foreign states who had been arriving throughout the night and the morning.

The route followed was very much the same as that along which Gandhi had made his last journey. Past the grandiose Government buildings erected by the British in the last years of their own rule, the procession moved slowly. Past the Parliament House, down the great ceremonial way of Rajpath, down the Tilak marg, named after another Indian nationalist long dead, and finally to the cremation ground with its plain brick plinth, five feet high and ten feet square, surmounted by a pyre of sandalwood.

Along the way the vast crowds, as many as three million people according to some reports, pressed against the police and troops lining the route. It was very much an Indian crowd, boisterous, inquisitive, with tears and laughter intermixed, reverent but undisciplined. At one place the bier and the first couple of cars were cut off from the remainder of the procession as the crowd surged across the road. But at last, at four o'clock, the cortège arrived on the banks of the river. To the sound of muffled drums the body was placed on the pyre. Hindu priests began the magical rites for the dead, holy water from the River Ganges was sprinkled, a small group of leaders filed past, each placing a piece of sandalwood on the pyre. The Indian flag was replaced with a white scarf and flower petals. Sanjay lit the pyre and the body of Jawaharlal Nehru, socialist, agnostic, prophet of Indian secularism, went up in flames like that of a Hindu king.

The whole affair had appeared to many as a display of bizarre incongruities. Nehru's Will, written ten years before his death, had laid down that no religious ceremonies should be associated with his funeral. Among those who placed a final piece of sandalwood on his pyre were such Muslims as the Vice-President of India, and Sheikh Abdullah, the Kashmir leader. And, as the sacred *mantras* droned on, there was a volley of rifle shots and twenty-four bugles blared out the *Last Post*. Yet none of these contradictions was without its point or its relevance to Nehru's own life and personality. The Eurasian overtones of the funeral, those elements of east and west which some saw as being in execrable taste, had been as much a part of the living Nehru as they were of his death. The Muslims who willingly took part in a Hindu ceremonial represented not only the special place the Muslim world had occupied in Nehru's political life but also his antecedents, for his family background had been significantly influenced by the pre-British Muslim rulers of India – the Mughals.

Even when everyone except the priests and a few soldiers had left the cremation ground – the family, the cabinet ministers now more concerned with the succession, and the foreign dignitaries anxious about the outcome – the apparent paradoxes of Nehru's death were still not complete. On the following day, the Indian President with several Cabinet ministers and members of the dead Prime Minister's family attended the collection of the ashes. These were put into copper urns, sprinkled with water from the Ganges, and taken to Nehru's house. There in the garden they remained while thousands of people paid them homage.

The final act took place on Tuesday 9 June, not at Delhi but near Nehru's birthplace of Allahabad. There the River Ganges joins the Jumna at a spot particularly sacred to Hindus. In his Will, which had been read over the radio by the elder of his sisters a few days before, Nehru had asked that some of his ashes be thrown into the Ganges. He disclaimed any religious implication. For him, he said, the Ganges was 'a symbol of India's age-long culture and civilization, ever changing, ever flowing, and yet ever the same. She reminds me of the snow-covered peaks and deep valleys of the Himalayas which I have loved so much and of the vast plains below where my life and work have been cast'. The remainder of the ashes should, he wrote, 'be carried up into the air in an aeroplane and scattered from that height over the fields where the peasants of India toil, so that they might mingle with the dust and soil of India and become an indistinguishable part of India'.

The ashes were brought by train from Delhi and crowds lined the tracks. A huge assembly awaited them at Allahabad. With Nehru's ashes came an urn containing those of his wife, Kamala, which Nehru had kept in his room for the twenty-eight years since her death. At Allahabad the urns were placed under a tree near the house where Nehru had spent his childhood. Again, there were flowers and quiet adoration. Then, surrounded by soldiers and priests they were taken to the bank at the sacred spot and ferried out to the confluence of the rivers. There they were scattered. A helicopter showered flower-petals, guns boomed out, *mantras* were chanted, buglers blew the *Last Post* again, and a military band – its members almost certainly all good Hindus – played *Abide with Me*.

The superficial absurdity of Nehru's funeral proceedings angered many Indians. The secular intelligentsia considered the flouting of Nehru's own desires as a cynical attempt by the Government to milk all the emotion they could from the death of one whose place in the hearts of the Hindu masses owed much to traditional values. As for the weakness of his family in agreeing to it all, this was charitably excused on the grounds of their grief. To foreigners, and especially those who had seen in Nehru a leader free from what they believed to be the essential bigotry and superstition of Hindu beliefs, a modern man in their western sense of the word, there seemed to be firm grounds for these opinions. Though Nehru had certainly been born a Hindu, his whole education had been western in form and content. He had escaped from the net of Hindu society and religion to become a western-style liberal democrat, forward-looking, constantly criticizing the weight of Indian tradition as he tried to drag his country into the twentieth century.

But were they right? Nehru's will, with its repeated disclaimers of any religious feeling, was a decade old. In the last few years of his life, there had been a change in his attitude to the Hindu world from which he had emerged. Through all the years of independence, Hindu occultism had had its devotees in governing circles. Astrologers made a comfortable living as advisers to ministers, officials and politicians. For most of the time, Nehru had chosen to ignore the soothsayers on the backstairs of the palace, but in the last months after his stroke in January 1964, months almost Byzantine in character, the occult had been allowed to penetrate the palace itself.

There were others, too, who complained. The ceremonies were, said some, not in the traditional form at all. And the scattering of Nehru's ashes from the air should never have been allowed to happen. The orthodox – and orthodoxy can be found in some unexpected places in India – had a spokesman in Dr Rammanohar Lohia, the Berlin-educated socialist leader who had been an outspoken and sometimes virulent political enemy of the late Prime Minister. 'Whatever Mr Nehru might have written in his Will,' he declared at a public meeting, 'whatever he might have said about his attitude towards religion, the fact remains that Mr Nehru was born a Hindu, he had his [sacred] thread ceremony performed in the Hindu way, he lived a Hindu, died a Hindu, and was cremated according to Hindu rites. All his ashes should have been immersed.'

That statement and the events to which it was a response are important clues in the complex plot of Nehru's life as, indeed, they are to an understanding of the India for whose freedom he fought and over whose destinies he presided for the seventeen years from its gaining independence from British rule to his death.

Chapter 2
Canal and Court House

Early in the eighteenth century a distinguished Sanskrit and Persian scholar named Raj Kaul left his home in Kashmir for the Mughal imperial capital of Delhi. He was very much following the tradition for men of his caste and country, for he was Brahmin, a man of the élite in the Hindu social order. Kashmiri Brahmins, men both of learning and ambition but no great wealth, had for centuries left their mountainous but economically arid home-land to occupy places of authority and trust in the administration of the Mughal empire and in those of the Hindu princes in alliance with it. They made up a small community, very conscious of the ties of kinship and of their superiority of learning. Their pride was only matched by the handsomeness of their men and the beauty of their women. Like the Scots, away from their birthplace they were ever mourning their exile.

Raj Kaul, however, even though he had been invited to Delhi by the Mughal emperor himself, had chosen a time when the imperial patronage was weakening. Yet Raj Kaul would hardly have noticed it. In the usual manner he was given a grant of land, with a house situated by a canal on the outskirts of Delhi. From this location and to differentiate him from the other Kauls, he added 'Nehru' from the Urdu word for a canal, *nahar*, and for some years the family was known as Kaul-Nehru. Despite the vicissitudes of the imperial house, as long as it reigned – though by the middle of the century it no longer effectively *ruled* – a Kaul-Nehru occupied some official position. But not always with the Mughals. One Lakshmi Narayan Nehru (by this time the family had dropped the 'Kaul') perhaps sensing a change in the wind, became the first *vakil*, a sort of combination of legal adviser and representative of the English East India Company at the court of the virtually powerless Mughal emperor.

The Indian Mutiny of 1857, that first and unsuccessful revolt of traditional India against British rule, ended the Nehrus' connexion with Delhi. Pandit Ganga Dhar Nehru had been the chief of police in the city before the terrible events that led to the final extinction of the Mughals. After the collapse of the revolt, the Nehrus left Delhi for Agra, once the second city of Mughal India but by then somewhat tattered. Even the glorious marble monument of the Taj Mahal had been turned into an armoury. Early in 1861 Ganga Dhar died. A few months later, on 6 May, his son Motilal was born.

With his father dead, Motilal became the responsibility of his elder brothers. One was in Government service, the other, Nandlal, after a period in the employ of a petty raja, qualified in law and began to practise at the Agra Bar. It was upon Nandlal that the active responsibility for Motilal's upbringing was placed and when the High Court was moved from Agra to Allahabad the Nehru family also moved to this quiet provincial town. Allahabad was and still is a holy place, for there the sacred River Ganges meets the River Jumna for all to see, while every Hindu knows that the legendary River Saraswati also joins, even though it does so below the level of consciousness. Even the Muslims seem to have been conscious of Allahabad's special position, for the name they gave it means 'city of god'.

For the first twelve years of his life, Motilal was educated at home. His lessons were mainly in Arabic and Persian, the languages and the literature of the once-ruling Muslims. This might seem an eccentric cultural emphasis for a Brahmin, the highest of the Hindu castes in a part of India that is so much the heartland of Hinduism. The United Provinces of Agra and Oudh (now the state of Uttar Pradesh) not only contains the junction of the sacred rivers at Allahabad, then the provincial capital, but also the mecca of Hinduism, Banaras. To the north are the Himalayas, where on Mount Kailas dwells Shiva, the most important of the gods. At Ayodhya was the capital of the hero of the *Ramayana*, Rama the golden king of a golden age. And the area around Mathura had been the scene of many of the escapades of that most popular of Hindu deities, the divine cowherd Krishna.

The nearness of gods and heroes had preserved Hindu values from the threats of a succession of non-Hindu conquerors. The mass of the population remained faithful to their tradition, but it did not command the allegiance of the élite. They became steeped in a culture whose inspiration was Muslim. Some of the Hindu élite also took the religion of the Muslim conquerors, but many Brahmins and members of the influentially placed writer-caste, the *kayasthas*, while remaining Hindus adopted much of the Islamized culture. Among the smaller groups who accepted this Indo-Persian culture were the Kashmiri Pandits. The position of members of these groups, men in effect of two cultures, reflected their relationship with the Muslim rulers. That relationship was one of service, of intimacy but not identification with whatever Government was in power. With the coming of the British these groups welcomed the opportunities they offered for western-style education. They found service in the administration as they had done before, or took employment with those elements such as the large landlords whose position had been enhanced by British rule. Many retained their two-culture allegiance to which they added another, that of the west.

Motilal Nehru followed such a course. From private tuition in Arabic and Persian, he moved to an English education at the Government High School at Cawnpore (Kanpur) and the Muir Central College, Allahabad. There he acquired a deep admiration for western ideas and also for the western manner of life. But Motilal did not take his degree. Doing, as he thought, badly in the first paper of his B.A. examination he stayed away from the rest. On the surface it was a foolish decision, for at this time a university degree was the only passport to a well-paid job in Government employ. Fortunately, this moment of weakness passed and turning to the study of law, Motilal took his examinations, topping the list of successful candidates. In 1883 he went to serve his apprenticeship at Cawnpore and three years later returned to Allahabad to begin practice at the High Court.

No sooner had Motilal begun to establish himself at Allahabad than tragedy struck the Nehru family. Nandlal, who had built up a lucrative practice, died in 1887 at the age of forty-two, leaving a widow, two daughters and five sons. Motilal now found himself the head and sole support of a large family. He was twenty-six years old. He himself was married but had no children. It was Motilal's second marriage. There had been a child of his first, but both mother and child had died. For Motilal the tragedy was not yet over for a boy born to his second wife was also to die in infancy. Under the circumstances it is hardly surprising that when a second son was born on 14 November 1889 his arrival was an occasion for particular rejoicing. Motilal named his son Jawaharlal, the red jewel.

Chapter 3
A Passage to England

For the first three years of Jawaharlal's life the family lived deep in the city, not far from the central market. But the direction of Motilal's life was towards great financial rewards and increasing westernization in his style of living. The family moved to a bungalow in what were known as the Civil Lines, a residential area mainly for Europeans, reflecting both their aloofness from the India of the crowded city and their desire to show their superiority to it. Even though the bungalow on Elgin Road was not particularly luxurious compared with some of the mansions of the British which surrounded it, the move was significant. Motilal Nehru's choice was not just that of a man earning large sums of money who moves into a better house in a more fashionable district. Though the Civil Lines and the city were only separated by a few hundred yards, mentally and socially they were worlds apart. Motilal Nehru was following the tradition of his community and attaching himself to the values of the conqueror.

But not to the exclusion of all others. Motilal's wife Swarup Rani remained a Hindu wife with little interest in anything but her home and her family. Motilal himself did not reject tradition. The atmosphere in the Nehru home, however, was more English than Indian, and increasingly so as Motilal's earnings at the Bar rose higher and higher. In 1900 Motilal purchased a large house with extensive grounds in Church Road and named it Anand Bhawan – Abode of Happiness. A great deal of money was spent on making it a palatial home.

Anand Bhawan symbolized the three cultures which had come to dominate the lives of the Nehrus. The house itself was Indian in style. A big rambling house with large rooms and many terraces, which gave the impression of great height. The rooms were built around a courtyard with a fountain in the centre. There was also a swimming pool and the house was the first in Allahabad to have electricity and piped water. Motilal, like his son later, was attracted by science. But Motilal's interest was mainly in the practical. In this sense he was very much the Victorian polymath. Among the law books and the English classics in his library were manuals on such subjects as *Practical Bell-fitting* and a detailed work, *A Practical Treatise upon the Fitting of Hot-Water Apparatus.*

Still, the house was divided between the Indian and the western. In the Indian part, the women and children lived a comfortable but essentially traditional life. The kitchens were in the charge of Brahmin cooks and the servants were all Hindus. On the first days of every month large quantities of rice were cleaned and wheat ground in stone handmills on the kitchen floor. In the western part, there were cooks and servants who had been trained to work in English homes; Goans or Mughs from Bengal were in charge of the kitchens, while the other servants were Muslims, for no Hindu would handle meat. Motilal ate in the western dining-room sitting on a chair at table. Most of the family ate in the Indian dining-room sitting on mats upon the marble floor. To point the ambivalence, Motilal always wore European clothes outside the house but the traditional kurta and pyjamas of the province – wide trousers and knee-length shirt of fine muslin – inside. For ceremonial occasions he would wear a long black or white coat – the *achkan* which his son was to make famous throughout the world – and close-fitting, almost legging-like trousers.

This catholicity of behaviour embraced religious festivals. The Hindu calendar abounds with them. All were observed. But so was the Muslim *Nowroz* – the celebration of the New Year – which in Kashmir was as much a Hindu festival as a Muslim. Members of the family would also join Muslim friends to eat bowls of sweet vermicelli scented with rose water and decorated with gold and silver leaf at the end of the fast of *Ramadan.* Christmas, it seems, was not observed in Anand Bhawan, but the children were allowed to go to parties given by their Christian friends and baskets of flowers were sent to decorate the church of the Holy Trinity which stood next door. Anand Bhawan itself occupied sacred ground, for according to legend the hero Rama had been greeted by his brother Bharat at the end of his long exile at a spot in the garden. Every year, that meeting was celebrated by a procession which ended at Anand Bhawan.

It was in this atmosphere that Jawaharlal, an only child and lovingly spoilt, spent his early life. For his education there were private tutors, most of them British. To balance them Motilal employed learned Brahmins to teach the boy Hindi and Sanskrit, apparently without much success. Motilal, indeed, seemed determined to turn his son into an English gentleman. The Indian part of the household was merely an annexe to Jawaharlal's life. His father's personality dominated everything. Motilal's sense of pride was enormous and there was absolutely no doubt who ruled. He demanded unquestioning obedience, and if anything upset him the household was battered by his ferocious temper. Not an intellectual, he adored the practicalities; yet there are signs of uncertainty in his constant pursuit of the very latest gadget – the first electric light, the first motor car.

The presence of this almost protean figure, the absence of children of his own age in the house, and the stifling privacy of his education wrapped Jawaharlal in a profound loneliness which he carried with him to the end of his life. Jawaharlal had great admiration for his father and there are many of his character traits in the adult Jawaharlal. But they did not include the self-confidence and absence of doubt which Motilal showed in all his actions. Perhaps this was due to the constant presence of older people. Without friends of his own age Jawaharlal could, in effect, only take instruction and advice. There was no escape from the pressure of mature minds and achievements. For some years Jawaharlal saw little of his father, and there was no one of his own generation with whom to exchange ideas and confidences. His mother gave him uncritical love and later he admitted that, though he would go to her to pour out his frustrations and fears, he received nothing *but* love in return.

If Anand Bhawan was in some ways a prison it was one without bars. Jawaharlal enjoyed sport. His father's stable was extensive and he did a great deal of riding. There was swimming in the pool at Anand Bhawan, cricket and tennis. There were visits to temples and festivals, even dips in the Ganges surrounded by the unsubtle piety of the pilgrims. Among the women of the Nehru family there was a real sense of traditional religion. With Motilal there was respect but no belief. Jawaharlal with his English tutors, his English books and his English clothes absorbed both his father's tolerance and his agnosticism.

Among the tutors who guided Jawaharlal's mind along the lines of any English schoolboy and most upper- and middle-class Indian boys of the time, only one seems to have had any lasting effect. When Jawaharlal was ten Mrs Annie Besant, the theosophist leader and Indian nationalist, recommended a young man of twenty-six to Motilal as a suitable tutor for his son. F. T. Brooks, son of an Irish father and a French mother, was an ardent believer in theosophy, a hybrid belief in which Hinduism is dressed up in traditional Christian terms. Brooks held meetings of local theosophists in his rooms and his pupil attended. To the amusement of his father, Jawaharlal at the age of thirteen became so interested in the teachings of the theosophists that he was initiated into the Theosophical Society by no less a person than Annie Besant herself. Soon afterwards Brooks left – he seemed to Motilal to have too much influence upon his shy and intellectually receptive son. Jawaharlal's interest in the occult over-world of the theosophists did not survive Brooks's departure but the three years of the tutor's stay left certain indelible strains in Jawaharlal's mind. Under Brooks's inspiration he had acquired a taste for serious reading which never left him and only became more refined with the years. And of course it was the reading of an English boy of his own age. There were Lewis Carroll, and Rudyard Kipling, whose *Jungle Books* and *Kim* were great favourites. There were Scott and Dickens and Thackeray. The romances of H. G. Wells shared the appeal of stories of real-life explorers. There were the English poets for whom Jawaharlal was to retain a deep attachment.

It was also to Brooks that Jawaharlal owed his first interest in science. A small laboratory was fixed up in one of the rooms at Anand Bhawan and the simple experiments carried out there

were a thrilling introduction to science. The long and interesting hours spent working out experiments in elementary chemistry and physics probably decided Nehru's choice of natural
sciences when some years later he went up to Cambridge.

After Brooks's departure it was becoming clear that the
young Nehru had exhausted the range of knowledge that could
be given through private tuition. For Motilal there was only
one choice. Jawaharlal must go to an English public school
and then to university. The special hopes that from the first
Motilal had placed in his son had been reinforced. In 1900
Swarup Rani Nehru had given birth to a daughter also named
Swarup. As Mrs Vijaya Lakshmi Pandit she was later to play a
minor role in the history of independent India. But there had
been no son. Jawaharlal was still the only one who could
maintain the continuity of the family name – and add to its
lustre.

Motilal had first visited England in 1899. On his return he
had refused to submit to a purification ceremony which the
Kashmiri Brahmin community insisted was the only way to
wipe out the sin of going outside India. This refusal in fact had
not only confirmed his own westernization but by polarizing
the unorthodoxy of other members of the community helped
to destroy what he called the 'tomfoolery' of the whole business. He had found his stay in England very pleasant, had made
friends there and had discovered the dominating role in English
society and public life of the alumni of the great public schools.
Only the most exclusive would do for Motilal's son.

The family – Motilal, Swarup Rani, Jawaharlal and his four-
year-old sister – sailed from Bombay on 13 May 1905. With the
help of some English friends Motilal had been able to get his
son into Harrow. Jawaharlal left little impression upon Harrow
but the school left its own upon him. He played cricket, joined
the Rifle Club and the Cadet Corps and absorbed the general
feeling of superiority of the Edwardian upper classes. His responses were essentially emotional. While accepting the class-
conscious values of the English, he resented the discrimination
those same English displayed in India towards Indians equally
class-conscious. The winning as a prize of the first volume of

Trevelyan's life of the Italian patriot Garibaldi created in him the romantic vision of liberating India. It was not quite the sort of attitude he could discuss with other English boys or indeed with the few Indians, sons of princes, who were also at Harrow. An interest in the new science of aviation hardly lessened the frustration.

It seemed to the young Nehru that great events were taking place that might change the world. On the day of his arrival in England the Japanese had destroyed the Russian fleet at the battle of Tsushima, the first blow Nehru thought against the white man by an Asian people. In India too it seemed that a violent nationalism was flexing its muscles. To all these Jawaharlal reacted, not intellectually but with the emotions, an attitude which was to become the leitmotiv of his political life. In 1907 he looked for a wider world than Harrow and persuaded his father to let him leave and go up to Cambridge.

At Trinity College, another forcing house of the English establishment, Nehru studied the natural sciences, chemistry, botany and geology. He began to read widely in other fields, in literature, Greek poetry, politics, history and economics. It was a time when socialism, the romantic socialism of the Fabian Society, was very much the fashionable thing. Nehru responded in his dilettante way but the groundwork was laid for a future attachment to socialist ideas. As Motilal was becoming more and more involved in politics so his son chose to give him advice. Motilal was a moderate, a constitutionalist. His son fired with idealism leaned towards the revolutionary element among the nationalists.

Yet even these enthusiasms were peripheral to Jawaharlal's life. His father's wealth meant that he could live a life of pleasure and he did so. There was always, of course, the question of what he was going to do after he had graduated. In the light of the later activities of both father and son it seems almost incredible that Motilal wanted his son to go into the Indian Civil Service and that Jawaharlal saw no reason to object. But there were reasons against it. Jawaharlal would probably have to remain in England for a further two years before he reached the required age, and the examinations were held in London.

Then, too, his father's somewhat possessive love had been re-inforced by the death of another son in infancy while Jawaharlal had been in England. A career in the I.C.S. would mean that Jawaharlal would be sent to posts always remote from the family at Allahabad. For Motilal any further separation was unthinkable. Jawaharlal must study law and on his return to India take up practice at Allahabad.

Jawaharlal took his degree in the summer of 1910 – a second class honours in the natural sciences tripos. In the autumn he left Cambridge to read for the Bar at the Inner Temple where some twenty-two years before an Indian of very different type and social class, Mohandas Karamchand Gandhi, had also been admitted to the study of law. There was no parallel in the lives of the two men. Gandhi was poor. Nehru was rich. Though Gandhi dressed himself up as an English gentleman it was in essence an act of defeat, reflecting a desire for status and acceptance. The handsome young Nehru with his light skin wore his Bond Street clothes as of right. While Gandhi searched for vegetarian restaurants, Nehru frequented the right clubs, the theatres and the proper social functions. He took trips to the Continent, almost drowned on a walking holiday in Norway, went to Ireland and took a romantic view of the Irish national-ists. It was a frivolous life which ended with his being called to the Bar in 1912.

Apart from two short visits Nehru had been away from India for seven character-forming years. The passage to England – a journey essentially in the mind – was complete. He was, he admitted later, 'a bit of a prig'.

Chapter 4
Armchair Politics

The India Nehru returned to in the late summer of 1912 was quiet. The drama of revolutionary nationalism which had occasionally excited him in England had come to an end, drowned in the apathy of men of moderation. The British had responded to terrorism with repressive legislation which not only silenced the revolutionary leaders but inhibited orthodox political activity. The imperial Government, after a moment of panic, seemed as powerful, as remote and as immutable as it had ever been. The Indian National Congress once again in the control of moderate men had reverted to its old, cautious and submissive role. Nehru attended the annual session at Bankipore in December 1912 and found it depressing. An English-speaking upper middle-class social gathering of men in morning coats and well-pressed trousers.

At its beginning in 1885 Congress had had the approval of the British Government who saw in it a way of neutralizing the political activity of the Indian middle class. Its leaders, too, saw Congress as a sort of loyal opposition, a pressure group for their own minority interests. Its members were essentially conservative, coming as they did from those elements in India which had profited from British rule and thought only that they should profit more. In 1899 40 per cent of the 13,839 delegates to the annual Congress meeting came from the legal profession, by training and inclination respectful of the law and legitimate means of agitation. The other big groups consisted of large landowners and businessmen. The remainder was made up almost entirely of journalists, doctors and teachers.

The classes who supported Congress were those who benefited from the meagre measure of reforms doled out from time to time by the British in order to keep them quiet. They had no concern for the mass of India's people. In fact Congress was strongly against any attempts made by the Government to better the lot of the peasants. The large landlord and commercial element which supplied most of Congress funds was no friend of the peasant or the industrial worker. As the years went by the landlord element declined, finding other outlets for its political ambitions. But the businessmen remained and it was their financial support for the non-violent Gandhi rather than a leader who might create commercial chaos by a revolutionary programme, which had a profound effect on the progress towards Indian freedom, and on the life of Jawaharlal Nehru.

Motilal Nehru had been drawn to Congress in 1888 and his name appears in the list of delegates for the session held that year at Allahabad. For Motilal joining Congress was more a social than a political act, a gesture of identification with men of his own kind. He attended the meeting at Nagpur two years later and was the secretary of the reception committee when the session was once again held at Allahabad in 1892. But afterwards his name disappears from the lists of delegates. He was too busy building up his law practice to give time to active politics. But he was not out of touch. Indeed, there was every reason why he should not be. Congress was the trade union of his class – the westernized bourgeoisie. Among its leaders Motilal particularly admired Gopal Krishna Gokhale, another Brahmin though this time from Maharashtra. Gokhale was highly westernized, a constitutionalist by conviction and a loyalist of principle, who was to say that if the British were to leave India, Indians would call them back before they reached Aden.

Gokhale was to become the voice of moderation. His appeal to Motilal was an appeal of the two cultures. He reconciled a real Indian patriotism with loyalty to England. The two he believed – and so did Motilal – were necessarily compatible. But there were others who did not. After 1870 there had been a considerable expansion of English education. New social classes found themselves with a primarily literary education in the western style and with no outlet, because there were simply not enough jobs for them either in Government or in commerce. Inadequately educated in an alien cultural tradition, they found themselves uneasy in that of their fathers. With their ambition halted by the dominance of the fully westernized upper middle class they were ripe for the attraction of new forms of cultural nationalism.

Their frustration produced a new synthesis of east and west. Their reading had revealed to them that the secret of European revolution was militant populism not cooperative reform. The evolutionary approach of Congress was not only too slow but when reforms were granted they only benefited those who had successfully turned themselves into bastard Englishmen. These men began to represent for the educated unemployed the foundation of a new tyranny almost as alien as the one they might some day replace.

As the first reaction to western ideas had been towards identification so the second was to be that of rejection. New leaders emerged who saw in a refurbished tradition a political weapon not only against the British but against the westernized Indian upper middle class. As most of these leaders were Hindus it was to the Hindu tradition that they looked. In a sense this was nothing new – early in the nineteenth century there had been an attempt to reform Hinduism so that it might resist the flood of western ideas and values. But this movement, however intellectually stimulating, had been primarily defensive. In 1875 however Dayananda Saraswati had founded the Arya Samaj, a reformist society which sought to cleanse Hinduism of superstition and give it an aggressive political direction. The British, Dayananda maintained, had imposed upon traditional Hindu society a vast superstructure of western law, economic organization and administration which had continually assaulted long-cherished customs and attitudes to life. For good Hindus there was no possibility of reconciliation in the face of cultural aggression. Cultural and religious freedom could be attained only through political freedom.

The message of Dayananda was of considerable appeal to those who, while not wishing to surrender to western cultural values, had received sufficient western education to be unwilling to accept the rude superstitious Hinduism of the mass of Indians. Dayananda had attempted to show that behind popular Hinduism lay a body of thought and belief of extreme sophistication which would more than bear comparison with whatever the west had to offer. The pseudo-intellectual praise of Hinduism by the founders of the Theosophical Society helped in the rehabilitation of the Hindu past. Cultural self-confidence is the first step in national self-assertion. To its growth another major figure contributed a sense of purpose. Vivekananda, a religious teacher and propagandist, called for an active involvement in reform and social service. In his speeches he urged young Indians to dedicate themselves to changing the lives of millions of their poor and starving fellow-countrymen, to regain faith in their ability to act independently and to repudiate the self-assumed right of the British to think for them. 'What we want is strength' was his message in 1897, '. . . believe in yourselves. . . . What we want is muscles of iron and nerves of steel. We have wept long enough. No more weeping, but stand on your two feet and be men.' How much more inspiring this all seemed to the alternative offered by the moderate leaders of Congress constantly on their knees begging for entry to the administrative machine and wasting their rhetoric in the powerless legislatures.

The first to unite religious and cultural sentiment with positive political action was Bal Gangadhar Tilak, like Gokhale, who was to be his principal antagonist, a Brahmin from Maharashtra. Western educated, he first supported the moderate elements in Bombay but realizing that they had no mass support turned to creating it for himself. Acquiring a newspaper he sponsored two festivals, one dedicated to the Hindu god Ganesha – known in western India where he was held in particular popular esteem as Ganapati – and the other honouring the Maratha hero Sivaji who in the seventeenth century had been the most consistent opponent of the Mughal empire. Tilak was extremely successful in arousing mass support and militant action. He never hesitated to distort some perfectly reasonable Government action into a dire threat to the Hindu religion and social order.

Tilak's success led to his arrest and imprisonment and a wider dissemination of his ideas. His call was for *swaraj*, complete independence and no compromise, 'militancy not mendicancy' was his rousing slogan. For moderate Congressmen he seemed to sum up the most atavistic forces. His allies were the Hindu gods and heroes and his army the illiterate and the superstitious. But to the young Tilak offered action, identity and a hope of triumph. They responded enthusiastically and waited for some great issue with which to arouse primitive passions. In 1905 the British supplied one. In that year the Government decided for the best of reasons to divide the immense and un'wieldy province of Bengal. This act was taken by the Bengalis as the climax of a policy of humiliation. All their frustrations were released in an unprecedented wave of protest in which religious revivalism and Bengali nationalism combined to make it explosive.

The young who had formed secret societies dedicated to the violent overthrow of British rule erupted in terrorist activities. The Government replied with instant repression. New methods of protest were put into practice. There was a boycott of British goods and a general shut down of business. The moderates in Congress now found themselves trailing behind what became more and more a popular movement. The new militant leadership while not condoning violence did call for action and not words. Boycott, not only of British goods but of Government-controlled educational institutions, of courts of law and the rest of the apparatus of alien rule. The people should support *swadeshi*, goods produced in India by Indians. For the first time the phrase 'passive resistance' appears in the vocabulary of Indian nationalism. It meant, wrote Aurobindo Ghose in 1907, the 'lawful abstention from any kind of cooperation with the government'.

It seemed that the conflict between the Moderates and what were now called the Extremists would soon break out in Congress itself. In spite of the revolutionary overtones of the Bengal agitation there was no *Indian* revolution. This was in part due to the lack of an organization by the Extremists. Congress offered such an organization and yet its leaders were strongly against any militant struggle which might jeopardize their vested interests best served by *association* with the Government. The possibility of a head-on collision between Moderates and

Extremists at the 1905 session of Congress brought Motilal Nehru back as a delegate. On this occasion a clash was avoided but the Moderates were determined to stifle the opposition as their militancy might prejudice the chance of reforms then being contemplated by the British Government in London.

As part of the campaign against Extremism, a provincial Congress was held in Allahabad in 1907 with Motilal as its president. His son, romantically identifying with the Extremist position, gave only qualified approval to his father's address to the meeting. In the same year there were serious disturbances in the Punjab. An important Extremist leader, Lala Lajpat Rai, was arrested and deported to Mandalay jail in Burma. Back in England Jawaharlal was aroused by this new oppression and after a trip to Ireland had seen in the nationalists there an extremist posture which should be a lesson for India. Motilal, however, did not think so and found himself being drawn more and more into active defence of the Moderate position. At the meeting of Congress at Surat in December 1907 the Moderates triumphed and the Extremist leaders were expelled.

Extremist activities were slowly eroded. Without Congress there was no organization. The Government was as oppressive as ever. In 1911 the emotional fire of partition was doused by the reunification of Bengal. But Extremism was by no means dead. It had gone underground into the hearts of the young who now clearly saw Congress for what it was, a pressure group for a minority. There had also been the sinister by-product of communalism. The agitation in Bengal had been almost entirely the work of Hindus. The Muslims had gained through partition a new state with a largely Muslim population and the campaign for reunification seemed yet another example of the Hindu majority determined to dominate all. In 1906 conservative Muslims founded the Muslim League and in the same year sent a delegation to the British Viceroy appealing for the guarantee of a separate electorate in the coming reforms.

There was no wonder that the young Nehru found politics dull. The excitement had evaporated by the time of his return from England. He joined the United Provinces provincial Congress in 1913 but took no active part. Two years later after the outbreak of the First World War he did become secretary of a fund being raised to help Indians in South Africa. But his politics were armchair politics, comfortable and placid as was his life. He was not particularly interested in practising law – he was not a good speaker and the vibrant personality of his father continued to overshadow him. Perhaps for the same reasons his father was the prominent figure in Congress. In 1916 Nehru married Kamala Kaul, the pretty seventeen-year-old daughter of a prosperous Kashmiri businessman of the same caste as himself. Like Nehru's mother, Kamala was educated in the traditional Hindu manner and in an endeavour to narrow the intellectual gap between herself and her future husband she spent a few months with the governess of Motilal's two little girls, Swarup and Krishna, who had been born in 1905 while Jawaharlal was in England. In November 1917 Kamala gave birth to a girl, Indira Priyadarshini, now better known as Mrs Indira Gandhi. It was in the same year that Nehru left his armchair for more active politics.

A change had come over Congress. In 1914 it had loyally declared its support for the war in Europe. But in the following year three of the most influential Moderate leaders, including Gokhale, died and the Extremists began to return. In 1916 Moderates and Extremists united and in the same year Congress and the Muslim League joined together in a demand for Dominion status for India. The Lucknow Pact, as the scheme was called, was conceived at Anand Bhawan. Taking an important part in the discussions was a highly westernized Muslim lawyer, Muhammad Ali Jinnah, who was later to become the creator of Pakistan.

In the light of history it is ironic that the Congress meeting which led to a display of Hindu-Muslim concord also saw the triumph of the Extremists. In 1916 Tilak and Annie Besant, in an endeavour to break the immobility of political life, had independently founded Home Rule Leagues. Though the movement had the appearance of revolutionary vigour it was essentially conservative. Tilak's experience of British repression, which by 1914 had given him six years in jail, had turned him towards caution. Mrs Besant's aim in entering Indian politics had been primarily to bring India and Britain together, a reflection of the Eurasian nature of her religious beliefs. She was against violence and had even denounced Tilak's advocacy of passive resistance. But now she believed that Tilak had had a change of heart and her purpose was to unite in Congress all shades of nationalist opinion so that together they might engage in agitation. As she conceived it, agitation would not be violent or terroristic. Such methods would only invite the full weight of British power to crush it. Mrs Besant had in mind the classic British campaigns for reform – for the abolition of slavery, the repeal of the Corn Laws, and for Irish Home Rule. Monster public meetings, newspaper articles and pamphlets would produce widespread support and such agitation would compel the British to grant self-government. 'British politicians,' she maintained, 'judge the value of claims by the energy of those who put them forward.' Only in the dull climate of political India in the middle of a war would such thoughts have been considered revolutionary.

Yet they were. The younger nationalists frustrated by efficient Government suppression were inspired by the new call for action. Tilak, who disliked Mrs Besant, set up his own Home Rule League in Maharashtra in order to get ahead of her. For her own organization she relied on the branches of the Theosophical Society which produced the initial cadres. But many others responded to this rather faint light in the general gloom. One was Jawaharlal Nehru, who was already acquainted with Mrs Besant and perhaps even emotionally drawn to this surprisingly dynamic and vigorous woman of sixty-nine who had played a not inconsiderable role in his early life. In June the Government of Madras interned her and six days later a branch of the League was formed in Allahabad with Jawaharlal Nehru as its secretary.

Yet in spite of everything, the aura of excitement and what was in effect the capture of Congress by the Extremists, Jawaharlal's involvement was by no means total. At the Congress session of December 1917 Mrs Besant was swept into the office of president. But once there she seemed to express a view not far from that of the Moderates. It looked as if she was advocating caution and had decided to await the outcome of new reforms which were foreshadowed in August of that year by the announcement that new advances were to be made towards responsible government in India. At the session of 1918 Mrs Besant's leadership was rejected by the young men of Congress as well as by the Extremists. But she had succeeded in changing the whole character of the organization. The Moderates began to leave the movement they had dominated so long with their constitutional approach to change. The overwhelming majority of Congress members by 1919 were young men and Extremists. Even the offer of new reforms had been basically a response to the fact that the British Government in London had realized that its failure to answer the demands of the Moderates had driven them to support the Home Rulers.

Mrs Besant's legacy to the new Congress which discarded her was an all-India organization and an agitational style. Tilak had foreshadowed it, so had the Extremists in the Punjab and in Bengal, but the Home Rule activity of the years 1915–18 had aroused a wide range of interests to a sense of solidarity and shared impatience. It was upon this basis that a new leader Mahatma Gandhi was to build a new sort of national movement. He was also by the peculiar force of his complex personality to attract Jawaharlal Nehru from a partial involvement in politics to a wholehearted dedication to the fight for India's freedom.

Chapter 5
Enter the Mahatma

Only British-ruled Hindu India could have produced such a figure as Mohandas Karamchand Gandhi. By caste he was born a Vaisya, next to the lowest in the Hindu social scale, in Porbandar, a tiny princely state in Kathiawar in western India, in 1869. Though educated in the western style at Bombay and London he remained fundamentally an unreconstructed Indian. One effect of his western education was to supply words for his political vocabulary to be used occasionally as a Hindu peasant would use a railway train – as a means of communication. Another, which was to have a profound effect on his strategy in the fight for freedom, was the conviction that the British were a moral people believing in justice. If they could be persuaded to recognize the unrighteousness of their rule in India they would willingly abdicate power.

After an unsuccessful period practising law in Bombay, Gandhi had gone to South Africa in 1893. There, under the pressure of a racial discrimination which he shared with the Indian community, he blossomed from a diffident and tongue-tied lawyer into a persuasive advocate. Finding little protection from the law, he evolved a device of mass protest which he called *satyagraha*, or non-violent non-cooperation. For nine years – 1906 to 1915 – Gandhi and his followers waged a sort of war against the South African Government. The sufferings of the Indian community, members of which were imprisoned and flogged, aroused not only opinion in India where the Government brought to bear what pressure it could, but in Britain. Combined they forced the South African Government to right many of the wrongs. When Gandhi returned to India in 1915 he was received as a hero. The Government gave him a medal in the New Year's Honours list. His name had become widely known.

Gandhi's peculiar approach to political action, however, seemed irrelevant to both strains of nationalist thinking. The

Moderates, relying on rational argument to make their case, could not approve of mass protest as a means of persuading the British. His ungrudging and unequivocal support of the British Empire at war had no appeal for the Extremists and the impatient young men. Gandhi made some impression at meetings of Congress but he did not inspire more than respect for his achievements in South Africa. Gandhi was not worried for he sensed that his time would come. Observing the scene, he recognized the impotence of the essentially urban-oriented Congress.

The opportunity for Gandhi to arouse the rural masses came in 1918 when he was invited to champion the cause of indigo workers at Champaran in Bihar and was successful. He also took up the grievances of mill-workers in the industrial city of Ahmadabad in Gujarat. It was there that he first used the fast as a political weapon. While in Gujarat he also supported a no-tax campaign by peasants in the Kheda district. For Gandhi all these were experiments in arousing mass action. They were also significant in bringing two very different men into Gandhi's orbit. The Kheda affair brought Vallabhbhai Patel, the son of a poor farmer but by then a rich and successful lawyer in Ahmadabad. Patel was to become the organizer of the Congress campaign against the British and after independence the most powerful force in Indian politics until his death in 1950. Champaran, which displayed Gandhi as a man of action, came to Jawaharlal Nehru as a revelation, and prepared the way for his commitment not only to the nationalist cause but also to Gandhi.

The times were certainly ripe both for revelation and commitment. The initial enthusiasm of Indians for the war, which in the light of later events now seems so improbable, had drained away as the fighting dragged on. The Home Rule League agitation had worried the Government and there were growing signs that terrorism was about to emerge once again. The country was uneasy. An influenza epidemic originating in Europe spread to India and resulted in some twelve million deaths. The year saw a failure of the monsoon in some parts and floods in others, both producing a poor harvest. Food prices rose steeply. Indian soldiers who had been hastily demobilized in case they should use their weapons against their officers, had taken their grievances back to the villages. In the cities, despite the enormous profits made by industrialists both British and Indian, wages had been kept low while the conditions in which the worker had to live became progressively worse.

Even the certainty of political reform had contributed to apprehension. In October 1917 the then Secretary of State for India, Edwin Montagu, a liberal of almost classic naïveté, had visited India and the consequence had been that the British Government had decided upon a series of reforms unprecedented for a colonial power. Earlier constitutional changes had been based upon a limited representation for the expression of Indian opinion but none for legislative authority. The new reforms, though they were decried by Indian nationalists and socialists in Britain, were sensational in their implication. For the first time an imperial power had declared that some of its non-white colonial subjects were capable of operating self-government.

The reforms, when their contents were revealed, did not, of course, include *complete* self-government. But they did grant a division of powers. The central executive remained responsible only to the Secretary of State in London, but legislation was, in theory anyway, to be the function of a new legislative assembly and a council of state with elected majorities but also an 'official' or nominated bloc. To balance this there was the proviso that if the legislature refused to pass an important bill the Viceroy had the authority to bring it into effect by an executive act. The provinces were also to have legislative councils and the central government would give up some of its powers to these bodies. This devolution covered both finance and administration and to a certain extent the provinces would become self-governing. But again, that government was a division of power. The actual administration was apportioned between the elected council and the governor. Finance, justice and the police remained the governor's exclusive field while the elected ministers were to be given such things as education and public health. The electorate was to be increased from that granted by the 1909 reforms, though it was still subject to a sliding scale of property qualifications. The number who would be able to vote for the provincial councils would be about five million, for the central legislative council nearly one million and for the council of state a select group of some seventeen thousand.

In spite of the encumbrance of so many checks and balances the reforms were a real move forward. Many nationalists, including Gandhi, thought the changes reflected a new British attitude to India. Others however were not so sure. Among these the Muslims in Bengal were, for example, already angry and anxious over the reunification of Bengal. After the partition they had been given many concessions by the British in order to build up opposition to the almost entirely Hindu agitation against it. A larger proportion of posts in the provincial civil service had been allotted to Muslims and substantial funds had been made available for Muslim education. In 1909 they had received the grant of separate electorates in order to protect their community interests against the Hindu majority. Then in 1911 the British had seemed to capitulate to Hindu extremism by reuniting Bengal. It was this as well as other factors, in particular the death of the most influential old-style Muslim leader in 1915, which had led to the alliance between the Muslim League and Congress at Lucknow in the following year.

In order to achieve the Lucknow alliance Congress had agreed to the principle of separate electorates for minorities in any future reforms. But Bengal had a Muslim majority, as did the Punjab. There the Hindu minority was to be protected by what in fact was over-representation for the minority. When agreed, this concession had seemed only academic but with the announcement of new reforms, the Muslims of Bengal realized that they would suffer. Bihar, which presented Gandhi with his first exercise in agitation in India, had also a few months before given Muslims a foretaste of the future. In September 1917 the Hindus of the Shahabad district had attacked Muslims performing their traditional cow-sacrifice and the result had been communal violence on a scale previously unknown in British India. It seemed to many Muslims that this was a fore-taste of Hindu raj; the rule of the majority. Coupled with statements by the Viceroy and the Secretary of State that separate electorates were incompatible with parliamentary de-mocracy, Muslims in Bengal became convinced that the new reforms were a threat not only to their communal identity but to their lives.

The reaction of some Muslim leaders was of great conse-quence to the future of the freedom struggle. In September 1918 a Muslim mob was incited to attack the houses of non-Muslim moneylenders and others, in a district of Calcutta. The ground had been prepared by stories of offensive references to Islam in Hindu newspapers. An attempt to stop a mob marching on Government House to present a petition dissolved in violence. In the end Calcutta was given over to three days of lawlessness, loot and arson. It was perhaps the first time in British India that a violent mob had been organized for specifically political purposes. The aim of the leaders was to direct violence against the non-Muslim community for the sole purpose of influencing the British. Their success in arousing mob violence revealed that there was mass discontent which could be manipulated by unscrupulous politicians for personal or communal advantage. The techniques for the communal disturbances of the coming years had been established.

Overwhelmed by a feeling of insecurity, the Government of India decided to protect itself by taking special powers. The report of a commission of inquiry under Mr Justice Rowlatt into what the Government called 'criminal conspiracies' was published shortly before the report of the Secretary of State on the proposed reforms. The Rowlatt Report advocated sweep-ing security measures including the trial of political cases without a jury and the weapon of preventive detention without any trial at all. The report was received with dismay by virtually every level of informed opinion in India – except, of course, the British. Of the nationalist leaders only Gandhi took posi-tive action. He called upon the Viceroy to refuse to authorize the security ordinances. When this appeal went unheeded he formed a Satyagraha Society whose members would take a pledge to disobey the law as an act of passive resistance.

It was this call coming on top of the revelation of Champaran which suddenly caught the imagination of Jawaharlal Nehru. His reaction, he wrote later, was 'one of tremendous relief'. It was as if Champaran had built up an intolerable tension awaiting some release. The satyagraha pledge supplied that release, though why, it is difficult to see. Yet even this did not draw Jawaharlal into action. His natural inhibitions were reinforced by the disapproval of his father who saw in the technique of non-cooperation the negation of everything he believed in. There was a coolness between father and son which lasted for nearly a year and a half. But events took place in the Punjab which were to destroy Motilal's faith in British justice and bring the two together in the hope of creating a new India.

Chapter 6
Amritsar and After

The protests against the new security measures took place on two levels. Gandhi, in order to give drama and a nexus to acts of non-cooperation, proclaimed 6 April 1919 Satyagraha Day. There would be a *hartal*, or total suspension of business; protesters would fast and mass meetings would be held. On another level, and probably without Gandhi's knowledge, Congress workers were spreading alarmist propaganda. Rumours were set about that the Government would be empowered by the new laws to 'inspect' a man and a woman before marriage. Another provision, it was said, restricted to two the number of plough-bullocks a peasant could own. Such rumours grew and multiplied especially in the Punjab, the province from which a large majority of the rapidly demobilized soldiers had been recruited. Soon there were outbursts of popular indignation.

Most of the rioting, which was virtually confined to the Punjab and parts of western India, was spontaneous and characterized by racial and communal hatred. The Government over-reacted to Satyagraha Day and on 9 April Gandhi was arrested, though soon released. His detention provoked serious rioting in Bombay and Ahmadabad, and Gandhi, horrified by the violence that broke out, called off the campaign. But, as he was to learn again and again, violence once begun could not be called off. In the Punjab the administration, determined upon a show of force, arrested two popular Congress leaders on 10 April and when a crowd began a protest march on the European section of the city of Amritsar, the police opened fire. Turned back, the crowd looted two banks and burnt the railway station. Four Europeans were murdered by the mob and others beaten up, including a woman missionary who was left for dead. The military commander, Brigadier-General Dyer, managed to restore order and all public meetings and assemblies were banned.

Despite the ban, on 13 April a large crowd estimated at

some 20,000 men, women and children gathered in an enclosed space known as the Jallianwala Bagh. When he heard of this General Dyer went personally to the spot with ninety Gurkha and Baluchi soldiers and two armoured cars. As the entrance was too narrow for the armoured vehicles to pass through he used them to block the only exit. He then ordered the crowd to disperse. It does seem likely that Dyer, who was a stranger to Amritsar, did not know that there were no other convenient exits from the Jallianwala Bagh, and that, when the crowd did not disperse because it could not, and he panicked. Without warning, Dyer ordered his soldiers to shoot into the crowd. He admitted later that he fired all the ammunition he had with him and then withdrew, leaving, according to official estimates, 379 dead and 1,200 wounded. The armoured cars were left blocking the entrance so that no one could leave and no medical aid could get in. Dyer's action was given the approval of the governor.

The following day, a mob rioting and burning at another spot was bombed and machine-gunned from the air. On 15 April martial law was declared and not lifted until 9 June. During this period Indians were forced to walk on their hands and knees past the spot where the woman missionary had been attacked and, according to the report of the Hunter Commission which inquired into the disturbances, public floggings were inflicted for such minor offences as 'the contravention of the curfew order, failure to salaam to a commissioned officer, disrespect to a European, taking a commandeered car without leave, or refusal to sell milk . . .'. The commission which was set up in October 1919 with four British and four Indian members only criticized Dyer's actions in the mildest terms as 'unfortunate' and 'injudicious'. Indians considered them a profound insult to their self-respect and pride.

It took some time for the news to reach the rest of India as the Punjab government had imposed a strict censorship. But when it did there was a thrill of anger and resentment. In some there was also a terrible disillusion. Those, like Jawaharlal Nehru, who had admired British justice and liberal idealism, those, like Motilal, who had believed, in spite of everything, in

British promises of a growing participation for Indians in the running of their country, found their faith irrecoverably shattered. After Amritsar there could be for them no compromise, above all, no trust. Amritsar occupies a special place in the martyrology of the freedom struggle – and it is not difficult to see why.

Gandhi's response was immediate and precise. There could be, he declared, no 'cooperation with this satanic Government'.

Champaran had been for Jawaharlal Nehru a revelation of technique. The massacre at the Jallianwala Bagh filled him with bitterness. But it still did not drive him to action. His hesitation at that time displays two character traits which are the clues to his subsequent political behaviour: lack of decisiveness and dependence on older and dynamic personalities. His inability to break from his father over the technique of non-cooperation led him to allow Gandhi to make the decision for him. Gandhi advised him not to upset his father.

Nevertheless the massacre brought Jawaharlal into contact with the outstanding nationalist leaders of the time. Early in June 1919 Congress established its own commission of inquiry into the troubles in the Punjab. As a distinguished lawyer and an important figure in Congress, Motilal was a member. So were Gandhi and the Bengali Congress leader, C. R. Das. The younger Nehru became assistant to Das, who was in charge of investigations in the Amritsar area, and it was there at the epicentre of administrative violence that he first approached reality, the reality both of an India he had never known and of the dark face of the British whose civilization had moulded his life and thought. He also came into close contact with Gandhi for the first time.

At the end of 1919 Congress held its annual session in Amritsar. In this emotive atmosphere the call was for positive action once again and the rejection of the forthcoming reforms. But Gandhi, who had been horrified by the violence that had emerged out of his campaign against the security laws, surprised and even shocked the delegates by calling for moderation, the acceptance of the reforms and participation in the working of them. Congress members had not yet learned the essential elements of the Gandhi style. Indeed there was no reason why they should have done, for they had only once been displayed in the hurried calling off of the satyagraha campaign earlier in the year.

It was to be some time before the more astute Indian nationalists grasped the fact that the Mahatma had no policy, that he did not look to the future with logic and carefully formulated plans. His response was only to the present. For him the future consisted only of a present that had not yet presented him with its problems. Gandhi was never aware of the reality of historical development. True to the Hindu spiritual tradition, he was consciously aware of *eternity* but *time* was of no consequence. This was both his strength and his weakness. He was abnormally sensitive to the temporary and unpredictable mood of the Hindu masses. They learned to recognize this mysterious gift and gave him their allegiance. But his constant reaction to the shifting and disconnected elements that made up the present was to give to the Indian National Congress a spasmodic, unexpected and unforeseeable movement which disconcerted both the British and his own more intellectual followers.

In January 1920, true to his style, Gandhi again changed his mind. One of the reasons was the hero's welcome given to General Dyer on his arrival in England even though the Government of India had disowned him and forced his resignation from the army. Another reason was the rejection by the British Government of Indian Muslim protests over the terms of the Turkish peace treaty. Indian Muslims, growing more conscious of their minority status in their own country, had begun to look outside India to the wider Muslim world in the hope of gaining some sense of a larger identity. The highest religious office in the Muslim world was that of the Caliph of Islam, a title held by the Sultan of Turkey. The decision by the Allies to abolish the office of Caliph aroused considerable anger in India for it was taken as an insult to the faithful as well as being a violation of a pledge given by the British Prime Minister, Lloyd George.

The emotional effect of this was canalized into the formation of a political organization by two brothers, Muhammad and Sharkat Ali. The Khilafat movement, as it was called from the Indian word for caliphate, attracted widespread support but more important still was its alliance with Congress. Gandhi recognized that the Khilafat issue could be used as a means of uniting Muslims and Hindus in common cause against a Government which had shown so much disregard for the feelings of Indians of both religions. Gandhi was able to bring the two separate issues of the Amritsar affair and the campaign against the abolition of the Caliphate together and direct them towards the shared goal of *swaraj* or independence.

Gandhi convinced the Khilafat leaders more quickly than he did those of Congress. Most were with him on the matter of non-cooperation but many were against both his bid for leadership and his technique of non-violence. To some Gandhi appeared to be both obscurantist and reactionary. Just as many nationalists had taken their life-style from the west, so they had taken their political vocabulary too. Gandhi was now using Indian words and Indian images to describe the aims of the freedom movement. He spoke always of *swaraj* and not of 'self-government'. He called not for the acceptance of the institutions of the British, even if their working was handed over to Indians, but for national reconstruction. He wanted new institutions created to take their place. He demanded not the boons of western reforms but a reformation of Indian society. This, he claimed, could best be achieved by Congressmen leaving the cities and helping to set up cottage industries. The local manufacture of cotton goods should be revived and the spinning wheel become the symbol of India's new life. The wearing of homespun cloth would be a gesture of rejection as well as an affirmation of Indianness.

Gandhi's approach was frankly anti-intellectual. He demanded that imported European ideas be given up in the same way as imported European cloth. In 1920 he was proposing a complete reversal of the previous trends of Indian nationalism. He held up his own life and commitment as the *only* example to be followed. Back to simplicity of living so that the individual could be free from the tyranny of material possessions, the renunciation of non-essentials so that there could be a total dedication to the struggle against foreign rule. Naturally, he was opposed inside Congress by those who disliked his views or believed them to be the wrong ones for India. But Gandhi was already attracting the allegiance of groups who had never participated in the nationalist struggle before and more significantly was doing so on an all-India scale. The majority of his opponents drew their support from specific regions and no others. Congress had hitherto been an alliance of regional leaders. Gandhi demanded something new – national leadership and a leadership without question. 'So long as you choose to keep me as your leader,' Gandhi told a meeting early in 1920, 'you must accept my conditions, you must accept dictatorship and the discipline of martial law.'

Jawaharlal Nehru played no significant part in the conflict between Gandhi and his opponents. He had already made his commitment to the Mahatma. But 1920 was for him another year of revelation. Amritsar had opened up a vista of an unknown India, now he was to learn the harsh world of the peasant. In May 1920 he and his wife had spent a holiday in the hill-station of Musoorie. In the same hotel was staying a delegation from Afghanistan, negotiating the terms of the peace after the war of 1919. There was no contact between the two parties but such was the fear of the British authorities that Nehru was instructed by the local magistrate to give a formal promise that he would not approach the Afghan delegation. Nehru, on principle, refused and he was ordered to leave the district.

Returning to Allahabad earlier than expected, he was present when a group of peasants from a nearby district marched into the city in the hope of gaining the support of local political leaders. Nehru agreed to return with them to their villages to see the subject of their grievances for himself. There for the first time he saw the grinding poverty of the Indian countryside. 'A new picture of India seemed to rise before me,' he wrote later, 'naked, starving, crushed and utterly miserable.' He felt an immediate emotional identification with the peasants: in response to the childlike faith they seemed to have in this

visitor from the city, his shyness left him. It was the beginning
of that special empathy which was one of the keys to his later
dominance of the Indian political scene.

While Nehru was expanding his awareness of the peasant
masses – for the next months were times of continuous agrarian
unrest – Gandhi was preparing both for a campaign of civil
disobedience and for the control of Congress. It was, however,
not Gandhi but the leaders of the Khilafat movement who
took the initiative. The beginning of non-cooperation was set
for 1 August 1920. Gandhi and Nehru were on a tour of the
province of Sind when news reached them that the great Extremist leader Tilak had died on the very same day. Tilak was
perhaps Gandhi's only serious rival for the leadership of
Congress and both men hurried to Bombay to pay their last
homage to the man who had first used the rousing slogan of
swaraj.

A month later Congress met in special session at Calcutta.
The opposition to Gandhi was all the stronger because much
of it had originated in Bengal. Those who opposed included
Mrs Besant and Muhammad Ali Jinnah, then still an active
member of Congress. But Gandhi claimed an unexpected ally.
Motilal Nehru had at last given up his disbelief in satyagraha.
His defection helped to sway the balance in favour of Gandhi
but it was by a very small majority that non-cooperation
became the official policy of Congress. Gandhi's triumph was
still to come. The proof of the policy was in the performance
and none of his critics expected it to work. Gandhi called for a
simple boycott of the coming elections under the Government
of India Act of 1919, of Government educational institutions,
and of the law courts. To the surprise both of Gandhi's opponents in Congress and of the British almost two thirds of the
electorate did not vote in November 1920. After this, criticism
remained but opposition faded away.

At the regular annual session of Congress held at the end of
1920 in Nagpur, Gandhi managed to win over even his most
vocal opponents. The Congress goal was changed from self-
government within the British empire to *swaraj*, though Gandhi
refused to be tied to a precise definition – Dominion status or

complete independence. He was now the acknowledged leader and Congress began to take on the images and the symbols he had made so peculiarly his own. But the session at Nagpur drove one important member away never to return. Muhammad Ali Jinnah left for the political wilderness out of which he was to emerge in later years as the leader of the Muslim League and the architect of India's partition.

Jinnah's going was a minor affair compared to what was about to happen to Congress. From its limited, almost parochial, organization was to emerge a new unified *national* movement. If Gandhi was to lead there had to be an apparatus that put the power of leadership into his hands. Congress was reorganized from top to bottom. India was divided into twenty-one areas known as provinces. In these at the apex was the Provincial Congress Committee. Below, the organization was subdivided into districts, towns and cities with each committee electing members to the one above it until the final tip of the pyramid was reached in the All-India Congress Committee. The AICC with a membership of some three to four hundred carried on the business of Congress between meetings of the supreme legislative body, the annual session. It also elected the real source of power and decision, the Working Committee which was made up of the Congress president, the general secretaries, the treasurer and about twelve others. The president was elected annually. Until independence Gandhi remained above all, often without formal office but always both the conscience and the guide of the movement.

The non-cooperation campaign for all the hopes and the effort placed in it got off to a very poor start. The boycott of schools and colleges was ineffective – most students were not prepared to risk their future employment by missing their studies. Government servants stayed at their posts and there seemed to be no lessening in the amount of litigation in the courts. There were meetings, exhortations, an occasional strike but no mass involvement. The Government helped to fan a flame of action by arresting the Ali brothers in September 1921 for inciting Muslims in the army to mutiny. Gandhi came to their support and ordered Congress workers to read out

Muhammad Ali's seditious speech, which had led to his arrest, at special meetings on 21 October.

On this occasion the Government considered arresting Gandhi but decided not to. It was becoming fairly clear that the Mahatma's reputation among ordinary people had grown to such an extent that his arrest might cause a popular rising. Or so the Government was advised. The exact nature of the challenge presented by Gandhi was not yet understood by the Government. Nevertheless it was better to play safe – at least for the time being. The British were not the only people in India who found the Mahatma confusing. Jawaharlal Nehru, though drawn to him by his personality and unorthodox approach, was still not totally reconciled to the obscurantism of his methods. But he put his doubts aside and as general secretary of the United Provinces Provincial Congress Committee directed all his energies into the campaign.

In the autumn of 1921 the Government in an attempt to divert attention planned a visit to India by the Prince of Wales. The glamour of a tour by the heir to the king-emperor would be sure to attract that peculiar respect for royalty which it was believed inhabited every Indian heart. Gandhi proclaimed a nationwide boycott of the visit. To everyone's surprise the call was heard and the prince found himself driving through empty streets to meetings consisting only of his fellow-countrymen and those Indians now divorced from the mainstream of Indian political life. As always there was violence. Terrorism was by no means dead and there were many political activists who totally rejected Gandhi and his ideas.

This time however the Government had no qualms about taking action – though they left Gandhi alone. Congress volunteer organizations were declared illegal and mass arrests of Congress workers followed. Among those taken into custody where the two Nehrus – on 6 December at Anand Bhawan. Both were sentenced to six months' imprisonment, Motilal for being a member of a banned organization and Jawaharlal for distributing leaflets calling for a boycott. This turned out not to be an offence within the meaning of the existing laws and Jawaharlal was released after serving three months.

While the Nehrus were in Lucknow jail Gandhi was still calling for more and more demonstrations. This time students responded by leaving their studies to take part in the campaign. To dramatize the boycott of foreign goods, European clothes and cloth were ceremoniously burnt and shops selling foreign liquor ostentatiously picketed. Arrests continued until there were some thirty thousand under detention. At this stage violence again broke out. In a remote village in the United Provinces a police station was burnt down with the police still inside. Horrified, Gandhi issued an order on 4 February 1922 calling off the civil disobedience campaign throughout India. The people, he claimed, were not yet ready for the kind of struggle he had in mind.

Both the arrogance and the apparent naïveté of Gandhi's decision shocked other Congress leaders. To call off a campaign when despite the Government's actions it was going well seemed foolish to say the least. Jawaharlal was outspoken in his criticism. Surely if India had to wait until all its people were fully trained in the techniques of non-violence there was little chance of success in anybody's lifetime. Yet he was still prepared to trust the Mahatma's judgement, an index of how much he had surrendered of his own.

On 3 March 1922 Jawaharlal was released and hurried to Ahmadabad where Gandhi was on trial for sedition. The Government noting the disarray in Congress caused by Gandhi's decision to call off the campaign had taken advantage of it to arrest him. The British had in fact learnt something important about Gandhi. They now believed – and retained their belief – that they had nothing really to fear from him. While Gandhi was in control of Congress they had an unofficial ally. As long as civil disobedience remained non-violent the Government had little to worry about. Who was hurt by non-cooperation anyway? Only the Indians. Gandhi's aim was to minimize violence. So was the Government's. Small-scale violence was easily suppressed, but if once Gandhi ceased to dominate Congress other more dynamic and violent men might use the machine he was building up to incite a full-scale rebellion. Henceforth the Government would leave Gandhi free as long as possible, arresting him only when it seemed that he was losing his influence which could only be refreshed by a small martyrdom. Meanwhile the Government would take more positive action against the terrorists and the western-style revolutionaries whom they really feared.

Among those was Jawaharlal Nehru. The British completely misunderstood Nehru's character. They took his revolutionary words at their face value and acted towards him as if he was a dangerous opponent. Gandhi knew otherwise. The Mahatma was a particularly shrewd judge of men. He saw Nehru's weakness and used it for his own purposes. As the years went by he built up the 'revolutionary' Nehru, the 'progressive' Nehru, partly to impress foreign well-wishers such as members of the British Labour Party but also to polarize behind an ineffective leader those genuinely progressive elements within Congress who posed a threat to Gandhi's own position. To the image of the revolutionary Nehru the British contributed the essential accolade of frequent arrest and imprisonment.

This time Gandhi was sentenced to six years' imprisonment but was released after serving almost two. The grounds were his ill-health, the reason – Congress was riven by factions, the thin thread of Hindu-Muslim alliance had parted and the non-cooperation campaign stifled by apathy and disillusion. Nehru too was rearrested after only six weeks of liberty. On his return to Allahabad he had organized a boycott of foreign goods and when some shopkeepers refused to cooperate their shops had been picketed. Nehru was charged with criminal intimidation and, refusing to plead, was sentenced to eighteen months in jail.

Release came in January 1923. Nehru had not enjoyed his stay in jail even though he had not been badly treated. The lack of privacy had irked him but there had been time for reading and reflection. Imprisonment had endorsed his commitment to the struggle for freedom.

Chapter 7
Father, Son and Holy Ghost

Nehru had gone to jail proudly claiming that it was his good fortune to serve India in the battle for freedom. On his release he found the battle-ground deserted, allies no longer allies and his own troops divided amongst themselves. The Khilafat movement was in a state of collapse. The Turks under a new revolutionary leader had expelled the sultan-caliph and were planning themselves to abolish the caliphate. The movement no longer had a purpose. Hindu-Muslim tensions had been revived by a particularly ferocious rebellion of Muslim peasants in south India in which the violence had been directed not at the British but at Hindus. The year 1923 was to see the outbreak of serious communal disturbances which were to set a pattern for the future. For Muslims it was a year of despair made all the blacker by the euphoria which had raised hopes so high.

Congress too in its disillusion had broken into factions. Without the commanding presence of the Mahatma his policies and his behaviour were attacked as failures. Of course he still had his supporters to whom on his release was added Jawaharlal. But on the opposite side, the 'pro-changers', as they came to be called, were Motilal Nehru and a number of others including C. R. Das. Gandhi's supporters, the 'no-changers', advocated waiting until the climate of apathy and disillusion had cleared away and a new campaign could be started. Their case was eroded by a commission of inquiry set up by Congress which toured the country. From their report it was obvious that no new campaign could be mounted without the Mahatma.

The pro-changers were anxious to contest the general elections due to be held in November 1923. The Congress boycott of the last elections had meant that the councils were dominated by the moderates who had left Congress to form their own Liberal Party. Motilal had never given up his genuine attachment to the constitutional approach even though he had accepted non-violence and given up his luxurious way of life in order to please Gandhi. The pro-changers represented the old opposition to Gandhi. They thought they should use the new quasi-parliamentary institutions in order to further the cause of Indian freedom. The pro-changers did not however propose to work the institutions, only to prevent them being used by moderates.

The no-changers insisted on a total boycott of the elections and concentration on Gandhi's programme for reconstructing Indian society. Led by C. Rajagopalachari and Rajendra Prasad the no-changers had triumphed at the annual session held at the end of 1922 even though C. R. Das had then been president of Congress. After the session Das announced his resignation and his intention of forming a Swaraj Party to contest the elections. It looked as if Congress was bound to split. In an attempt to retain unity Das was persuaded to hold off his decision for a few months. Jawaharlal Nehru and Maulana Azad, a Muslim who was to become an important Congress leader, emerged as mediators between the two factions. A reconciliation was agreed but it could be no more than superficial for both sides were absolutely convinced that they were right.

The younger Nehru considered his father mistaken in his views but was mainly concerned in avoiding a split which could only damage Congress, perhaps irretrievably. With others he formed a Centre Party within Congress and it was largely because of the efforts of its members that an open split did not take place. What was produced instead was a compromise solution which permitted both sides to get what they wanted. The no-changers would concentrate on Gandhi's programme, the pro-changers would contest the elections. The compromise was to set a precedent. Congress unity was to be frequently threatened by the diverse groups of which it was a sometimes uneasy alliance. In the coming years Jawaharlal Nehru was to play a special role as a neutralizer of conflict. The present compromise in which he played a not inconspicuous part was his first introduction to the domestic politics of the nationalist movement.

Soon after the compromise had been reached and confirmed

by a special session of Congress held in Delhi in September 1923, Jawaharlal was arrested for the third time. Not on this occasion by the British but the police of a princely state. The Maharaja of Nabha had been forced to abdicate by the British because of his continuous quarrels with the ruler of the adjoining state of Patiala. Both were Sikhs. This martial race, which had never forgotten that it had once ruled the Punjab before the British took it away from them, had responded to Gandhi's non-cooperation campaign with enthusiasm; particularly so a militant Sikh group known as the Akalis which had been agitating for control of the Sikh temples, some of which were administered by the British Government. The Akalis resented the deposition of the ruler of Nabha, who had been friendly to their cause. They decided to send parties of men across the state frontier to make their way to the capital. The Akalis who had merged their movement with Congress invited Jawaharlal Nehru and two others to observe this unarmed invasion.

When the observers reached Jaito just inside the state frontier they were served with an order requesting them not to enter the state or if they had already done so to leave at once. When they explained that they were not demonstrators but observers and that in any case they could not leave immediately as the next train was not for some hours, they were arrested and placed in the local lock-up. In the evening, with his left wrist handcuffed to one of his companions' right and a policeman holding a chain attached to the handcuff, Nehru and his colleagues were marched through the town's main street to the railway station. This was very different from the almost courteous treatment he had received from the British. So too was the cell they were lodged in for three days when they arrived at the state capital. Not only were they left handcuffed but the cell was small, insanitary and alive with rats.

The three men were finally taken into court and charged with illegal entry into the state. The judge appeared to be illiterate and the case dragged on until one day, without warning, the accused were taken into another court room complete with another magistrate. Here they were tried on another and much more serious charge – that of criminal conspiracy. As even the archaic state laws of Nabha required four persons to make up a conspiracy, the court generously supplied another person to stand in the dock with Nehru and his two companions. Both court and procedure were farcical. The accused refused to take part in the proceedings though Nehru did submit a statement. The sentences when they came however were by no means a laughing matter. After a fortnight all four were condemned to eighteen months on the conspiracy charge and Nehru and his two colleagues to a further six months for not obeying the order to leave the state.

This was Nehru's first experience of the 'law' in the princely states and he realized, probably for the first time, that the fight for freedom from the British must also include the princes whose medieval rule was permitted only because the British considered their states as bulwarks of conservatism.

Fortunately Nehru was not to suffer prolonged imprisonment in a princely jail. After the deposition of the Maharaja the state had been put under a British administrator. The evening of the day on which they had been sentenced, the three Congressmen were informed that their sentences had been suspended by the administrator. They were then escorted to the railway station and set free. What happened to the fourth man Nehru never found out.

Nehru left Nabha with a new awareness of yet another India. He also took with him what developed into a virulent attack of typhoid fever. Many years later he wrote that his illness was 'in the nature of a spiritual experience'. He believed that after it he was no longer so emotional about politics and could see the objectives more clearly. Certainly for the next few years, while being just as active in the cause of Indian freedom, he seemed curiously detached.

Not so the pro-changers of the Swaraj Party. In November 1923 they won forty-five seats in the Central Legislature which with the support of other nationalist groups gave them a majority. The party did not do quite so well in the provincial elections but won a majority in the Central Provinces and were the largest party in Bengal. In these provinces they refused to form ministries or to assist in the formation of them by others, so bringing the reforms to a halt. They were also able to hinder the function of the Central Legislature. Not that this really upset the administration, which merely used its reserved powers to push through legislation. But it was an effective protest, a show of real strength and a warning that constitutional reforms insufficiently progressive might always be nullified by the use of the democratic vote.

The success of the Swarajists in effect split Congress into two parties. On paper the compromise remained, its obvious contradictions ignored in order to maintain an appearance of unity. Jawaharlal was still committed to the reconciliatory middle way of the Centre Party though he played no significant role in the discussions which led to the reaffirmation of compromise at the annual session of December 1923. His only public act at the session was to advocate the formation of the Congress Volunteer Organization, the Hindustani Seva Dal. On the acceptance of the proposition Nehru was himself appointed president of the All-India Board of the organization.

Jawaharlal was also persuaded by Muhammad Ali, the Muslim president of Congress for 1924, to take the post of Congress general secretary. Nehru did so with reluctance. He felt that he was disliked by members of the Working Committee and was told by the president that that was the main reason why he should accept! He was neither worse nor better at his job than anyone else. His only act of defiance was an attempt to abolish the use of honorifics such as 'Pandit' and 'Mahatma' and was surprised at the depth of feeling aroused by it.

In the middle of January 1924 the news of Gandhi's illness – an acute attack of appendicitis – was released. It caused a flow of love, affection and anxiety from such diverse quarters that it demonstrated once and for all the special status the Mahatma held in the minds of the many. When it was announced that he would be freed from prison both the Nehrus went to Bombay where the Mahatma had gone to convalesce. With the imminent return of Gandhi to the political arena the Swarajists wanted his support for what they were doing. A word of condemnation from him and either Congress would split or the Swarajists would feel compelled to give up their assaults on the legislative apparatus. Gandhi was uncompromising. The legislatures should be boycotted. The function of Congress was to return to the grass-roots, not to give credibility to British institutions by trying to destroy them.

Fortunately Gandhi was persuaded, in the interests of unity, not to condemn the Swarajists openly. He suggested instead that they should try to assist his programme by forcing through legislation that might help. Meanwhile his supporters would respect the right of the Swarajists to continue their activities. Characteristically, for Gandhi was convinced that the Swarajists were in the wrong, he proceeded to undermine them in Congress. It was a technique he was to use over and over again, sometimes with the assistance of Jawaharlal. But not this time. At prayer meetings Gandhi praised the virtues of hand-spinning which he appeared to view as not so much an economic device as a spiritual one. In the summer of 1924 he moved a resolution at the All-India Congress Committee to make the spinning of a quota of yarn – two thousand yards *every month* – an indispensable qualification for membership of Congress. Motilal Nehru and C. R. Das taking it as an attack upon the Swarajists walked out of the meeting. The younger Nehru, fearing that Congress would be finally split thereby leaving the main body in the control of fanatical Gandhians, submitted his resignation as general secretary in protest against the resolution.

The resolution was passed but later withdrawn for it had become clear even to Gandhi that Congress could not afford to split on such an issue. Many members of Congress considered the spinning qualification ludicrous. So too did others. When Gandhi wrote to the great Bengali poet and nationalist, Rabindranath Tagore, advising him to use the spinning wheel for half an hour a day, he replied icily 'Why not eight and a half hours if it will help the country?' By the end of the year reacting as usual to the demands of the immediate present Gandhi backed down and at the December session of Congress the Swaraj Party was recognized as the official constitutional arm of Congress and as such Congressmen must give it their full support.

The decision was pragmatic but its consequences were to affect the course of Indian history. The Swarajists without absolute majorities were compelled to tone down their policy of total disruption of the legislative processes in order to acquire the necessary allies. In the Central Legislature they made an alliance with the Moderate and Muslim groups. But the situation outside the legsislature had begun to influence the parties in the coalition. Hindu-Muslim conflict, most of it bloody, was now becoming commonplace. Politicians outside the main leadership of Congress had taken advantage of the collapse of non-cooperation to return to the communal activities which they had always believed to be their passport to power.

Naturally they were most successful in those provinces in which their community was in a minority. Muslim communalism steadily grew in the United Provinces, Bihar, Bombay, Madras and the Central Provinces. Hindu communalism flourished in the Punjab, Sind, Bengal and the North West Frontier Province. Though Congress leaders were in the main revolted by communalism they did not understand either its sources or its dangers. Most of them came from Hindu-majority provinces and had no experience of what it was like to be a member of a religious minority. Furthermore they assumed that communalism was solely a product of British rule and would go away with it. Tragically they refused to take communal differences seriously.

In 1924 there were riots in Delhi, Nagpur, Lucknow, Allahabad and Jubbulpore. But the worst of all was at Kohat in the North West Frontier Province. Gandhi decided on a twenty-one day fast. A Unity Conference was called in Delhi and for a moment the tensions were quieted. But blackmail was no substitute for understanding. Congress was concerned with its own factional strife which had not been settled by the ostensible compromise with the Swarajists. The field was left to the communalists and they carefully sowed their seeds of hatred.

A recent census had revealed that Muslims were increasing in numbers. This was partly due to the incidence of more live births but another factor was Muslim missionary work among the Untouchables, the lowest level of the Hindu social order. To this the Hindu communalists responded with alarmist propaganda. As a counter to the Unity movement, essentially half-hearted though it was, and to the threat of Muslim conversion, such organizations as the Arya Samaj began their own missionary campaign. Most Indian Muslims had Hindu ancestors. They had been converted to Islam because once it had been the religion of the rulers. Now, the Hindu missionaries maintained, Indian Muslims should return to the faith of their ancestors. Very soon the whole texture of ordinary life in northern India was suffused by communal fears and hatreds. Naturally this affected those members of the legislature who had been elected on what was in effect a communal ticket under the separate electorate clauses in the Act of 1919. Their suspicions of the Swaraj Party grew and the alliance began to fall apart.

Jawaharlal Nehru viewed the scene with distaste. His slide towards religion which had taken place under the influence of the Mahatma had been quickly reversed. At least Nehru's attitude to *orthodox* religion had changed. He had never been happy with the religious overtones of Gandhi's campaigns but he had been driven to read once again such works as the *Bhagavad-gita* and had been attracted by what he thought was its message. Now, in his revulsion at communal violence, the West reasserted itself in a disgust for religion in politics. But his dislike of communalism was instinctive rather than intellectual. Gandhi, an essentially communal politician, hated the violence to which he continually contributed. That too was instinctive. Neither men understood or chose to understand the *cause* and therefore helped to keep violence alive.

Jawaharlal turned away into local politics. Congress was anxious to control the municipalities as part of its policy of infiltrating every aspect of Indian life. In the autumn of 1923 Jawaharlal had been elected chairman of the Allahabad Municipality. Memoranda on every conceivable issue flowed from his pen though with little effect. He found himself as he was to do later as Prime Minister of independent India, hamstrung by nepotism and corruption. His colleagues were more concerned in getting their relatives into lucrative positions than in making Allahabad a model city. Nehru decided to resign, was persuaded not to by the British Commissioner for Allahabad but finally gave up in February 1925.

Just before his resignation a foreign journalist, observing that Motilal Nehru had been appointed leader of the opposition in the Central Legislature, his son head of the municipal government of the capital of one of the most important of India's provinces, and that Gandhi was back again as the *animateur* of Congress, had coined a phrase. Indian nationalism, he said, had its Trinity of Father, Son and Holy Ghost.

Chapter 8
Rediscovering Europe

Despite Motilal's dedication to the cause and the cutting down in consequence of the luxury of life at Anand Bhawan the politics of both father and son was still the politics of the affluent. Motilal had given up much of his law practice but by no means all of it. He could still, as he told his son, make enough in a week to keep them all for a year. Jawaharlal, perhaps realizing how much his own as well as his father's status in the nationalist movement depended upon their freedom from want, grew to resent his dependence on his father's bounty. As a gesture he had begun to wear patched homespun and started living on what he thought to be a poor man's diet. He also imposed the same regimen on his wife, whose health was not improved by it. There was a suggestion that the general secretaries of Congress should be paid a salary out of organization funds and that Jawaharlal should take up full-time work. But it was not approved of by Motilal who insisted that freedom from money worries was a genuine contribution to the cause. Jawaharlal gave in and fortunately so, for his wife's health was now such that it was necessary for her to go to Europe for treatment.

In November 1924 Kamala had given birth to a son who died after a few days. A year later her doctor diagnosed tuberculosis. The only hope was to go to Switzerland, the mecca for sufferers from that disease. Gandhi, when consulted, agreed. Jawaharlal was pleased at the decision. The torpor that lay over Indian political life had only increased his sense of isolation. 'I welcomed the idea, for I wanted an excuse to get out of India myself. My mind was befogged and no clear path was visible, and I thought perhaps if I was far from India I could see things in better perspective and lighten up the dark corners of my mind.'

At the beginning of March 1926 Jawaharlal, Kamala and their daughter Indira sailed from Bombay for Venice. On the

same boat were his sister Vijaya Lakshmi and her husband
Ranjit Pandit. Their destination was Geneva, where Kamala
was to have some months of treatment. While Kamala remained bed-ridden, Nehru read books, explored the rather
dull city which was now the seat of the League of Nations,
and went off on visits to such eminent people as the French
novelist and admirer of Gandhi, Romain Rolland. He found
the great man's thought too rarified for him. He also met some
of the Indian revolutionaries who had made their home in
Europe and thought he saw behind them the shadow of the
ubiquitous British Secret Service. He found these isolated
people pathetic, living in a world long dead.

Europe at this time was alive with tensions. The effects of
the First World War upon the social and economic order were
emerging in the form of radical discontent at both ends of the
political spectrum. Fascism was already entrenched in Italy; it
waited in Germany. Socialists and communists hawked their
panaceas for the people while the reactionaries assembled their
visions of discipline and order. Jawaharlal who had only known
a Europe apparently stable and resonant with racial superiority
found it now harassed with doubts and anxieties. The Indian
scene seemed in contrast saturated with pettiness.

For one whose emotional responses frequently overwhelmed
his intellectual appreciations the appeal of socialist ideas was
considerable. In India Nehru had already succumbed to a
vague populism in his identification with the grievances of the
peasants in the United Provinces. He had also been inspired
by Vivekananda's doctrine of service to the poor and oppressed.
His mind was therefore receptive to the evangelical elements in
international socialism.

Though only intending to stay in Europe for a few months,
Kamala's condition and lack of response to treatment gave
Jawaharlal more time to absorb the new ideas presented to
him. In February 1927 he attended as a delegate of the Indian
National Congress, the Congress of Oppressed Nationalities
held in Brussels. There he met communists, left-wing socialists,
nationalists from Asia and Africa, a radical League of Nations.
Indeed most shades of left-wing thought had their representatives

at Brussels. Strong moral support for the meeting had come from Moscow and there was a powerful delegation of orthodox communists. But there were others less orthodox too. The principal finance had come from the Mexican Government and the Kuomintang, the latter still presenting a radical front. The British Labour Party was represented among others by George Lansbury who was elected president of the Congress primarily to show that it was not dominated by revolutionary communists. Later Jawaharlal was to join him on the executive of the League Against Imperialism, which was one of the outcomes of the Congress. Among the other members of its executive were Madame Sun Yat-sen, Romain Rolland and Albert Einstein. There were others at the meeting who were later to emerge as genuine revolutionaries. Not the least was a certain quiet-looking Vietnamese named Nguyen-Ai-Quoc, better known as Ho Chi Minh.

On the eve of the conference Jawaharlal issued a statement awash with Marxist jargon. It was an attack, not unnaturally, on British imperialism and appealed to all subject peoples to cooperate in the world struggle against alien rule. This was followed by a passionate speech to the meeting which ended with his prophetic belief that as soon as India became independent the British empire would fall. There was a great deal of emotion and quite a lot of rhetoric but very little ideological understanding. In his report to the Indian National Congress, Nehru emphasized the new vistas that had opened before him. For the first time he became aware that India's problems were not completely unique. He had learnt about the problems of Latin America of which he had known nothing, about the Sanskrit influences in Indonesia which were a relic of India's cultural expansion. He commented on the revolutionary passion of the Chinese delegates, on the iniquity of the British using Indian troops against the Chinese and the support for China's national movement by British Labour. As for the League Against Imperialism it would be an invaluable vehicle for Congress propaganda.

Nehru's enthusiasms were received by most of the leaders and members of the Indian National Congress with the same indifference they were always to show to Nehru's socialist creed. They had no interest in his internationalism or his world-view. In one sense it did not really matter. Nehru now had a set of household gods to which he could make obeisance while acquiescing constantly to the anti-radical bias of Congress leaders. Nehru's attachment to radical ideas was to be used by Gandhi to defuse radical elements in Congress because he knew that Nehru's emotional attachment to the idea of Congress unity was greater than his emotional attachment to socialism. In time Nehru's radicalism was drained of any reality it may have had and became mainly a collection of fine-sounding words and irrelevant phrases.

But while Jawaharlal was still in Europe and away from the enervating influence of Congress and Gandhi, the excitement was genuine. He found the British Labour Party weak and was not impressed by the record of the Socialist International. Though he found communism as practised in Russia rather vulgar, he was attracted by the way this great underdeveloped country was coping with its economic and social problems. He was however worried at possible Soviet influence on the activities of the League Against Imperialism. In the end radical criticism from the League of the blatantly non-radical Congress policies and an attempt by the executive of the League to incite anti-Congress sentiments among the members of workers' and peasants' associations in India led to Nehru's expulsion from the League and the severing by Congress of relations with the League in April 1930.

In September 1927 Motilal Nehru arrived in Europe. In the same month that Jawaharlal had himself left India the Swarajist Party had walked out of the legislatures as many of its members had succumbed to the temptation to take office. The walk-out was in effect a triumph for Gandhi, for Motilal now pledged himself to support full non-cooperation. It did not however stop the rot. Another election was approaching and the communally minded Hindus in Congress and the Muslims outside it were preparing to arouse religious feelings. Under their influence rioting increased. Virulent attacks were made on Motilal for being anti-Hindu and he was even accused of once plotting to introduce legislation legalizing cow-slaughter. From this time onwards communal politics were to dominate the nationalist scene. Though the majority of its exponents were to be outside Congress they had the only inadequately disguised sympathy of many inside. The nationalist struggle was about to move out of its heroic age into one of tragedy.

Motilal's arrival coincided with Kamala's recovery and the Nehrus departed on a grand tour staying at the very best hotels on the strength of Motilal's substantial fees from a difficult court case concerning the legitimacy of an heir to an important estate. The tour did, however, include a trip to the Soviet Union. Motilal himself had not been enthusiastic but he gave in to Jawaharlal's insistence. The visit was very short, only four days, but it had a considerable effect upon Jawaharlal.

The Nehrus arrived in Moscow, after a tedious train journey from Berlin, to be welcomed as important visitors. At the station to meet them with the Russian reception committee was an Indian, Shapurji Saklatvala, a communist member of the British Parliament whom Jawaharlal had met at Brussels. The Nehrus had been invited to the celebrations of the tenth anniversary of the Bolshevik Revolution but arrived too late for the great parade through Red Square. They were however taken to see the shrines of communism. At Lenin's tomb Jawaharlal saw on the lips of the embalmed body of the Soviet leader, a smile and the 'suggestion of pugnacity, of work done and success achieved'.

He was particularly attracted by the fact that the Soviet Union was not a European country but a Eurasian one, and faces in the Moscow streets confirmed his opinion. Another appealing characteristic was the simplicity of the life of the Soviet leaders, such a contrast to that of the British proconsuls in India. Even the prisons seemed to be designed for rehabilitation rather than punishment. Though he had his doubts that *all* Soviet jails were like those he visited, he was still prepared to believe that life in a Soviet prison was preferable to life in an Indian factory.

The visit to the Soviet Union though short, left a lasting impression upon the younger Nehru. He was not uncritical of

Soviet communism and his criticism grew over the years. But he saw in the Soviet experience a genuine similarity with that of India. Emerging out of tsarist autocracy was a country with very much the same problems as those which faced India. The Soviet Union too was a land of peasants, backward looking, once caught in the grip not only of tradition but also of reactionary landlords. He recognized that India had nothing to fear from the Soviet Union even though the British in India looked upon the Bolshevik government with just as much apprehension as it had once looked upon that of the tsars. Nehru's visit added yet another black mark to his security file.

But the British need not have worried. Nehru did not become a revolutionary communist though for twenty years Marxism influenced his thought and vocabulary. Nehru's study of Marx and Lenin which was directly inspired by the visit to the Soviet Union produced, he wrote later, 'a powerful effect on my mind and helped me to see history and current affairs in a new light. The long chain of history and of social development appeared to have some meaning, some sequence and the future lost some of its obscurity.' Part of the attraction undoubtedly lay in Marxism's powerful anti-capitalist message. Nehru saw a counterpart to this in Indian civilization which, at its highest, despised money-making and the selfish accumulation of worldly possessions and separated money power from prestige.

Nehru's Marxism was never much more than a sentiment. It gave a sense of universality to the ideas he had absorbed from Vivekananda whose message influenced him more than that of Marx. It was not just Vivekananda's vision of Indian unity but of his ideal of selfless service as a means of redeeming the poverty-stricken Indian masses that had fascinated Nehru. Under the influence of Gandhi he had discovered the terrible world of the peasant and because of it he now rejected the Marxist thesis that revolution lay with the urban proletariat. This enabled him to accept the fact that the Indian National Congress was financed by indigenous capitalists because his radical activities were directed not against industrial capitalism but against landlords.

This experience however was still to come. The effects of

Nehru's visit to Europe needed the Indian context to make themselves known. He had been away from India for nearly two years and felt certain qualms about the fact. Kamala was well again. His own doubts and despairs had disappeared in the excitement of a new discovery of Europe. Leaving his father behind he sailed for India at the beginning of December 1927.

Chapter 9
Out of the Midnight Gloom

After the Swaraj Party had left the legislatures in November 1926, and observing the growth of communal tensions, Gandhi had declared that Congress was 'passing through midnight gloom'. At the end of 1927, when Jawaharlal arrived back in India, the darkness was still enveloping. Only a month before, the *Times of India* had commented on 'the completeness of the Congress collapse, the utter futility of the Congress creed, and the total absence among Congress supporters of a single responsible political idea'. Jawaharlal was determined to fill that gap.

Congress met in annual session at Madras at the end of December. Nehru put forward a number of resolutions reflecting his experiences in Europe. There were resolutions on independence for India, on the dangers of a world war and on many other subjects. To his surprise they were all agreed to with acclaim. Nehru suspected that they had been passed because they were not understood, and he was probably right. But the Mahatma did understand and was disapproving. 'Congress,' he wrote, 'stultifies itself by repeating year after year resolutions of this character when it knows that it is not capable of carrying them into effect.' This was not the way to win freedom but it could win contempt. In a letter to Nehru he warned him not to go too far and suggested that he had lost touch with Indian realities during his stay abroad. Much more realistic from the Mahatma's point of view was the resolution passed at the same time to boycott the Simon Commission.

The commission was the result of a clause in the Government of India Act of 1919 which provided for a review of the working of the reforms after ten years. The date for an inquiry had, however, been brought forward because it seemed to the Conservative Government then in power in Britain that the Labour Party might come into office in 1929 and at least one member of the Conservative cabinet believed that Labour meant what it said when it talked – as it had recently started to do – about India's right to self-government. The then Secretary of State for India, Lord Birkenhead, considered it a wise move to set up a commission of inquiry ahead of time. Significantly, Birkenhead had been the only member of the cabinet to oppose the reforms of 1919. As far as he was concerned, there would be no more concessions if he could help it. To ensure that the commission would see things his way, it was decided that it would consist only of members of the British Parliament. Even the Labour Party cooperated with him by choosing obscure back-benchers as their representatives. One of them was a certain Clement Attlee whose experiences were to have a direct effect on his decisions nearly twenty years later when he was himself Prime Minister. The chairman of the commission was to be Sir John Simon – a lawyer who had once been a liberal but who had relapsed into a pedantic and frigid conservatism which would find any radical solution totally repulsive.

The news that the commission would visit India was announced in November 1927. The all-British composition of the commission was welcomed by the British in India. To nationalist Indians it looked like the old recipe once again. No Indian could possibly be thought mature enough to contribute anything constructive to an inquiry into India's future. It seemed as if the British Government had learned nothing from the immediate past. Naturally the composition of the commission aroused resentment in India and did so throughout the whole spectrum of Indian opinion. Muhammad Ali Jinnah, who was still attempting to bring about some sort of alliance between Hindus and Muslims forcibly expressed his support for a boycott. 'Jallianwala Bagh was physical butchery,' he declared, 'the Simon Commission is the butchery of the soul.'

The appointment of the Simon Commission shook political India out of its torpor. But it also intensified the appeal of communalism. With the possibility of reforms the Muslims began to think once again of their own interests. Jinnah, still aloof from communal politics, had persuaded Muslims to accept the end of separate electorates and fight with other nationalists on a single ticket. But this was before the British Government's announcement that a commission of inquiry would arrive in India in February 1928. The communal-minded among the Muslim leaders who had agreed to Jinnah's suggestion in March 1927 revoked their agreement in November. It seemed that most nationalists would boycott the commission but would not be willing to cooperate with each other.

To Jawaharlal, however, fresh from Europe and irradiated with Marxist thought, communalism seemed to be a product of middle-class ambitions and thus utterly divorced from reality. The Muslim and Hindu masses, he was convinced, only gave in to communal appeals for economic reasons. Bankers and money-lenders were usually Hindus while Muslim peasants were always debtors. In these circumstances religious conflict was merely a disguise for economic grievance. Settle the grievance and the communal appeal would disappear. It was a dangerous view for it ignored other, more visceral motives. Nehru was discounting the appeal of religion on the grounds that it was irrelevant to the real issues.

Nehru was now clamouring for action. Boycott the Simon Commission certainly but it was time for more than that. Gandhi disagreed but astutely suggested that Nehru should outline his differences in a correspondence which Gandhi would then publish in his weekly newspaper *Young India*. It is an index of Nehru's surrender to the Mahatma that he did not accept the challenge. But the surrender was neither absolute nor silent. Nehru recognized the pull of the leash but Gandhi ensured that it would always be a long one allowing Nehru a wide area of activity. This relative freedom was used to the maximum. Nehru was still a General Secretary and as such in great demand as a speaker. He was elected president of the All-India Trade Union Congress though he felt it not altogether seemly for one who was not a worker. But it gave him a platform and he talked – of socialism and the necessity of complete independence for India.

Nehru's speeches at this time had all the overtones of revolutionary fervour, much of which went clear over the heads of his audience. But he still denounced violence – a contradiction indeed but the tribute he always paid both to his own dislike of violence and to the paramountcy of Gandhi. He stressed the point that socialism could never be achieved without national unity and only after national independence. Violence would only destroy national unity and was therefore counter-revolutionary. When coldly analysed, it appeared as a confused doctrine and there were many activists who found it so. But it was Nehru's rhetoric, his view of the Indian struggle as part of a world struggle, that impressed Indian youth. He seemed to give to the Congress movement a modernist appeal. With him the essentially obscurantist Gandhian approach acquired a progressive gloss. The socialism Nehru preached, though linked to a wider world, was firmly rooted in the ideals of Indian life, and cultural integrity need not be sacrificed to alien doctrine.

As Nehru travelled throughout India he was convinced that he was witnessing a new awakening. The dawn was imminent and the dark night soon to end. Again it was agrarian discontent that was to shatter the passivity of Indian political life. The place was obscure but the issue of universal appeal. Bardoli is a small district in Gujarat, then a part of the province of Bombay. A revision of the land tax brought an increase of 22 per cent over the previous assessment. The small peasant proprietors of the district in their dismay appealed to Vallabhbhai Patel, who after his first introduction to nationalist politics had stayed in the area and had previously organized a no-tax campaign in 1922 only to abandon it after Gandhi had called off the non-cooperation campaign.

Bardoli, however, was prepared to take action and so was Patel. With Gandhi's approval and support he organized a small-scale satyagraha after the Government had refused to accept a reasoned and well-documented case against the enhanced assessments. The Government's response to the refusal to pay tax was wholesale arrests and the confiscation of property. But still the peasants would not yield and the story of their resistance, heightened with heroic overtones, flashed around India. The campaign lasted for six months and ended in victory for the peasants. It had been entirely non-violent at least on the part of the protestors. The assessment was reduced to an increase of only seven per cent. It was at Bardoli that Patel received the title of Sardar (leader). His name became known throughout India and a new figure emerged into national leadership.

When the Simon Commission arrived in India it was greeted, surprisingly, with only half-hearted demonstrations and if the personality of its chairman had been warmer it is possible that the commission might have got through its task without serious opposition. But it was not in Simon's nature to display friendliness. He was even convinced that the Government of India was against him because it did not prevent the few protests that did take place. Very soon, however, the situation was to change. When the commission visited Bombay a time-bomb was set off in a train and the police became more active against demonstrators.

Meanwhile, at an All-Party Conference held in May 1928, it was agreed that the nationalists should prepare their own constitution for India. As a consequence a committee was set up under Motilal Nehru, who had recently returned from Europe. The 'Nehru Report', as it almost inevitably came to be called, was published in August. It was an extremely able document and for its recommendations it drew on a wide variety of sources including the American Constitution. Two of its suggestions turned out to be highly controversial. One recommended the ending of communal electorates with no official reservation of seats in the legislatures for minorities. The second demanded that India be immediately made a self-governing Dominion. Both were concessions, the first brought about by pressure from the Hindu communalists who resented separate electorates, the latter was a sop to the moderate nationalists who felt that India was not yet ready for total independence.

Jawaharlal's reaction to this retrograde step was angry and vocal. In fact there was very little about the report that appealed to him. There was one clause that particularly offended his socialist conscience. It contained a recommendation that the rights of the great semi-feudal landowners of Oudh should be guaranteed. But this was only a minor issue compared with the substitution of Dominion status for independence. At another meeting of the All-Party Conference held in Lucknow in August, Jawaharlal spoke strongly against it. He wanted, he said, to have nothing at all to do with an Empire that only exploited its subjects. But he was in a minority. Soon after the conference a number of dissidents, headed by Jawaharlal and a young Bengali of about the same age, Subhas Chandra Bose, who had been appointed a General Secretary of Congress while Jawaharlal was in Europe in 1927, announced the formation of an Independence for India League. The League was open only to members of Congress and its sole purpose was to exert pressure against anything less than full independence.

The agitation of the League was not successful. It concentrated upon an issue which seemed to the majority of Congressmen comparatively unimportant. Nevertheless, there was every possibility of a genuine split between the old guard and the young over the question of independence. Both Jawaharlal and Bose worked hard to enthuse real life into the League but the only people who were really impressed by their activities were the British. Motilal Nehru, however, convinced as always that the constitutional approach should always be tried, was anxious about what would happen at the annual session of Congress at the end of 1928.

The elder Nehru was now president-elect of Congress. When the question of who should preside at what was obviously going to be a meeting of particular importance had come up, Motilal had suggested Vallabhbhai Patel, then at the height of his reputation after the Bardoli affair. Failing Patel, he suggested Jawaharlal. Gandhi did not want the younger Nehru. He had strayed too far away in a direction the Mahatma disapproved of. With Motilal as president Gandhi would be publicly endorsing the Nehru Report while at the same time making it difficult for Jawaharlal openly to attack his own father. This manoeuvre was a miscalculation, one of the very few made by the Mahatma in his relations with the younger

Nehru. Both Bose and Jawaharlal were determined to press their opinions.

At the meeting of the All-India Congress Committee early in December a resolution was passed which gave the impression of a compromise. The Madras resolution on complete independence was endorsed but the sections of the Nehru Report dealing with communal problems, the essential issues in fact, were hailed as a great step forward. This was not a compromise acceptable either to Motilal or Gandhi. They had seven weeks in which to persuade that all-powerful body, the Working Committee. At a meeting of the Committee Gandhi suggested that the whole of the Nehru Report including the Dominion status recommendation should become official Congress policy if the British Parliament would accept the Report as a constitution for India before the end of 1930. Should Parliament refuse he proposed another civil disobedience campaign.

Jawaharlal spoke out strongly against the suggestion and was directly critical, though in mild terms, of both his father and Gandhi. Instead of the Mahatma's resolution he put forward another – if a demand for independence was not conceded by the end of 1929 then a civil disobedience campaign should be started. There seemed no chance of compromise and the meeting broke up without a decision being taken. It was now up to Gandhi to exercise his influence on the younger Nehru. The Mahatma knew what the approach should be – the threat to nationalist unity and, by implication, the certainty that if Jawaharlal pressed his point to a split he would find himself in the wilderness outside the mainstream of the struggle for freedom. It was an irresistible appeal to both sentiment and vanity.

The compromise when it emerged was the reduction of the time limit for British acceptance of the Nehru Report to one year. In essence it was a total capitulation by the opposition and the younger Nehru was only too aware of it. He stayed away from the next meeting and suffered the humiliation of having the Mahatma explain his absence as the result of being 'a high-souled man'. With such a spectacular desertion, the opposition was emasculated. Subhas Bose also left the meeting but announced that he would not vote against the resolution when it came up at the open session of Congress. Bose however changed his mind and when the Mahatma personally moved the resolution he spoke against it, putting forward an amendment rejecting Dominion status. Shamed perhaps, Jawaharlal supported Bose. It was, however, essentially a pull against the leash and not a desire to break its hold. The younger Nehru was never to escape from his weakness, the need for someone – or something – to take the agony of major decision from him.

This time it was Gandhi. Once again, the Mahatma pulled out every stop in his vast repertoire of blackmail. In private conversations he had made it quite clear that he would once again withdraw from active political life if his way was not sanctified by approval. In the session he attacked his critics for deserting him! He impugned their honour. Had they not accepted a compromise in private and now chose to reject it in public? Was Congress to be shown up as a body that could not stick to its resolutions for even a day? Such immaturity was in itself a proof that India was not ready for independence. Bose's amendment was rejected but against considerable opposition for the vote was only 1,350 to 973, though many of those who voted against Gandhi did so for communal reasons.

Indeed communalism, after a period of quietude, was on the march again. Though the Nehru Report had come out in favour of joint electorates there had been a communal compromise. There would be no *official* minority representation but instead an unofficial division of seats amongst the minorities. The Report had also called for the redistribution of provincial boundaries which would satisfy linguistic as well as religious demands. The predominantly Muslim area of Sind should be separated from the province of Bombay and reforms were advocated for the North West Frontier Province. In the interests of a united front against the Simon Commission these proposals had been accepted by all but the then unimportant Muslim League. Unfortunately, by the end of 1928 dissatisfaction had grown up. At an All-Party Conference held almost simultaneously with the Congress session at Calcutta, the Muslims outside the League had gone back on the agreement.

Jinnah had put forward the claim that Muslims must be guaranteed one third of the seats in the central parliament. The claim had been rejected by the Hindu communalists and ignored by those, like Jawaharlal Nehru, who maintained that communalist fears were unfounded. Jinnah had left the Calcutta meeting broken hearted. With tears in his eyes he had said to a friend: 'This is the parting of the ways.'

The departure of Jinnah into a silence which was to last until 1934 was not the only significant by-product of the meetings in Calcutta at the end of 1928. Subhas Bose, a genuine and dedicated radical, had learned that Jawaharlal Nehru could not be trusted. 'We in Bengal,' he said to an Indian journalist, 'represent the real revolutionary force. Jawahar only talks. We act!' Soon these two men were to become rivals not only for the allegiance of Indian youth but also for positions of power within the Congress movement.

While the intrigues and counter-intrigues inside Congress had been acquiring momentum the world outside had been bubbling with activity – some of it bloody. The Simon Commission when it arrived at Lahore had been met by the usual demonstrators among whom was the veteran nationalist – and Hindu communal leader – Lala Lajpat Rai. For some reason – or none – he had been beaten across the chest with a baton by a British police officer. Rai was already suffering from heart disease and some weeks later he died. Naturally, his death was attributed to the beating, for which there was no justification as the demonstration had been entirely peaceful. Not long afterwards Jawaharlal himself was to feel the batons of the police on his body.

When the Commission visited Lucknow, Jawaharlal led a procession to a protest meeting. On the way the party was attacked by a patrol of mounted police. As the horses bore down upon them the procession scattered leaving Nehru alone in the middle of the road. A policeman gave him two heavy blows with a *lathi*, a long and very hard bamboo stick. Nehru found the experience more exhilarating than painful. Next day he was to have a more serious encounter with authority. Troops had been called out and when the crowd began to press forward they were charged. Nehru, once again among them, had felt a terrible desire to hit back but restrained himself with the thought that once violence started the troops would probably fire.

Violence, however, was once again in the air. Terrorism, now the only formal rejection of Gandhi's leadership, reappeared. In Lahore a police officer, believed to be the one who had struck Lajpat Rai, was murdered. In April 1929 two bombs were thrown in the Legislative Assembly in Delhi. No one was hurt but the two men responsible were hailed as heroes. A wave of terrorism broke out in Bengal, that epicentre of extremism and the Government took to itself wide-ranging powers of arrest and imprisonment. There were strikes, not always peaceful, in the Bengal jute mills and in Calcutta the scavengers stopped work. In Bombay one hundred thousand workers walked out and brought the cotton industry of that great city to a standstill. The Government responded by arresting the labour leaders and charging them with conspiracy and sedition. The trial, which was an attempt to crush a nonexistent communist menace, went on for four and a half years and was conspicuous for its perversion of the law of British India, let alone of natural justice. Nehru as president of the All-India Trade Union Congress organized a defence committee and drummed up interest from outside India, though even with his father's help he found it difficult to find both funds and lawyers willing to take up the defendants' case.

While the Government's executive arm was suppressing in one way or another the most militant opposition, the Viceroy attempted to neutralize the more moderate elements headed by Gandhi. The Viceroy, Lord Irwin, was a deeply religious man who reacted emotionally to what he believed to be the essentially moral content of Gandhi's ideas. He was, he said, prepared to meet Gandhi – critics called it 'taking tea with treason' – and discussions did take place. Gandhi seemed to think that Irwin's piety overruled his political sense and his loyalties, which were those of any other member of the British ruling class. Irwin was not in fact a free agent. The ultimate power of decision rested with the British Government in London. Nevertheless Irwin's gesture – unprecedented in the history of British India – was taken by Gandhi to be not only an indication of his own stature but of British weakness.

Irwin, however, was by no means a fool. Whatever the more blinkered of the British community in India might say, any evolutionary approach to constitutional change in India depended upon Gandhi, the apostle of non-violence. In what seemed to be a revolutionary situation it was only sensible tactics to encourage one who hated revolution and could carry the masses with him. It was necessary, Irwin thought, to strengthen Gandhi's hand. The Viceroy's first step was to make a public statement of the sort that no Viceroy had ever made before. He had, he said, a double duty to perform: to carry on the king-emperor's Government and to serve as an intermediary between India and Britain. Privately Irwin suggested to London that a declaration should be made immediately that Dominion status for India was also the goal of the British Government. This was too much for Lord Birkenhead, the Secretary of State.

Changes however were in the air. The Conservative fears that a Labour success at the polls was imminent were proved correct. In the summer of 1929, the second Labour Government in Britain's history took office. The Prime Minister was Ramsay MacDonald, who a few months before taking office had declared: 'I hope that within a period of months rather than years there will be a new Dominion added to the Commonwealth of Nations, a Dominion which will find self-respect as an equal within the Commonwealth. I refer to India.' Gandhi, responding to the call of the immediate present, had welcomed the statement. Others, including Jawaharlal, had been sceptical. In August 1928 he had referred to 'the sanctimonious and canting humbugs who lead the [British] Labour Party' and saw no reason now to change his mind. For a while it seemed that Nehru was wrong. In October 1929 Irwin made a rather vaguely worded statement which confirmed that the goal was indeed Dominion status. Gandhi praised Irwin's sincerity and joined a conference of leaders from all parties called by the Viceroy at the end of December. The morning it met, a bomb destroyed part of the viceregal train. The Viceroy was unhurt.

The terrorists showed a greater awareness of reality. When Gandhi insisted that Congress had only agreed to join in the conference on the understanding that another conference would be called in London to frame a Dominion constitution for India, Irwin told him that he was not empowered to make such a promise. The Congress delegates left Delhi realizing at last that the British Labour Party was just like any other political party. Promises made in opposition had a habit of losing substance when office was achieved. The Viceroy did, however, invite Congress leaders and others to attend a Round Table Conference in London in the following year.

Much now depended on the attitude of Congress. The 1929 session was to take place at Lahore in the Punjab. Its president was to be – Jawaharlal Nehru. This almost dynastic succession had been engineered by Gandhi essentially to neutralize the young and the leftist inclined. In preparing for the election of a president for what was believed to be the crucial year of 1930 most provincial Congress organizations had turned to the Mahatma for guidance. Out of eighteen of these organizations, ten had nominated Gandhi, five Patel and three Jawaharlal. Despite heavy pressure Gandhi refused to be nominated; he did not want office, only power. To many members' surprise he threw his support behind Nehru and was quite open about his reasons for doing so. Nehru, he said in a public statement, represented the youth of the movement (Nehru was then thirty-nine) and would rally the radicals to the cause. Responsibility, he maintained, 'will mellow and sober youth'. To those inside Congress who disagreed with Nehru, Gandhi gave his assurance that it would be like having himself in the chair – a revealing statement if ever there was one. In any case the president of Congress could not do what he liked, he was only a constitutional monarch.

Nehru was not altogether pleased by Gandhi's steam-roller methods of getting what he wanted. That he could not be elected on merit and without the rather obvious interference of the Mahatma wounded his sense of pride. In his autobiography,

Nehru claimed that he almost felt 'like handing back the honour'. But he did not. Gandhi knew him better than he did himself. 'A soothing letter from Gandhiji and three days of reflection calmed me.'

Congress met in an atmosphere of tension. Terrorists were still active and the whole country was uneasy. The Government was anticipating trouble and preparing for it. Congress too was not united and the session seemed headed for dissension. Nehru had only with some reluctance accepted Gandhi's conditions for attending a conference in London. In doing so he had once again forfeited the support of radical elements. Fortunately the attitude of Conservative spokesmen in the British Parliament and the absence of any reassuring statement from the Labour Government had come to his aid. At an All-Party Conference held in Allahabad on 16 November 1929 Nehru had attacked nationalist leaders for being taken in by the Viceroy. When Irwin was unable to give Gandhi an assurance that Dominion status would indeed be a product of the coming conference, Nehru and the radicals felt they would be able to push their views through Congress.

Over thirty thousand delegates had gathered in a great tented camp on the banks of the River Ravi at Lahore. The new president riding a white horse headed a long procession which included a herd of elephants. The handing over of office from father to son had all the appearance of an apostolic succession, one who was present alleged later. It was certainly the end of an era, for just over a year later Motilal died. As he stepped aside, with him seemed to go the constitutionalist approach, though in fact in a few years time Congress was to take political office under new reforms. To many at Lahore, however, it seemed that all Motilal had stood for was to be abandoned.

A substantial number of delegates, realizing that the issue was whether Congress would go to war with the British raj or not, still advocated caution. Gandhi however was now committed to independence and to the resolution of the Calcutta session that after a year without response to the demand for Dominion status, Congress must mount a civil disobedience campaign. Jawaharlal left the going to Gandhi and the radical voice was that of Subhas Bose. The Mahatma proposed a resolution congratulating the Viceroy on his escape from death when his train was bombed. It was passed by a very narrow margin, thanks to Bose who was in no mood for empty politenesses. Gandhi then put forward the major resolution. Congress would not attend the Round Table Conference in London. *Swaraj* was the only goal and *swaraj* meant complete independence. The first step was to be a boycott of the legislatures and the All-India Congress Committee was to be given the power to start a programme of civil disobedience whenever it thought the time was ripe.

The cautious pressed for delay. Bose called for a complete break and the setting up by Congress of parallel administrative and legislative institutions. 'I am an extremist,' he shouted, 'and my principle is – all or none.' It was a direct challenge both to Gandhi and to Nehru. Nehru was silent throughout this debate and his presidential address had made it quite clear to Bose that Nehru would not support the radicals. It was in fact a radical speech, full of sound socialist views expressed in the rambling way which was to become Nehru's particular style. There was talk of social and economic change, of the predatory nature of Indian capitalism. He disagreed with the Mahatma on the absolute value of non-violence – 'violence is bad but slavery is worse'. But, Nehru assured his listeners, if they were capitalists they had nothing to fear from him at least as long as the struggle for freedom went on. Independence first, socialism afterwards, was the message. For Bose the speech confirmed his opinion that Nehru was all talk.

Bose, however, was in a minority. Nehru's speech was to inspire many a young man who associated the words with the campaign that was to follow so that in retrospect they seemed to be a call to valour. In reality, Nehru was as ever a captive of the Mahatma. The Congress meeting though not supporting Bose was not completely on the side of the Mahatma. Gandhi had to exert every bit of influence and prestige to get his resolution passed. As almost a last resort he claimed that his policy had the confirmation of mysterious powers. 'I have but followed the Inner Voices,' he proclaimed, and in the end there were not enough who dared question whether he had heard them aright.

The decision taken, no one seemed quite sure what to do. Again Congress displayed its utter dependence upon Gandhi. On 1 January 1930, as if to underline the fact, the AICC met to elect a Working Committee in whose hands the campaign would lie. Gandhi put forward ten names and when there were suggestions for others, Nehru, as president, ruled them out of order claiming that it would be wrong to elect men to the Working Committee who had voted against Gandhi's resolution. The following day Gandhi's hand-picked committee decided that 26 January would be celebrated as Independence Day when the Congress tricolour would be raised at mass meetings and an Independence pledge recited.

Before the day arrived Congress legislators had with admirable discipline resigned their seats in the various Assemblies leaving them to the Liberals, the Hindu communalists and the Muslims. It also meant leaving the forthcoming Round Table Conference to them too. The meetings on 26 January showed that the rank and file were firmly behind the Mahatma. At gatherings throughout the country thousands repeated the pledge: 'We believe it is the inalienable right of the Indian people, as of any other people, to have freedom and enjoy the fruits of their toil. . . . We believe also that if any Government deprives a people of these rights and oppresses them, the people have a further right to alter it or to abolish it. . . .'

The raising of the Congress flag and the solemn words of the pledge aroused little enthusiasm outside Congress. Even the Government did not seem to be particularly impressed. Soon after the celebration of Independence Day Gandhi formulated eleven points which if they were granted, he said, would allow him to call off the civil disobedience campaign. Nehru found it almost incredible that they did not include any mention of independence. But the eleven points were actually a series of offers designed to win the sympathy of every social group in India – except of course the British and even they were offered a sop in the very absence of a call for independence.

There was a demand for total prohibition – a direct appeal

to the old-fashioned and the orthodox. The suggestions for an amnesty for political prisoners and for the abolition of the security police were directed towards politicians of all persuasions. For the commercial classes there were demands for a reduction in the exchange rate between sterling and the rupee, that coastal shipping be reserved for Indian-owned vessels, and for the imposition of a protective tariff on foreign cloth. The points calling for the reduction of military expenditure by a half and for a cut in the salaries of British civil servants were directed at the professional middle class. Calculated to win over the peasants were demands for a reduction in land revenue and the abolition of the tax on salt.

Unfortunately none of Gandhi's points seemed resonant with a call to action. Without some rousing issue the civil disobedience campaign was unlikely to attract the support of the masses. Economically the country was reasonably stable, the harvests had been good. The Government did not seem willing to oblige Gandhi with some spectacular act of oppression. At the end of February the answer came to him – he would break the salt laws. Salt was a Government monopoly and half its selling price was a Government tax. It was not a particularly onerous one, so little so that there was no attempt at illicit manufacture and consumption was rising every year. Gandhi realized that it was the *form* the tax took not the burden which gave it an impact on the majority of Indians. No one can go without salt, especially in a tropical country. Furthermore nothing would be easier to break than the monopoly. Salt could be picked out of the earth or distilled from sea water. It would be as if Gandhi had rallied to his side the forces of nature.

Despite the initial incredulity of Jawaharlal Nehru and others, Gandhi, whose skill in dramatizing issues for the masses was unsurpassed, wrote a letter to the Viceroy – addressing him as 'Dear Friend' – on 2 March. In it he informed Irwin that if his eleven points were not accepted by the Government he intended to take action against the salt monopoly. Irwin was not impressed and in reply merely expressed his regret that Gandhi thought it necessary to violate the law.

On 12 March Gandhi and seventy-nine chosen followers set out from his spiritual retreat near Ahmadabad to walk a distance of some 240 miles to the Arabian Sea and there solemnly make salt.

As the Mahatma made his slow and deliberately circuitous march to the sea he expected to be arrested. But the Government had no intention of cooperating with him. When he actually broke the law, then would be the time to take action. Even then only Gandhi's lieutenants were to be arrested. Vallabhbhai Patel, known to the authorities as the organizer not only of the march to the sea but of Congress itself, was quietly arrested before Gandhi set off, perhaps in the hope of disrupting the campaign. Other leaders were left alone. Finally, Gandhi reached the sea on 5 April and after prayers picked up salt lying on the shore. This act received great publicity abroad, especially in America where it took on some of the overtones of the Boston Tea Party. In India the message was taken up by Congress workers all over the country and at great public meetings attended, Congress claimed, by more than five million people, salt was ceremoniously made. The Government took no overt action and the demonstrations were almost all completely peaceful.

Jawaharlal who had been active in the organization of the campaign in Allahabad was himself arrested on 14 April and given a sentence of six months for breaking the salt law. Gandhi, however, remained free, even though the Government called his behaviour an act of rebellion. No attempt was made to restrict Gandhi's activities or threaten his control of Congress after the principal leaders had been arrested. He was not prevented from using the mails and the telegraph service. There is little doubt that the Government once again sought to protect Gandhi's authority over the civil disobedience movement by eliminating those like Nehru whom it thought might choose to give the movement a more revolutionary character.

This policy was partly successful. Gandhi's campaign, with its immense symbolic appeal to the masses, had for a time inhibited other action. The Government ordered that no provocation of any sort was to be given. The military were not to be used to disperse crowds. There must be no more Amritsars. The police too were to use minimum force. Congress would, of course, claim 'police brutality' – and did – but there were to be no bodies in the streets crying out for vengeance.

Unfortunately, there were men upon whom the techniques of Gandhi had no effect other than an extra incitement to militant action. These men were preparing to strike a blow. In Bengal with its hallowed tradition of revolutionary violence, an armoury was attacked and eight men were killed trying to defend it. This time the Government replied with vigour and a number of demonstrators were killed by police fire. There were disturbances too in Bombay province where local Congress leaders took over the town of Sholapur only to be ejected by the military with some dead.

The most disturbing outbreak of all took place in the North West Frontier Province after the arrest of Abdul Ghaffar Khan, later to be known as the 'Frontier Gandhi'. The city of Peshawar exploded into violence and troops had to be called in. Naturally there were heavy casualties on both sides. But worse still in its implication was the refusal of two platoons of the Indian army to go to Peshawar and shoot their Muslim brethren. The ugly spectre of another mutiny in the army like that of 1857 began to rise again. By 24 April conditions in the city were such that the British had lost control and it was not until twelve days later with the arrival of British troops and aircraft that the city was reoccupied.

The Government finally decided that the time had come to arrest the Mahatma. His campaign had in spite of everything degenerated into violence but it was only the violence of the dedicated revolutionary and not of the masses. The peasants who were both the backbone and the object of the civil dis- obedience movement were mainly busy in the fields reaping the spring harvest. Early in the morning of 5 May Gandhi was discreetly taken into custody. When news of his arrest became known there were demonstrations – serious ones in Delhi and Calcutta – and the remaining Congress leaders called for an intensification of civil disobedience. The Government, freed from the necessity of moderation now that Gandhi was in jail,

replied with an instant and heavy hand – five years' imprisonment for failing to give information to the police, seven years
and a large fine for carrying a Congress flag.

For a while the Government's attention was concentrated
on the troubles in the North West Frontier Province and the
responsibility for suppressing Congress activity was left to the
provincial administrations. The frontier areas, always tense and
regularly tattered by tribal risings, had been further inflamed
by the troubles in Peshawar. For a time it looked as if a new
frontier war was about to break out. While the army and the
air force tried to take care of the tribesmen the Government
decided to make some concessions to the people of the province
in case they decided to join their Muslim co-religionists and
attack the British. Local self-government was offered – the
province had been excluded from the 1919 reforms for security
reasons – and an intensive propaganda campaign was begun to
discredit Congress by labelling it a purely Hindu body. The
Government chose to believe, though there was never any proof,
that Congress had incited the tribesmen to rise and had paid
them large sums of money. This belief and the discovery that
the arrest of leaders did not prevent Congress from functioning
led to a Government order declaring the All-India Congress
Committee an illegal organization. Its chairman, Motilal
Nehru, was sent to join his son in Naini Central Jail.

The arrests did not, of course, halt the violence. They merely
cleared the way for it. But terrorism is something all Governments understand. There is only one course of action to take
and as the level of violence was not outrageously high, it could
be controlled and suppressed. There was a continuing boycott
of foreign goods; Indian businessmen, who knew that with it
they were on to a good thing, saw to that. There was nothing
very much the Government could do about it. In any case the
only people who were getting hurt were the cotton workers of
Lancashire and the makers of cigarettes. However the Government could try to get a little of the lost revenue back. In
Bombay the administration sequestered Congress property.
Other provinces followed suit. The British were now so sure
that they had broken the back of Congress opposition that

they began a recruiting drive for the police – and there were plenty of applicants. With the velvet glove finally off, collective fines were imposed and young offenders whipped.

Congress had certainly emerged out of midnight gloom but only into a twilight more deadly than the dark.

Chapter 10
'Not with a bang but a whimper'

In jail Jawaharlal spent his time reading, spinning and weaving. He was treated with some deference by the prison administration. He had plenty of books and writing material, and food could be sent in to him. As there were very few political prisoners he found himself alone. Though restricted, it was a comfortable life and he began to feel that he had no right to be comfortable while others were suffering outside. To his surprise, his wife Kamala, though unwell, had thrown herself into the civil disobedience campaign and in Allahabad had virtually taken over leadership from her husband. And she was not alone. The campaign had brought into the streets an unprecedented number of women – in India traditionally withdrawn from events. Nehru felt all the more frustrated.

With the arrival of his father, Jawaharlal found pleasure in trying to make the older man's life as easy as possible. Now seventy, Motilal was unwell and the conditions in the jail led to a rapid deterioration in his health. But before this became so serious that the British decided to release the elder Nehru, they were to be both involved in an event which could only have happened in British India. No other imperialist tyranny would have allowed its principal political prisoners to confer together and even put a special train at their disposal so that they could do so. At least it can be said of the British government of India that it was an authoritarian government disguised by good manners.

The meeting – between Gandhi and the two Nehrus – came about because the British Government in London was determined that the Round Table Conference it had gone to so much trouble to stage-manage should not be without its principal actors. The Government had already made a series of gestures. When the Simon Report had been published in June 1930 it had been received in silence. The Labour Government announced that Sir John Simon would not be attending the conference and did not even bother to consult those Labour M.P.s who had been on the commission. It was a gesture of repudiation that was not lost upon certain elements in the nationalist movement. Gandhi, in an interview with a British journalist who somehow got past the jailors, indicated that there was still a possibility of agreement if only there was a guarantee that the conference would be empowered to frame a constitution which gave the *substance* of independence. This seemed a distinct retreat from *total* independence. Then just before his arrest, Motilal, the eternal constitutionalist, had elaborated this offer. Negotiations he said were possible if the Government of India was prepared to give a *private* assurance that it would support a demand for full responsible government. Motilal was later to regret what he had said, claiming that he had done so without adequate thought, but it was enough to inspire two liberal nationalists, Tej Bahadur Sapru and M.R. Jayakar, to approach the Viceroy with a suggestion that they should act as mediators between the Government and the jailed Congress leaders. To this suggestion Irwin gave his blessing in words that appeared to be a paraphrase of Motilal's own.

Sapru and Jayakar made their way to Yeravda prison near Poona to consult with the Mahatma. There he stated his terms. He was prepared to call off civil disobedience if in return the Government would release political prisoners other than those convicted of crimes of violence, return sequestrated property, refund fines and not enforce the salt laws. Apart from these special conditions he still stuck to his original eleven points. The mediators, however, sensed a willingness to compromise though Gandhi insisted that he thought the time was not ripe for negotiations and in any case he could not act on his own initiative. As Congress President, 'Jawaharlal's must be the final voice.'

The mediators, carrying a letter from Gandhi, arrived at Naini jail to discuss the matter with the Nehrus on 27 July. For two days there were arguments and discussions. But just as Gandhi was apparently unwilling to commit himself without the Nehrus, they were certainly not prepared to make any

decision without consulting Gandhi. When the mediators conveyed this to the Viceroy he startled the prisoners by agreeing.
A special train was laid on to take the two Nehrus from Allahabad to Kirkee near Poona where they would meet with Gandhi.
Their meeting which was later to include Vallabhbhai Patel
and other Congress leaders must be one of the most extra-
ordinary political conferences on record. What was in effect
the Congress cabinet met in secret session inside a jail with the
full cooperation of the Government it was openly conspiring
to destroy. The conference lasted three days and roused
Winston Churchill, one of the leaders of the diehards in the
British Parliament, to declare with some claim to truth: 'The
Government of India has imprisoned Gandhi and they have
been sitting outside his cell door begging him to help them out
of their difficulties.' Gandhi indeed might have been willing
to do so. The Nehrus and the others were not. So they were
shuttled back in their special train to Naini jail.

Soon after these talks, the Government decided to release
Motilal on the grounds of ill health. The old man did not want
to go but it was obvious that he was very sick and the Government had no intention of letting him die in jail. Just over a
month later, early in October, Jawaharlal having completed
his sentence was also free once again. But not for long. The
Government had convinced itself that he was a really dangerous
irreconcilable whom it would be wise to keep out of harm's
way. No doubt he would soon supply them with an excuse.
This turned out to be true. Almost immediately after his
release, Jawaharlal was calling once again for defiance of the
salt laws and, more significantly, for a no-tax campaign.

Before he could be rearrested Jawaharlal joined his father in
the hill-station of Musoorie. Also there were Kamala and her
daughter as well as the three daughters of her sister-in-law
Vijaya Lakshmi. It was a pleasant break and Motilal seemed
very much improved. After three days Jawaharlal returned to
Allahabad to attend a conference he had called to organize the
no-tax campaign. On his arrival Jawaharlal was served with an
order forbidding him to address public meetings. Naturally he
had no intention of obeying the order. On the evening of

19 October while returning from a meeting the car in which he was travelling was stopped and he was taken into custody.

At this trial the conviction was a foregone conclusion. This time the sentence was to be longer – two years and four extra months for refusal to pay a fine. Jawaharlal's conviction was just what was needed to help revive the civil disobedience campaign, somewhat flagging for want of an inspiring issue. Motilal, though now gravely ill, rose from his sick bed and called for countrywide demonstrations at which passages from his son's last speech would be read out in the hope that the authorities would consider this too an act of sedition. The response was tremendous and at meetings which were held on Jawaharlal's birthday, about five thousand people were arrested. 'A unique birthday celebration' was his comment. It was not long before Kamala was also to receive that essential graduation prize of the successful nationalist, a prison sentence.

In the same month of November 1930 in the more august surroundings of St James's Palace, London, the first Round Table Conference had begun. The Indian delegates had been carefully selected and represented all the special interest groups from the princes onwards – except the major expression of nationalism, Congress. Oddly enough the conference was not merely a collection of yes-men. All the delegates made it perfectly clear that they wanted responsible government for India. Even those who might have been thought allies of the British were in agreement. This unanimity, which was not particularly welcome to the British Government, had been brought about by the influence of Sapru, who managed to convince the delegates where their best interests lay. It was perhaps the last triumph of the Moderates but the results were of great consequence not only to Congress but to independent India. The reforms that finally emerged were later to become the foundation of the constitution of the Indian republic.

This, however, was far in the future. Immediately it was obvious that Congress could not be excluded from the next session of the conference. The British Government seemed to have made considerable concessions to what was in effect the Congress standpoint. It was prepared to concede full provincial autonomy and the gradual introduction of responsible government at the centre. An attempt had been made at settling the problem of communal representation – joint electorates but the reservation of seats in the Assemblies – though this was soon sabotaged by communal politicians and their friends in the British Conservative Party. Nevertheless it appeared to Irwin – and the British Government – that there were some grounds for making a new appeal to Gandhi.

The appeal when it came was specially keyed to attract the Mahatma. He had called for a 'change of heart' on the part of the British. He was given an indication that such a change had taken place, that hate was to be put aside. The understatement in the Viceroy's words almost screamed a spirit of compromise. Irwin invited Gandhi to put 'the seal of friendship once again upon the relations of the two peoples, *whom unhappy circumstances have latterly estranged*'. As a gesture of goodwill Gandhi and the Congress leaders were released on 25 January 1931. To many of the British both in India and in Britain this seemed an act of treason for it implied that sedition had become respectable. Yet it was a sensible move designed primarily to reinstate Gandhi as the impresario of the nationalist movement.

The releases were welcomed by Congress and by Gandhi who declared: 'I am hungering for peace, if it can be had with honour.' Jawaharlal was not convinced either of the wisdom of Gandhi's acceptance or of the good faith of the British. But there were other things to occupy his mind. Motilal was obviously dying. He was confined to bed in the new and smaller house he had had built when he changed his way of life to that of comparative austerity. The old house had been given to Congress as a headquarters and renamed *Swaraj Bhawan*. Now, as Motilal lay dying, the Congress leaders were gathered there to decide on their next move. Motilal was well aware of his condition. 'Mahatmaji,' he said to Gandhi, 'I am going soon. I shall not be here to see *swaraj*. But I know that you have won it and will soon have it.'

On 4 February Motilal's condition seemed to be improved and he was moved to Lucknow for further treatment, but two days later the end came so quietly that Jawaharlal who was watching by the bedside thought his father was asleep. Motilal's body wrapped in the Congress tricolour was taken to Allahabad by road with Jawaharlal, Ranjit Pandit and Motilal's old servant, Hari, accompanying the body. Great crowds thronged the route. After lying in state at Swaraj Bhawan, the body was taken to the cremation ground by the banks of the Ganges and burnt. It was evening. Gandhi said a few words to the crowd and then everyone went home. 'The stars,' Jawaharlal recalled later, 'were out and shining brightly when we returned lonely and desolate.'

His father's death, though expected, affected Nehru deeply. For all their differences, some acrimonious, all fundamental, Motilal's dominant personality had never lost its pull. In fact until his father's death, Nehru had been frequently torn between the two dynamic figures of Motilal and Gandhi. Now he was to transfer to the Mahatma the special affection that up until then had been reserved for his father. And it was reciprocated. This alliance, whose foundation was dependence – on both sides for Gandhi needed Nehru almost as much as Nehru needed Gandhi – was reinforced by love. As such nothing could break it. When the tensions and conflicts came – and they were frequent – the sacrifices were always made by Nehru. It was to be an alliance with many consequences – not all of them for the better.

Motilal's death also seemed symbolic of the failure of Congress. Over the last ten months it had wearied of civil disobedience. The Government did not appear weakened by all these months of agitation. Authority, above all its ability to put down even the most violent of dissent, was apparently just as strong as ever. The death of the apostle of cooperation – for that is what Motilal stood for despite his support for satyagraha – seemed to release a strong desire to get Congress back into a position to negotiate with the British.

Again the initiative came from the liberals outside Congress. The delegates who had attended the Round Table Conference arrived back in India on the day of Motilal's death. Sapru, who had played such an important role in London, was determined not to lose the advantages he believed he had won.

Telegrams passed between the two sides and there were a number of meetings. Gandhi opened up a new phase by sending a letter to the Viceroy outlining his minimum terms: an amnesty, an end to oppressive measures, restitution of confiscated property, reinstatement of Government employees dismissed on political grounds, the end of the salt monopoly and an inquiry into police brutality. The Viceroy replied by appealing to Gandhi to forget the past and look to the future. The Government was not prepared to accept preconditions and there was really no reason why it should. Under pressure from Congress moderates and his own inclinations Gandhi agreed to visit the Viceroy for talks without an agenda.

He did not go with the full backing of Congress. The left wing, including Nehru, were not happy about the weakness of Gandhi's position. The members of the Working Committee, however, only asked him to be firm. They were rewarded by what to many radicals and others of a different persuasion like Vallabhbhai Patel appeared to be a surrender. 'I succumbed,' Gandhi wrote later, 'not to Lord Irwin but to the honesty in him.' On the morning of 5 March, at the sixth meeting between the two men, an agreement was signed. Gandhi had made no attempt either to consult with or to ask for the approval of the Working Committee. On the evening before, he had produced the substance of the agreement he was prepared to accept. Clause 2 came as a terrible shock to Nehru and rightly so, for its terms were not compatible with the Congress demand for complete independence. In fact it was the acceptance of the constitutional position as seen by the British Government and confirmed at the Round Table Conference.

This was something Nehru was totally unprepared for. But he said nothing and left the meeting. 'Was it for this that our people had behaved so gallantly for a year? Were all our brave deeds to end in this?' Apparently so, for Gandhi left for the Viceroy's palace to sign the agreement. On his return Nehru complained but when Gandhi offered to telephone the Viceroy repudiating the agreement, replied 'no'. It was a decision that Nehru was always to remember with anguish. As president of Congress, he had begun a war and now someone else had signed terms of surrender which he believed to be not only humiliating but also unnecessary. But Gandhi convinced him that there was no humiliation and no real surrender. His own common sense told him that the civil disobedience campaign could not be kept going as it had virtually come to a halt with news of the negotiations.

Gandhi had sensed the exhaustion of Congress, so had the Viceroy for the concessions he made were minor. Peaceful picketing would be permitted, prisoners would be released but not those convicted of murder, the salt monopoly would not be abandoned but villagers near the sea could make their own, though not for sale to others. As for the inquiry into the behaviour of the police, the Viceroy would make no concession. It was all very feeble but the Government *had* made a concession of real if more subtle substance. The very fact that the Viceroy had been prepared to discuss matters with Gandhi and to come to a formal agreement with him raised the prestige of Congress. The Gandhi-Irwin Pact, as it came to be known, appeared as one between equals and implied the acceptance of the claim that Congress spoke for at least a large proportion of the Indian people. Most British opinion recognized this immediately. The Conservative opposition in the House of Commons was vocal and an attempt was made to remove from office the party leader, Stanley Baldwin, who had given his support to the Viceroy. Winston Churchill, his rhetoric heavy with disgust that the representative of the king-emperor should parley on equal terms with a 'naked fakir', resigned from the Shadow Cabinet in protest, and prepared with other Tory diehards to fight the coming reforms.

The Government of India, however, remained unruffled even by criticism among its own ranks. In its desire to encourage Gandhi against possible opposition inside Congress the security ordinances were withdrawn *before* civil disobedience had been officially abandoned. Both sides, in perhaps a deliberate attempt to blur the implications of the pact, indulged in statements of considerable ambiguity. But one thing at least was clear: Gandhi had established a basis for Congress *cooperation* with the British and in spite of the events that followed the agreement, the

British Government was committed to cooperate with Gandhi. In the perspective of history the most significant outcome was that Gandhi had succeeded once and for all in diverting Congress from any truly revolutionary path.

Though this was apparent to some of the Congress radicals they chose not to embarrass him. Criticism of Gandhi came instead on an issue essentially irrelevant to the struggle for freedom. The refusal of the Government to grant an amnesty to those convicted of politically motivated murder had been resented by many. In particular the case of Bhagat Singh, who with others had been responsible for the murder of the police officer in Lahore believed to have beaten Lajpat Rai, had aroused a great deal of emotion. Songs were composed about his legendary exploits and pressure had been put upon Gandhi to get the Government at least to commute his sentence of death to one of life imprisonment. On this Irwin had refused any concession. An act of clemency would have been a wise political act but not a sensible imperial one. Irwin's mandate from the British Government was neither complete nor unchallenged and he could not risk arousing British opinion any more than he had already done by his settlement with Gandhi.

When Gandhi arrived at Karachi at the end of March to attend a special session of Congress called to ratify the pact, he was met by hostile crowds. Bhagat Singh had been executed a few days before and part of the demonstration was a condemnation of Gandhi for not saving him. There was also another though smaller demonstration of opinion. A Muslim crowd carrying black flags and shouting 'Gandhi, go back' showed that communalism was still very much alive. There was proof from elsewhere too. After the hanging of Bhagat Singh there were demonstrations all over the country. In Cawnpore they led to a Hindu-Muslim riot in which 166 were killed and nearly 500 wounded.

Though indignation ran high there was no real threat to the pact. Vallabhbhai Patel, already the spokesman of the Congress right wing and firmly installed in position as the third most important Congress leader, strongly supported Gandhi. Nehru, though still torn between principles and realism, offered no obstacle. In fact Gandhi insisted that he should move the resolution approving the pact! At the last moment Nehru agreed and the resolution was passed. Gandhi was to go to London and attend the next session of the Round Table Conference as the representative of Congress, with complete authority to do what he thought fit.

Nehru's submission was rewarded with Gandhi's approval of a resolution on Fundamental Rights and Economic and Social Changes. It was not a particularly revolutionary document – it would probably not have been accepted if it had been. But even with its cautious approach and its watered-down socialism it was to be a milestone on the road of India's political development. Though it was obvious to all that the resolution could not be implemented until independence and presented no threat to the entrenched interests of powerful factions in Congress, these early commitments, accepted partly because they were not fully understood and partly as a sop to Congress radicals, had by the time of independence taken on the inviolable nature of some ancient inheritance. This was to lead after independence to the endorsement by Congress of national economic planning and the 'socialistic pattern of society' as the natural fulfilment of the legacy.

Those sections of the resolution which showed mild socialist influence were the right of a living wage for all, the introduction of an inheritance tax and of a graduated income tax on agricultural income, rent reduction and the state ownership or control of basic industries. The other 'fundamental' rights were in the main taken over from Gandhi's own eleven points and from a list contained in the Nehru Report. They included such liberal necessities as the equality of all before the law, the protection of regional languages and cultures, the abolition of untouchability, total prohibition and free primary education. These too had their place in the development of India's political framework after independence. They were to become the main contribution of Indian nationalism to the Constitution of 1950.

The Karachi meeting was an undoubted triumph for Gandhi. The president of the session was Vallabhbhai Patel but the

dominant figure was that of the Mahatma. Nehru's own attitude was somewhat equivocal. He had sponsored the resolution
supporting the Gandhi-Irwin Pact but without really having
his heart in it. When Gandhi had first shown him the clauses
of the pact he had been certain that something very important
to India had been lost and recalled the lines from T. S. Eliot
which, in spite of the brave words of the resolution on fundamental rights, might well have applied to the Congress session
at Karachi:

> This is the way the world ends,
> Not with a bang but a whimper.

Chapter 11
Years of the Locust

The death of Motilal, the retreat symbolized by the Gandhi-Irwin Pact, the tension between intellectual inclination and emotional dependence, all had their effect on Nehru's health. After the strain of the Karachi conference his doctor advised him to take a holiday. It was an escape from the prison of nationalist reality. It was also a rediscovery of his own marriage. The Nehrus went to Ceylon and in the calm of this beautiful island, so apparently untouched by the great crises of its northern neighbour a new, and on Jawaharlal's side perhaps more respectful, relationship grew up between the husband and wife who had never really understood each other. From Ceylon they returned to India, visiting friends in a leisurely, almost tourist style. It was, of course, not to last.

The truce between the Government and Congress had begun to fray at the edges. The provincial governments, mainly in the hands of officials who had never approved of the Viceroy's concessions to Gandhi, were slow to implement the agreement. Many political prisoners were still in custody despite the recommendations of the central Government. Some of the more radical members of Congress headed by Subhas Bose were actively agitating against local grievances. There was continual trouble in the North West Frontier Province where the security ordinances had been left in force because of the tender situation with the frontier tribes. In April Lord Irwin had returned to England at the end of his tour of office. He had been replaced by Lord Willingdon whose sympathies were very different from those of his predecessor. An appeal to him by Gandhi for an impartial tribunal to investigate breaches of the pact was refused and it was only when Gandhi refused to go to London early in August 1931 that an attempt was made to patch up the differences between the Government and Congress. The effort was successful enough to allow Gandhi to leave for the new session of the Round Table Conference.

Nehru saw the Mahatma off from Bombay. Gandhi, who declared that he went with only God as his guide, arrived in London to find that the faintly progressive Labour Party was no longer in office, though the Prime Minister, Ramsay MacDonald, remained the head of a so-called National Government which was in fact under the control of the Conservatives. The conference itself he was to find preoccupied with the problems of minorities and in particular with those of the largest, that of the Muslims. Gandhi insisted that Congress would accept any solution which was agreeable to Hindus, Sikhs and Muslims but was against separate electorates for any other group, especially so for the Untouchables whom he vehemently maintained were part of the Hindu community. Indeed they were but only in a special sense. The Untouchables were the lowest class in Hindu society, so low that a caste Hindu could be utterly defiled by having their shadow pass over him. They did the unclean jobs, the tanning of leather, the clearing away of night-soil. They were denied entry to temples, the use of the same wells as caste Hindus, and were generally discriminated against both socially and religiously by the rest of Hindu society. The Simon Commission had estimated that Untouchables made up some 30 per cent of the population, and it was the British Government's intention to protect their interests by reserving seats in the legislative bodies exclusively for representatives of the Untouchables.

Gandhi, having spoken, made no effort to reconcile conflicting opinions and only succeeded in antagonizing everyone. The other delegates resented his assertion that only Congress spoke for India and that they were merely unreal figures representing themselves. If the compromising Gandhi had come out of the viceregal palace in New Delhi with an agreement, the arrogant Gandhi was uppermost at St James's Palace in London. As it became obvious that there was no possible basis for agreement, the British Government announced that it would make a decision on the problem of minorities itself. Gandhi's reply was to leave the conference with expressions of regret that it had neither taken his advice nor accepted his veiled ultimatums. The conference was officially adjourned on 1 December.

While Gandhi was in London, tension and unrest had increased in India as it became increasingly clear that he had failed in his mission. The Government of India also convinced itself that the pact was no longer worth the paper it was written on and made no attempt to restrain the more provocative and oppressive actions of the provincial administrations. In Bengal terrorism had revived and had been replied to with police brutality. In the North West Frontier Province Abdul Ghaffar Khan's Congress-aligned 'Redshirt' movement had been growing to such an extent that the administration feared an uprising. The police fired on unarmed crowds and many arrests were made. Towards the end of December the movement was declared an illegal organization and its leaders were imprisoned.

Nehru's homeland of the United Provinces was particularly disturbed. The no-rent campaign which had been abandoned as part of the Gandhi-Irwin agreement revived when the Government demanded payment. Before his departure for London and anxious to avoid a major agrarian revolt at such a time, Gandhi had advised the peasants to pay half the taxes. The Government, realizing the strength of the peasants' case, offered to reduce the amount, but not by a half. Under pressure from the local Congress Committee, Nehru and another United Provinces Congress leader, Pandit Pant, tried to negotiate a settlement between the two parties but the local revenue officials were hostile. The taxes, they said, must be paid before negotiations could take place.

Congress was now at a dead end. Its leader was away and no one seemed quite sure what to do. Gandhi appealed to, replied from London: 'Do as you think fit.' Nehru, who drew so much of his sustaining idealism from the plight of the peasants, exerted his own pressure on Congress, which finally decided to support a no-tax campaign. When the crisis came to a head in mid-December 1931, Nehru was in Bombay where he had taken Kamala, now ill once again, for medical treatment. There he heard that the United Provinces government had given itself sweeping security powers and had issued ordinances banning all agitation. At the end of the month Nehru, after a propaganda visit to south India and a return to Bombay, decided that he must go to Allahabad and support the peasants. The conference in London was over; it was now a time for action.

Leaving Kamala bedridden in Bombay, Nehru set off. A few miles outside Allahabad while the train was stopped at a station, a police officer served orders confining him within the Allahabad municipal limits, restraining him from addressing or attending public meetings, and from writing newspaper or other articles. On his arrival in Allahabad, Nehru acknowledged receipt of the orders to the District Magistrate, informing him that they were unacceptable and that he intended to go to Bombay to meet Gandhi on his arrival from Europe. With local Congress officials he boarded a train for Bombay on 26 December. A few miles down the line the train was stopped at a wayside halt. A police wagon was waiting and in it the party was taken to Naini jail. Nehru's sixth imprisonment had started.

Gandhi arrived at Bombay to be welcomed with the news of the arrests. 'Christmas gifts from Lord Willingdon, our Christian Viceroy,' he remarked. He telegraphed to the Viceroy asking for an urgent meeting. In reply he was told that the Viceroy would be prepared to see him only on the understanding that there would be no discussion of the security ordinances or of the arrests. As this was exactly what Gandhi wanted to discuss, the terms were naturally unacceptable. Gandhi who had still not realized that Willingdon was a very different Viceroy from Irwin also overlooked the fact that the situation had changed. After the failure of the London conference there was now no point in the British treating him with consideration.

Congress, though unwilling to break the pact, could hardly swallow the Viceroy's treatment of its leader. Gandhi was authorized to write to Willingdon threatening a resumption of civil disobedience with the proviso that 'if His Excellency thinks it worth while to see me, the operation of the resolution will be suspended pending our discussion'. Willingdon's reply was a refusal to talk 'under threat'. The next day, 4 January 1932, the Government took swift and crushing action. It arrested the Mahatma and Patel, and over the next four months, some eighty thousand Congress workers. On 10 January Congress was declared an illegal organization. The speed and efficiency with which the Government acted, the comprehensiveness of the security ordinances issued on the day of Gandhi's arrest, revealed that the Government had been preparing for some time to crush Congress. For a while it looked as if it had succeeded.

On the same day as Gandhi was taken into custody, Nehru came up for trial at Allahabad and was sentenced to two years' imprisonment. It was obviously a punitive sentence because a fellow-accused was given only six months on the same charge. The Government also moved against other members of the Nehru family. Jawaharlal's two sisters were each sentenced to one year in jail. The authorities threatened to seize Nehru's property because he had refused, as part of the no-tax campaign, to pay off the tax liabilities on his father's estate. In fact the personal aspect of the Government's new policy was particularly marked. Heavy fines and other economic penalties were designed to convince the nationalist businessmen and the professional classes that their support of Congress could lead only to bankruptcy.

Congress was ostensibly completely crushed. Its buildings seized and its funds confiscated, its records destroyed, its schools, dispensaries and hospitals closed, there was nothing much left of its organization. Even the women were harshly treated, some being given sentences of two years for merely shouting slogans. Those members who remained free tried to keep the civil disobedience campaign going but without funds: enthusiasm was not enough. By the middle of 1932 the campaign had subsided into minor outbursts, and a sullen peace descended on India.

All this was observed by Nehru with growing sadness. He had never really believed in the accommodation between Gandhi and Irwin. It was a delusion that had led only to disaster. And not only that but to personal suffering. During a demonstration in April Nehru's mother, who had insisted on joining the crowd, was beaten though not arrested – in fact a police officer discovered her lying in the road with head injuries and took her, bleeding, to her home in his car. Nehru was both angered and distressed. If he had been present he wondered how far his non-violence would have carried him. Not very far, he feared. There was little satisfaction in the news that rumours of her death led to demonstrations and more police brutality.

In February Nehru had been removed from Naini to the jail at Bareilly. There under rather closer confinement his health began to suffer. After four months he was again moved, this time to Dehra Dun where he remained for fourteen and a half months. Fortunately his health improved but that sense of detachment which all illness gives remained with him. He also had no visitors for the last seven months of his sentence because his mother had been insulted by a warder at Allahabad jail and he was unwilling to have a repetition at Dehra Dun. On the whole he was well and even courteously treated by his jailors. Others were not so lucky. Political prisoners of less eminence were placed with hardened criminals and whippings for minor infringements of jail discipline were not infrequent.

Nehru's enforced detachment from the events of the India outside his prison turned his mind to the world outside India. Once again he saw India's troubles as part of wider, a universal, drama. Fascism was on the march both in Europe and in Asia, for early in the spring of 1933 Japan had completed its conquest of Manchuria and Hitler had come to power in Germany. The effects of the Depression were still causing social and economic chaos in the western democracies. Only the Soviet Union seemed to offer a dynamic and forward-looking policy for mankind. Very soon, he thought, there would be a terrible clash between communism and fascism and India must in some way be ready for it.

What that way could be with the Mahatma as the animateur of the freedom movement was obscure. In September 1932 Nehru had been shocked to hear that Gandhi had gone on a fast to the death. The issue he chose for this dramatic gesture was the announcement by the British Government that it would grant a separate electorate to Untouchables. Gandhi's decision to fast was not that of a nationalist fighting for his country's freedom but of a religious leader. The Untouchables, for all the disgusting way in which they were treated by caste Hindus, were for Gandhi part of the seamless fabric of Hinduism. The suggestion that they should be cut out of it even politically was immoral. To prevent such a thing happening he was prepared to die.

For Nehru and many others it seemed hardly the right issue to die for however important it was in itself. Nehru's response was also confused by his fear that Gandhi might actually die. It was almost a personal affront to his affection and dependence that Gandhi should choose to risk his life, and to do so for something less than freedom. There is a note of genuine panic in Nehru's letter to his daughter in which he asks: 'And whom shall I go to when I am in doubt and require wise counsel? What shall we all do when our beloved chief who inspired us and led us has gone?' Yet no appeal for *political* common sense had any effect on the Mahatma. The struggle for independence had been subsumed in the desire for religious reform. The question of separate electorates gave way to an assault upon the Hindu conscience. Untouchability was an offence to Gandhi's concept of a clean and refurbished Hinduism. It mattered nothing to him that the Untouchables, constantly discriminated against, had through their leader, Dr Ambedkar, jumped at the chance separate representation offered to them to break away from the dominance of caste Hindus.

On 20 September the fast began. The British were not particularly worried about it though would not like to have Gandhi die in jail. They were prepared to feed him forcibly if necessary, or under certain conditions to release him on the principle that he was less dangerous alive than dead. The following day a conference of Hindu leaders met and some were allowed to visit Gandhi in prison. Attempts were made to put pressure on Dr Ambedkar who was quite unmoved by Gandhi's fast. On the fifth day of the fast, however, Ambedkar gave way and agreed to reject the British Government's award. He did so in return for a promise that the Untouchables would be given seats from those reserved for Hindus. By this agreement the Untouchables got twice as many seats as they would have had under the award! But for Gandhi, and for caste Hindus, it meant that Hinduism was preserved.

For a while, too, it seemed that Gandhi's hope of reform in the way Untouchables were treated would be fulfilled. Temples previously closed to them opened their doors. The wells and the pasture lands from which they had been excluded were now offered to them with all the appearance of genuine repentance. But it was not to last. The emotion drained away in the fear that thirty million Untouchables might threaten the vested interests of caste Hindus. The temple doors closed once again, tradition reasserted itself. The fast had indeed been a waste of time. It had also done real harm to the nationalist movement for it was a diversion from the narrow road that led to freedom. The British recognized that Gandhi had once again cooperated in taking the fire out of their opponents.

Nehru in his distant jail, his mind occupied with wider issues, soon forgot the anger and fear he had felt. But he was to be reminded once again of the, for him, irrational nature of Gandhi's approach to politics. On 8 May 1933, still in prison, the Mahatma announced yet another fast. The Inner Voices had spoken to him once again and this time they had even been precise about the period he must fast. It was to be twenty-one days, and the purpose – 'self-purification'. This time the Government had had enough. On the same evening a communiqué was published stating that in view of the nature and object of the fast, it had been decided to set the Mahatma at liberty.

No one was more shocked than Gandhi. Prison was an almost essential backdrop for his personal drama. Now with his mind adjusted to fasting he was to be virtually put out in the street. Reluctantly he allowed himself to be taken to a mansion outside Poona and there, despite the protests of followers and Congress leaders, went on with the fast. In return for his release he called off officially the civil disobedience campaign, which had already died of exhaustion. For some reason he still thought that he had something to bargain with and announced that he was only *suspending* the campaign for six weeks and would reactivate it unless the Government released the remaining political prisoners. But not even Gandhi could raise the Lazarus of civil disobedience and the Government knew it.

The drama now became a farce. Gandhi ended his fast after the divinely ordered number of days. In June he extended the 'suspension' of civil disobedience for another six weeks and in July formally ended *mass* civil disobedience. The Government was indifferent. Gandhi asked for a meeting with the Viceroy. It was refused. At the beginning of August now fully recovered he offered individual satyagraha, was arrested and released after three days with an order confining him to Poona. This he refused to accept and was arrested again and this time sentenced to one year's imprisonment. Back in his old cell he thought he could continue with his campaign against Untouchability. Previously he had been treated with considerable tenderness; this time he was told that he would not be allowed to dictate the terms of his imprisonment. His reply was to begin yet another fast.

The trivialization of the technique was now complete and even Gandhi was aware of it. The fast became an acceptance of failure. Within five days he was seriously ill and making no attempt to resist the effects of starvation. Again the Government decided to release him, to die, if he must, elsewhere than in a British jail. Gandhi was caught off balance. Again he was taken to the mansion outside Poona where his friends tried to convince him that he must really fight to live. The fast was over but the effects remained not only on Gandhi's shattered body but on his mind. He was in despair and wanted to leave Congress and politics. Many Congressmen thought this would be the best thing for the nationalist movement. Subhas Bose away in Europe for medical treatment – the British were never willing to allow their important political prisoners to die on them if they could help it – attacked Gandhi. He was, he said, 'an old, useless piece of furniture' and it was time for new leadership. Despite his disapproval of Nehru, Bose still considered him the best candidate for the job. Others of the same radical persuasion as Bose were not so sure. Neither was Nehru himself.

In August Nehru had been brought down from Dehru Dun to Allahabad to finish his sentence. There he learned that his mother was seriously ill and the Government released him, thirteen days before the end of his term, on 30 August. After a brief stay – and assured of some improvement in his mother's health – Nehru left for Poona and reunion with the Mahatma. It was a sad meeting. Congress was in the lower depths. Gandhi had withdrawn from political activity. Worse still no one seemed to be thinking about the future. The conversations that took place between the two men and the lengthy correspondence which followed reveals the deep gulf that lay between them in the field of ideas.

Away from the Mahatma, Nehru aired his socialist views in a series of articles which aroused considerable interest, not least because they contained an indirect attack upon Gandhi for not having a policy. But Nehru made no effort to answer the question of what should be done next. Certainly Congress was still a proscribed organization and existed only in the underground cells which some members had managed to keep going despite the security police and Gandhi's request that they be dismantled. For some time Nehru was preoccupied with family problems, with his mother's health and his younger sister's marriage, and with money matters as he fully expected to be arrested again and wanted to ensure his mother's financial security. Nehru made a few speeches, met occasionally with his colleagues of the Working Committee but there was no sense of purpose. Gandhi, touring the countryside on a new campaign against Untouchability, was drawing large crowds. He seemed quite happy doing this and to let the nationalist movement mark time. In a speech in December, however, he indirectly attacked Nehru's socialist ideas and because of this Jawaharlal considered resigning from the Working Committee.

In January 1934 Congress members were wondering how, as an illegal organization, Congress could celebrate Independence Day. If it did so defiantly, a wave of arrests would follow. Nehru issued a brief appeal in favour of celebrating the day but leaving the arrangements to local Congress leaders. He planned to make a trip to Calcutta, taking Kamala for a medical examination, but to return to Allahabad in time for Independence Day. The Government had already decided to arrest him and was only waiting for a good excuse. Two of his recent speeches had been considered seditious enough for a prosecution but no action had been taken before his visit to Calcutta. There Nehru made three highly provocative speeches which supplied even better grounds for his arrest.

On the day the Nehrus left for Calcutta an earth tremor was felt in Allahabad. The centre of the shock was Bihar in northeast India where whole towns were shattered and hundreds of villages destroyed. The area of devastation was over thirty thousand square miles with a population of about fifteen million. The final death roll was estimated at over twenty thousand and more than a million homes were damaged or destroyed. When the news reached Calcutta, Nehru decided that he must visit the area and spent a short time there on his way back to Allahabad. After getting a fund-raising campaign started, he returned to the scene of the earthquake.

The ten days he spent touring the area shocked him with the horrors of almost total devastation. He was vocally critical of the Government's relief measures. To add to his anger Gandhi announced that the earthquake was an act of punishment for the sin of Untouchability! Nehru was repelled by the essential vulgarity, the monumental indifference to human suffering, that Gandhi displayed. And he was not alone. Rabindranath Tagore, in a letter to the Mahatma, asked why God should have chosen the people of Bihar for His displeasure? Surely, no one had the right to assume that natural catastrophes were harnessed to moral ends? Gandhi remained unmoved. The earthquake was a punishment.

On 11 February Nehru, exhausted, returned home. The next afternoon just after tea a police car drew up at the door. There was a warrant for his arrest issued in Calcutta. He was taken to that city, tried and sentenced to two years' imprisonment. The jail at least was different and so was the space allotted him, a tiny cell because this was a city jail, though there was the usual veranda and high wall. He was allowed to have books and the *Manchester Guardian Weekly* but no Indian newspaper. He found himself better informed about what was going on in Europe than in India. But in April he learnt from a casual remark that Gandhi had decided to abandon all forms of civil disobedience and had approved a revival of Motilal's old Swaraj Party to contest the elections coming in November.

Nehru found the first decision immoral and the second heavy with menace. Gandhi's reasons for abandoning civil disobedience were so trivial as to be an 'insult to the intelligence and an amazing performance for a leader of a national movement'. The intention to revive the Swaraj Party showed that moderation had triumphed once again. Nehru's depression was so deep that he felt that his relationship with Gandhi was over and that for the future he would have only himself to depend upon. In fact the separation was many years off and would only be finally brought about by the death of the Mahatma.

In the midst of his depression, Kamala, though far from well, came to see him. Her visit cheered him immensely. His own health was beginning to worry him and the prison authorities. On 7 May he was transferred to his old prison at Dehru Dun. But it was not quite as comfortable as before. His old cell was occupied and he was put into a converted cattle shed. He could not even see the hills because of a fifteen-foot wall. Worst of all he was kept by himself. He was also allowed to have an Indian daily paper. The news it brought only added to his depression.

His estrangement from Gandhi and the knowledge that his wife, whom he had learned to admire, was now seriously and probably mortally ill with pulmonary tuberculosis made him feel particularly helpless in his lonely prison. There was nothing he could do either for her or for the freedom movement. The Government had allowed the All-India Congress Committee to meet and had removed the ban on many of its affiliated bodies though not upon the agrarian organizations and the 'Redshirts' of the North West Frontier Province. Two new groups had emerged inside Congress, one planning to enter the legislatures, the other trying to create a socialist party. In between stood Gandhi, who dominated the proceedings.

Nehru felt that Gandhi was becoming far too dictatorial. Moderate elements with all the caution of moderates seemed to be in control. Congress was becoming respectable and many new faces were appearing in the ranks of the leadership, people who would never have dared join when Congress was militant. The Working Committee even came out with an attack upon socialism and went on record as being of 'the opinion that confiscation and class warfare are contrary to the Congress creed of non-violence'. Socialists were branded as wanting to confiscate private property.

In August there was alarming news about Kamala's health and the Government decided to give Nehru a conditional release to be with his wife. He found her very frail and weak. His mother was also ill in the same house. All his suppressed emotion burst out in a letter to Gandhi condemning the road Congress was taking under his influence. In his reply Gandhi chided Nehru for his criticisms which he insisted were not well founded. In any case he fancied that he had 'the knack for knowing the need of the time', which was surely sufficient justification.

On the eleventh day of Nehru's freedom a police car came to take him back to prison but not to Dehra Dun. While his wife was ill he would be confined at Naini. For two weeks he received medical bulletins, then they stopped. A month later he was taken to see his wife and promised regular visits to follow but the promise was never kept and it was not until October that he was taken to see Kamala again. Before he left it was suggested to him that if he would agree to keep out of politics he would be released. This placed him in a terrible dilemma. Kamala was very ill and in a dazed condition but when he was leaving she whispered: 'What is this about giving an assurance to the Government? Do not give it!'

Soon afterwards Kamala was moved to a sanatorium in the hills at Bhowali in the eastern United Provinces. Nehru saw her before she left and found her bright and cheerful. Three weeks later he was moved to Almora jail close by the sanatorium, a concession that seems to have been motivated by heavy pressure from leaders of the British Labour Party and others in India for his release. At Almora conditions were less restricting. He was housed in a vast barrack and had ample room for walking about.

Nehru's main concern was with his wife's condition. Every third week he was allowed to visit her. The news from elsewhere was not inspiring. At the annual session of Congress held at Bombay in October attempts to introduce a radical economic programme had been soundly defeated. Congress was completely in the control of the right wing. Gandhi himself had announced a month previously that he would resign from Congress, ostensibly, as he wrote in his letter of resignation, because the more intellectual Congressmen 'were hampered' by an 'unexampled loyalty' to him which prevented them from opposing his policies! Of course Gandhi was not actually leaving Congress. As Nehru put it, Gandhi 'could not rid himself even if he wanted to of his dominating position'. Indeed, Gandhi had 'resigned' partly to demonstrate just that. The meeting confirmed their confidence in him, and his programme of spinning and community service became uppermost once again.

In the following month Congress triumphed in the elections by winning forty-four of the one hundred and thirty-seven seats in the central Legislative Assembly. With other nationalist groups it could muster a majority if it wanted to. Nehru was more than ever anxious to be about in the world.

In May 1935 Kamala's condition was so bad that it was decided that she should go to Europe for special treatment. After she had gone, Nehru found prison life especially wearing without his occasional visits outside the walls. He was anxious too, about his mother who in January had suffered a paralytic stroke. Then, quite unexpectedly, on 4 September he was released. It was an act of humanity for Kamala was critically ill once again. Five days after his release Nehru, who had travelled by air to Basle and from there to the little town of Badenweiler in the Black Forest of Germany, was by Kamala's side.

After about a month Kamala seemed considerably improved but it was too late for any cure to be effective. Nehru felt that he could leave her for a short visit to Paris and London. It was eight years since he had been in England and he was surprised at the welcome he received even from those who disagreed with his politics. Though he sensed among the British 'a vague pricking of conscience' about India, the general feeling was of indifference, even of boredom with Indian affairs. In August the new Government of India Act had received the royal assent and would come into force two years later. Why, he was asked did not Congress cooperate and take these reforms as a step nearer to its goal? He found it difficult to make his questioners understand his own attitude.

After a fortnight he returned to Badenweiler where he spent his time revising the text of his autobiography, the writing of which had occupied much of his time in prison. He had started it in an attempt to divert his mind and as an exercise in self-analysis. After a short relapse Kamala again seemed better. In January 1936 Nehru paid another short visit to London where he learned that he had been elected president of Congress once again and that he was needed back in India. The pressure to return was heavy though Nehru was reluctant to leave Kamala. At the end of January she was strong enough to be moved to another sanatorium at Lausanne in Switzerland and her doctors assured Nehru that he could safely spend a few months away from her in India. It was decided, with Kamala's approval, that Nehru would leave by air for India on 28 February. But for some reason Kamala appeared uneasy. A few days before the time of departure, her doctor urged Nehru to stay a further week or ten days. The change in Kamala was very clear and it was soon obvious that she was dying. Early in the morning with Nehru and their daughter Indira at the bedside, Kamala died peacefully. Her body was cremated and the ashes placed in an urn so that Nehru could carry them back with him to India.

On the journey home Nehru felt overwhelmingly lonely. At Rome he was told that Mussolini would like to see him personally in order to convey his condolences at his wife's death. It was a difficult situation. The fascist dictator was anxious to appear as a supporter of nationalist movements against the British and had already suggested that Nehru should visit him while in Europe. Nehru, remembering that the official fascist newspaper had printed a bogus interview with Gandhi, was not willing to risk a meeting even if he could get over his dislike for fascism. Despite the persistent arguments of a high official, Nehru refused to visit Mussolini and rejoined his plane.

When he landed at Baghdad, Nehru sent a cable to his publishers in London who had accepted the manuscript of his autobiography. The cable contained the dedication for the book – 'To Kamala, who is no more'. The years of the locust had eaten deep into his own life as well as into that of the nationalist movement.

Chapter 12
The Radical Mediator

A sad and weary Nehru returned to India with the consolation that though Congress was a mere shadow of its former self, its membership down to less than half a million, there were prospects of a new battle over policy. In preparing for it he could lose himself in the only therapy for despair that had ever worked for him – the struggle for Indian freedom. The coming battle had been heralded by the passing of the Government of India Act of 1935 under which elections would take place early in 1937.

The Act incorporated all the stages of constitutional development up to that date and added two new principles: that India should be organized into a Federation and that popular responsible governments should be set up in the provinces. Under the terms of the Act new provinces were to be created in India while Burma was to be separated and given a new constitution of its own not so advanced as that of India. The Federal provisions had been designed to incorporate the princely states into the new system of government but the rulers of the largest looked upon them with some suspicion while nationalists considered the whole affair as another Machiavellian attempt by the British to perpetuate their rule by playing on the divisions between special-interest groups. In any case the British had ensured they remained in power by an immense array of safeguards which left them in control of all the levers that really mattered.

But if India as a whole was to be denied freedom, parts of it were not. Except for some reserved powers, the provincial administrations were to be in the control of Indian ministers, themselves members of an elected legislature. The franchise was also to be considerably widened. In day-to-day affairs the provincial governments were to be entirely responsible. It was a very seductive offer of real power to those nationalist elements who were still prepared to cooperate with the British.

The right wing of Congress was in complete control of the organization and Nehru feared, rightly as it turned out, that it would be willing to take office. Nehru had no objection to fighting the elections. On the contrary, he was convinced that an election campaign could be used to revive the image of Congress in the eyes of the masses with which it had lost touch. But he was utterly against taking office and thereby becoming partner in the imperial system. The problem was how to fight the right wing's willingness to be tempted and still maintain the unity of Congress.

Some of Nehru's friends had advised him not to accept nomination for the presidency of Congress. The right wing was so entrenched that he would be able to do nothing. He had also been warned by a right-wing leader, Rajendra Prasad, that if he tried radically to change Congress policy there would be 'difficulties'. The warning was all the clearer because it was oblique. Gandhi, however, had pressed Nehru to accept office. He would have a free hand but again the Mahatma reminded him that in the final analysis it was he who controlled Congress. There was no question of Nehru rejecting the appeal. In the first place it came from Gandhi, whom he could never refuse. In the second, Nehru would never voluntarily give up leadership. In any case both Gandhi and Nehru were determined to keep Congress from splitting and in this they needed each other's special talents.

In particular, Gandhi needed Nehru. His own leadership, above all his *style* of leadership, was being challenged and especially by the young. Though the young men realized Gandhi's immense appeal to the masses, they believed it to be an atavistic appeal, essentially anti-progressive. Because of it they identified him with those right-wing elements, the businessman and bourgeoisie who now dominated Congress. In order to canalize this opposition both to Gandhi and to the right wing, a number of left-thinking Congress members had decided, while in jail, to form a socialist party.

The party was founded in 1934 while Nehru was himself in jail. His own writings and speeches had obviously influenced some of the group of young men who founded the party but its chief philosopher and guide was a scholarly Marxist of about Nehru's age, Narendra Deva. The significant thing about the new party was that it had no intention of separating from Congress. There was every reason why it should not. Congress was not a monolith, but a nationalist rally, incorporating a wide range of interests. The Congress Socialist Party, as it called itself, was designed to offer an alternative leadership to the nationalist movement and to give Congress policies a more revolutionary leftist bias. The attraction of its programme of western-style socialism was obviously deep for in the Congress session of 1934 the CSP controlled one third of the delegates.

It was in this situation that Gandhi needed Nehru. Though sympathetic to the views of the socialists, Nehru had been relieved of any responsibility in the founding of the new party by being in prison at the time. On his release he did not join the party, an omission which disappointed some of his admirers. Nehru rationalized his decision by pointing to the rigidity of the socialists' thinking and the western jargon in which it was expressed. There was, he said in a message to the CSP at the end of 1936, a great danger in not relating socialism to Indian conditions and, as for the jargon, 'merely to use words and phrases, which may have meaning for us but which are not current coin among the masses of India, is often a wasted effort ...' This was justifiable criticism but Nehru's real reasons for remaining aloof from the socialists were more personal. He wanted *national* not factional leadership. He had noted that as the CSP had increased its influence inside Congress so the right wing closed its ranks. He could best maintain his own position by identifying with neither but by retaining the support of both Gandhi and the socialists. This was exactly what Gandhi wanted – a mediator, a radical mediator, and Nehru was happy to play the role.

But what of the right wing? Were they prepared to accept Nehru in the part allotted to him by the Mahatma? They were certainly willing to take Nehru the man, for Gandhi had made it quite clear that Nehru was *his* choice, but Nehru the socialist was a different matter. The right wing, apart from dominating the leadership, controlled the movement's organization, and it had no intention of giving it up. This was made quite clear to Gandhi by Vallabhbhai Patel. The right-wing leaders were, however, not prepared to come out openly against Nehru but to outmanoeuvre him. When Nehru put up a number of socialist resolutions for the next Congress session there was no objection from the predominantly right-wing Working Committee. But the All-India Congress Committee when it met, rejected the most important and modified others and the full session of Congress confirmed the changes.

On issues of no consequence, Nehru was given his head. He wanted a foreign department so that Congress could keep in touch with the world outside India? Of course, it harmed no vested interest. A resolution that Congress would take no part in any future imperialist war? Certainly, nobody could suffer from that and it sounded politically mature. But on matters that threatened right-wing positions – the affiliation of trade unions and peasant leagues with Congress, for example – the leadership was adamant. A resolution on agrarian reform was so watered down that it offered no threat to landlords. And on the most immediately vital issue of all – that of boycotting the new constitution – Nehru was utterly defeated. The 1935 Act was formally rejected though it was agreed that Congress would fight the elections, but the question of whether Congress should accept office was significantly left undecided.

On the whole, by the use of methods which Patel was to make especially his own, the right wing had triumphed. Nehru's response was to consider resigning from office. Inevitably, he changed his mind and claimed he did so in the interests of unity. He had indeed helped to put it in jeopardy. Though Gandhi could define Nehru's role he could not write his lines for him. Nehru's presidential address had included an attack on the right wing because of its grip on every level of Congress organization. The existing Congress constitution encouraged authoritarianism and ought to be changed in the interests of the fight for freedom.

This attack was not unnaturally resented by the right-wing majority but worse still was the enthusiasm Nehru's speech aroused among the radicals. He had called rousingly for a united front of all mass organizations against imperialism. He had trounced the princes as props of 'an alien power' whose days must surely be numbered. As for the 1935 Act it was 'a new charter of slavery to strengthen the bonds of imperialist domination and to intensify the exploitation of our masses'. The speech had ended with an apocalyptic vision of an India after many privations and sufferings arriving inevitably at the promised land.

Even Gandhi, who was ill and not present at the opening of the session, was somewhat anxious at the tone of the speech and its effect on the younger men in Congress. There was an attempt to give the impression that Gandhi had broken with Nehru and had declared his life's work harmed more by Nehru's words than by the repression of the British Government! This was publicly denied by Gandhi but there are indications that he had deliberately set the rumour about himself in order to bring Nehru to heel. Whatever the truth there was no real question of a complete break between the two men. Nor indeed had the right wing much to fear. An inflammatory speech was for Nehru a necessary catharsis to surrender. When the time came, after the Congress session, for him to pick the members of the Working Committee he chose ten right-wing leaders and only four from the left!

No wonder his socialist admirers were shocked. It was unbelievable to them that having the opportunity to pack the most powerful body in Congress with radicals he would choose to isolate himself by creating a permanent majority in opposition to his ideas. From the beginning Nehru had displayed an ambivalent attitude towards the Congress Socialist Party. From now on, though he was always to have their support, this attitude was to be matched on their side. In the end it was to lead to the socialists leaving Congress after independence.

Nehru ignored the protests of his friends while freely acknowledging that he was outnumbered in the Working Committee and could get nothing done. He did not seem much concerned and had thrown himself into spreading the Congress gospel though in his own special socialist versions. He made a number of tours, drawing large numbers to his meetings. He attacked communalism – still scorching the peace of ordinary Indians – as the work of the British and of ambitious Hindu and Muslim politicians. He talked of protection for the peasant from exploitation by feudal landlords and greedy moneylenders. The fight, he said, was between classes not faiths, poor peasants and rich landlords, workers and capitalists, not between Muslim and Hindu.

Nehru's popularity with the masses, already high, increased with every tour. The crowds who attended his meetings understood him even less than the majority of Congress when he talked about socialism, but they knew exactly what he meant when he castigated landlords and factory owners. It was not long before those he attacked began to be alarmed and their fears were passed on to the right-wing Congress leaders. At the end of June 1936 six members of the Working Committee offered their resignations. The list was headed by the names of Vallabhbhai Patel, Rajendra Prasad and C. Rajagopalachari, a formidable triumvirate. Patel, the shrewd and subtle lawyer from Gujarat, Prasad, an orthodox Hindu and believer in pure non-violence, and Rajagopalachari, a Brahmin from Madras, intellectual with a cold reserve and a gift for biting sarcasm. In the tragi-comedy of Nehru's life these men were among the Eumenides.

The charges were simple and precise – Nehru as president of Congress was preaching socialism while Congress itself had rejected it! Such a policy was not in the interests of the struggle for freedom. Purely as a matter of discipline, the discipline which Nehru had accepted, the charges were undeniable but they cut Nehru on his sensitive skin. He protested that in the interests of unity he had put forward his ideas in the mildest possible way and now he was indicted for having behaved in a manner which was harmful to the Congress cause. There is an overtone of injured innocence about his letter to Gandhi in which these sentiments are expressed. He offered his resignation once again, pleading that his health had suffered because of the opposition inside the Working Committee. As usual with the letters between Nehru and Gandhi there is an air of unreality, as if they were always intended for publication. Nehru's are sharp, defensive, but with an escape clause. Gandhi's are warm, honeyed and absolutely rigid. In this case Gandhi had already intervened with the right-wing leaders and forced them to withdraw their resignations but not their criticism.

Nehru agreed to withdraw his own offer of resignation. The reason he gave to himself and the public was that with the outbreak of the Spanish civil war he saw the coming of a world conflict and could not weaken the Congress movement in the face of it. Nehru the internationalist, escaping from the problems that surrounded him into the wider and more amenable reality of 'foreign policy', was not an entirely new persona but it was one that would be more frequently assumed in the future. Wearing it, Nehru could ignore the parochial politicians and what he believed to be their petty concern with narrow domestic problems – let small men get on with small matters. It was an escape which hardly damaged the struggle for freedom but after independence Nehru's preoccupation with foreign affairs was to lead to an abdication of decision on internal matters to just those parochial politicians he so despised.

With the provincial election looming near, Nehru abandoned the fate of the world for that of the Congress campaign. With the approval of Gandhi, a slightly leftist manifesto was approved. It contained the usual Congress demands for complete independence and the abolition of Untouchability but there was also an appeal to the peasantry with a pledge of agrarian reform rather more precise than before. It was to pay off enormously. But first there was the problem of who should be president of Congress in the vital year of 1937. It was time Nehru stepped down, and he was perfectly willing to do so, so that he could give all his energies to the election campaign. The candidate of the right wing was Patel and he had considerable backing within the party. Gandhi, however, wanted Nehru, now certainly the second most popular Congress leader in the country. Under pressure Patel stood down once again though he reminded Nehru that in doing so he did not endorse Nehru's views. It was also made clear that the right wing had no intention of abandoning its grip on the organization.

It was as a Congress president who would succeed himself

that Nehru carried out an immense election tour. During some eight months of speech-making he covered more than 50,000 miles through all sorts of country, jungle and desert, plain and mountain. Every variety of transport carried him to the remotest village or through the streets of the great cities. Some ten million people heard him speak and millions of others caught a glimpse of him as he passed by. He carried the message of Congress, he said, 'not only to the thirty million and odd voters but to the hundreds of millions of non-voters too'. His themes were simple: fight for Indian freedom; build Congress into a mighty army of the Indian people; organize to remove poverty, unemployment, social and cultural degradation. Nehru drew strength from the vast crowds. They, seeing the heir of Gandhi, gave him their uncomplicated adoration. The empathy he had felt earlier for the peasants and the workers intensified in the warmth of the welcoming crowds. He convinced himself that he felt their fears and their hopes, their tragedy and their dreams. From the election campaign of 1936–7 another Nehru appeared, a figure created by the popular imagination.

When the election results were announced it was clear that Congress had won an overwhelming victory. The size of the Congress vote surprised everybody, including Nehru. Congress secured absolute majorities in five of the eleven provinces and was the largest single party in three others. Its main strength was in the Hindu-majority provinces and elsewhere it captured the Hindu vote. The rest of the votes went to a variety of communal and factional parties. In Bengal a government was formed by a Muslim-dominated coalition and in the Punjab, the Unionist Party, an agrarian alliance of Hindus, Sikhs and Muslims, swept the board. The Muslim League did very badly, drawing less than five per cent of the *Muslim* vote. Nehru was more than satisfied by the result. It proved, he thought, that communalism was dead, for Congress had not only won seats reserved for Hindus but a substantial proportion of those unallotted to any specific group. The appeal of communalism, he reckoned, had fallen as a consequence of the Congress campaign among the masses. All that was needed to destroy it altogether was further mass contact.

It was a dangerous assumption and played into the hands of the communal-minded Hindus inside Congress. Nehru for his own reasons was now not prepared to consider negotiations or deals with communal parties and in particular those of the Muslims. In this, and for their very different reasons, the right-wing leadership was in full agreement. A new arrogance, the arrogance of elected power, was soon to show itself. But first Congress had to decide what its next move was to be. It had fought the elections, would it now boycott the legislatures?

This, of course, was what Nehru and the left wing wanted but they were overruled. Somehow Nehru managed to reconcile himself to it. 'The opinion of the majority of Congress today,' he said in July 1937, 'is in favour of acceptance of office, but it is even more strongly and unanimously in favour of the basic Congress policy of fighting the new constitution and ending it. . . . We are not going to be partners and cooperators in the imperial firm. . . . We go to the assemblies or accept office . . . to try to prevent the federation from materializing, to stultify the constitution and prepare the ground for the constituent assembly and independence . . . to strengthen the masses and, wherever possible, in the narrow sphere of the constitution, to give some relief to them.'

Congress, however, would not take up office except under certain conditions. The governors of the provinces who in special circumstances had the right to veto legislation, must guarantee not to do so. This was refused by the Viceroy on the grounds that such a promise would be a violation of the terms of the constitution. Congress then refused to take office and interim provincial administrations were appointed by the governors. After three months a compromise was arrived at. The Viceroy made a public statement calling for cooperation between governors and ministers. Gandhi chose to consider this adequate, responding, as he said, to the honesty of motive which he had first seen in Lord Irwin. What had actually happened was that Congress, closely observing the working of the constitution during the three months it had been in force without its cooperation, had discovered that the ministers had exercised a large measure of real power. The majority of Congress members were not prepared to go on losing the perquisites of that power.

The decision to take office put into practice the Congress attitude towards communal parties. During the election campaign in the United Provinces, Congress and the Muslim League had cooperated and there was an unstated understanding that a coalition government would be formed. After victory at the polls Congress would have none of it. 'There are only two forces in India today,' was Nehru's arrogant way of expressing it in March 1937, 'British imperialism and Indian nationalism as represented by the Congress.' Members of the Muslim League in the legislatures should join Congress and in future by-elections the League should refrain from putting up candidates: in effect an invitation to the League to disband itself.

This was too much for Jinnah, now returned to politics as leader of the League. Jinnah, after the disappointments of the previous years, had left India altogether in 1932 and had gone to live, and practise law, in London. He had, however, never totally given up hope of returning to Indian politics. While in London he had been influenced by the life of the Turkish leader Kamal Ataturk and by the ideas of the Punjabi Muslim poet, Muhammad Iqbal, who in 1930 had put forward his conception of a Muslim state in India. Under their influence and of that of Liaquat Ali Khan, a politician from the United Provinces who was to become the first Prime Minister of Pakistan, Jinnah returned to India in 1935 with the aim of uniting Indian Muslims to fight the coming elections under the new constitution. Jinnah, who had once been the advocate of Hindu-Muslim unity still did not envisage the *partition* of India. He still believed in a partnership but a partnership that recognized that Muslims had a separate personality, that they were not just converted Hindus, who should return to the fold they had so foolishly left. Jinnah was still looking for a *personal* identity in the Indian political scene. Congress was to help him in finding it as a communal leader.

Nehru's attitude at the time was not unreasonable, taking his ideological standpoint. Congress did appear to him to have triumphed over communalism. Jinnah, too, was still essentially an *Indian* nationalist. Why then should he not be prepared to join Congress once again in the fight for Indian freedom? A correspondence between the two men, however, reveals something of the later Nehru's political style which was to end in the nadir of the Sino-Indian conflict. Nehru was prepared to *talk* about issues but not to *negotiate* them. His aim was not to compromise or even to learn the motives behind the other's point of view but to convince him that Nehru's position was the right one. There was an *appearance* of flexibility but Nehru's distaste for the point of view which he convinced himself was that of the other party would never allow him to accept its sincerity. This was a failing that was to lead in 1947 to the partition of India and in 1962 to the Chinese attack on India's north-eastern border.

The failure of negotiations and the generally pro-Hindu activities of Congress provincial governments turned Jinnah to the organizing of the Muslim League as the sole expression of the Muslim masses. He had seen what could be done with the Hindu peasants and workers and he took his own campaign to the people. The basis of the campaign was fear, fear of Hindu raj, and its language was essentially religious. It could hardly be anything else for this was the only common identity. The results of intensive propaganda were immediate. 'Islam in danger' was the recurrent theme and Congress was a Hindu organization. The call to faith was answered. Muslim leaders began to join the League, so did the Muslim peasant and worker. The League defeated a Congress candidate in a by-election in the United Provinces late in 1937. Very slowly Congress began to realize what it had helped to create. Offers of negotiations were now refused – by Jinnah.

Though Congress was perturbed by the growth of the Muslim League and the new stature of Jinnah, it was basically much more concerned with the fruits of office, and in building up discipline among its members. Congress was not a political party in any western sense nor when it took office did it operate in western democratic terms. It had declared its aim as not to work the constitution but to help to destroy it. Congress had, however, been elected on a platform which contained specific promises of social and economic reform. When ministries took office they found themselves under pressure to implement those promises. This created something of a dilemma. To institute *radical* changes would be sure to alienate one or more of the special-interest groups in Congress. Agrarian reforms would antagonize some elements; industrial legislation would upset those Indian businessmen upon whom Congress depended for its finance. Yet not to take some positive action would only disillusion the masses who had given Congress their support. Furthermore, if nothing was done it would seem to prove the contention of those who maintained that Indians were not capable of governing themselves. Congress was to be rescued from its dilemma by the outbreak of the Second World War which gave the Congress ministries an excellent excuse to resign. Yet in the two and a half years in which they remained in office, severe strains began to show inside Congress.

The right-wing leadership, however, managed to keep control over most Congressmen, even the most dissident. The organization built up with such care and attention by Vallabhbhai Patel facilitated the dictatorship of the Congress Parliamentary Board. In fact the Board was so powerful that it functioned as a sort of central government, dictating the policies of the provincial administrations. The authoritarian control exercised by the Board added further support to the Muslim League contention that should a federal India ever emerge with a Congress majority it would coerce the provinces whether they had a Congress government or not.

The Muslim League was not alone in its dislike of the activities of the Congress high command. Many Congressmen of the left resented being bullied from above and there were moves once again to try and give Congress a radical image. More significantly still, the lack of reforms were leading to an increase in the membership of the *kisan sabhas* or peasant leagues which Nehru had tried unsuccessfully, in the face of right-wing opposition, to affiliate with Congress. The leagues were adopting a militant attitude towards agrarian reform and challenging local Congress organizations. Nehru, the radical mediator, was called upon to reconcile the leagues to Congress policy. His appeal to rally behind Congress in the struggle for independence without which there *could* be no sweeping reforms was on the whole accepted. Congress governments did institute a number of reforms, admirable in their limited way, but on the whole they showed considerable caution.

Nehru was disappointed by what in one criticism he described as 'counter-revolutionary' tendencies in some of the Congress ministries. As Congress president he was constantly urging ministers not to sink to the level of ordinary politicians. Not much notice was taken of these exhortations – most of the chief ministers were of right-wing persuasion and in any case there was a strict limit on the amount of finance available for reform. Not greatly successful in inculcating socialist ideals into the ministries, Nehru was at least allowed to set up inside Congress a National Planning Committee to consider India's economic problems and needs. Again Congress leaders were to accept an essentially socialist institution of no immediate value or threat, according to one's point of view, which was later to become an inalienable heritage of the golden days of the free-dom struggle.

In the spring of 1938 Nehru turned away from the problems of India for another *tour d'horizon*, another trip to Europe. He was dissatisfied with the legislative record of the Congress ministries. Congress and the Muslim League seemed even more hostile to each other. He had once again come into conflict with Gandhi, this time over a resolution of the AICC con-demning the Maharaja of Mysore which the Mahatma would not accept. Nehru considered resigning from the Working Committee but decided against it because the next president of Congress was to be Subhas Bose and Nehru felt that he would need his support. A trip to Europe would 'freshen up my tired and puzzled mind', he wrote to Gandhi.

Nehru was obsessed by the coming conflict in Europe. Hitler had marched into Austria. Fascism was on the move. Was this the prelude to war? On his journey he paused at Suez to meet the leader of the Egyptian nationalist party, the Wafd. But his main interest was Europe. Joined at Marseilles by Krishna

Menon, then head of the India League in London, together they left for Spain. Nehru spent five days in Barcelona, the capital of the Republicans who were being assaulted by an indigenous fascism strongly supported by that of Germany and Italy. He was impressed by the idealism of those who were fighting for all the things he cherished most, for democracy and socialism, for human dignity and human rights.

In London and Paris, Nehru addressed meetings on behalf of the Spanish Republic. The cause of Indian freedom he linked in his speeches with that of anti-fascists everywhere. He visited Czechoslovakia and was horrified when that country was dismembered by the Munich agreement; 'the murder of another nation' was his description. Now he was sure that Britain had a pro-fascist Government. Imperialism and fascism could only be allies and yet there was some confusion in his attitude. He saw that it was possible that Britain and Germany might go to war with each other – a contradiction one might have thought. But he really felt that it might be two forms of fascism fighting each other and he made it quite clear in a letter to the *Manchester Guardian* that the Indian people were not going to be dragged into a world war at the dictation of the British Government. The letter reveals the dilemma of the nationalist who sees hope for his country in a war between rival imperialisms but at the same time prefers one to the other.

Returning to India in November 1938, Nehru moved out of one crisis into another but this time one with a personal edge to it. Subhas Bose had been strongly critical of Gandhi's role in the nationalist movement almost from the beginning. Though he was without Nehru's mass appeal, Bose's popularity among the left-thinking young outrivalled Nehru's, particularly in Bengal. Bose had his own view of India's future and that of the freedom movement. His activism had been rewarded with the persecution by the British and he had been forced to spend some years outside India. Returning in April 1936, having warned the British that he was coming, he was arrested immediately on arrival at Bombay. Bose's reputation abroad now rivalled that of Nehru and Gandhi, indeed on the surface anyway he was much the most attractive of Indian leaders. Through his writings and speeches Bose had also become a national figure.

At this stage Gandhi decided to use the same tactics he had used on Nehru. Give Bose the highest office in the movement and allow it to mellow his revolutionary zeal. It might also bring into the orthodox Congress organization those left-wing elements outside Congress who preferred Bose to Nehru. Although Bose was very conscious of the need for Congress unity he was not prepared to compromise his principles for it. He accepted the nomination for Congress president as a tribute to the ideas he represented so forcefully and was determined to use his period of office to free Congress from the 'dead hand' of Gandhi. Gandhi was fully aware of this. Unlike Nehru, Bose offered a real threat not only to the unity of Congress but to the Mahatma's dominant position.

Bose acted at first with great circumspection. His presidential speech contained no criticism of the Mahatma, no call for Congress reform. But he looked forward to the time when Congress would have achieved independence and for this Congress must plan now. Once at the centre of things Bose discovered that though he reigned as president he did not rule. The old guard were firmly in control and apparently immovable. He had the support of Nehru but Bose quickly realized that Nehru, too, was without effective power. Bose had been too long out of India. In his disillusion he felt isolated and useless. Gandhi had succeeded in emasculating this tiger from Bengal. Towards the end of 1938, however, Bose became convinced that war in Europe was not far off. He had always considered that should Britain go to war it was the duty of Indian nationalists to take advantage of its preoccupation elsewhere. Bose decided that he needed a second term as president.

Gandhi was not prepared to consider such a thing. He had avoided a direct challenge to his authority and it was now time for Bose to be put aside. Gandhi asked Nehru to become president once again. Nehru refused and suggested Maulana Azad. Bose, however, made it clear that he would contest the election and Azad declined. The right-wing leaders headed by Patel now put up another candidate and issued a statement condemning Bose's determination to stand for election as a threat to Congress unity. Bose refused to withdraw. Nehru then entered the affair with a conciliatory statement which only antagonized both sides. Gandhi, who had taken no direct part in the controversy although he had been very active behind the scenes, openly came out against Bose in an article in his newspaper *Harijan* on 28 January 1939. 'Out of the present condition of Congress,' he wrote, 'I see nothing but anarchy and red ruin in front of the country.'

To the surprise of the right wing, Bose won the election by a majority of just over two hundred votes. Gandhi took the result as a personal defeat. Bose was conciliatory, Gandhi firm in his opposition. Soon there came a pretext for all but three of the members of the Working Committee to resign, leaving only Bose, his brother Sarat and Nehru. Again Nehru attempted to mediate but this time Bose refused to cooperate. Nehru, though he did not officially resign from the Working Committee, now let it be known that he would not serve on a new one. He appeared to have joined, however obliquely, the right-wing opposition. In actual fact the right wing and the Mahatma had no further need of Nehru. They did not want a mediator, especially if he had a chance of success. Bose had to be crushed and Nehru's interference was merely an irritation.

Bose was now in extreme danger. If Congress had to choose between him and Gandhi it was obvious who would be the loser. Bose's attitude to Nehru remained friendly though critical. Bose still consulted Nehru about what he should do but the advice he received was not very helpful. He tried to approach Gandhi but – though the two men met for discussions at which Bose, realizing rather belatedly that there would be no national movement with any real popular support without the Mahatma, was conciliatory – Gandhi had no intention of co-operating with him. There was now no alternative for the rebel president but to submit his resignation. Nehru again tried for a compromise. Reappoint the Working Committee and when vacancies came up put in his own men – this was Nehru's advice. Bose refused and confirmed his resignation. The strongest challenge Gandhi had so far had to face was at an end.

The final humiliations, however, were still to come. The Bose faction organized a Forward Bloc inside Congress in an endeavour to unite all the left-wing groups. The Congress Socialist Party was reluctant to join. In July 1939 Bose called for country-wide demonstrations to protest against a directive from the All-India Congress Committee giving itself a wider measure of control over the provincial Congress organizations. In return Bose was removed as president of the Bengal Provincial Congress Committee and disqualified from holding elective office for three years. It was the end of Bose the politician. Early in 1941 he was to leave India in an attempt to fight for India's freedom with means more militant than Congress could offer.

For any aspiring rebel, the treatment of Subhas Bose was a lesson in practicalities. Here was a popular leader elected democratically in preference to Gandhi's own candidate. Those who had voted for him had known his views. Yet his mandate as president had been denied by intrigue, intrigue not only against Bose but against the democracy which had elected him. The message was clear – do not fight the Mahatma. Nehru saw the moral as well as most. He was also not happy about his own role in the affair. There is no satisfactory evidence that Nehru recognized Bose as a rival for the leadership of the socialists in Congress. Nehru was not willing to identify himself with any faction so he could hardly resent someone else wishing to do so. Nehru preferred an individual crusade to a group offensive. Nevertheless he seems to have felt that in some way his behaviour might have been different. Fortunately, there was an opportunity to escape from any pending crisis of conscience. He was to go to Nationalist China on an official visit as the representative of Congress. The invitation had been open for some time but now, with war threatening in Europe, it seemed the right time for someone to go. The obvious choice was Nehru.

On 20 August Nehru left India for China. He expected to be away four weeks. The outbreak of war in Europe cut down the actual length of time to less than a fortnight.

Chapter 13
The Mad World of War

Nehru had watched the slide to conflict in Europe with both fear and foreboding. He was strongly anti-fascist and hated the thought of fascism being victorious, yet the war would be between two sorts of imperialism, one of which ruled in India. He had already made it clear that India would not be prepared to fight in such a war, because it could do so only in defence of empire. Throughout the negotiations with the British that were to come Nehru consistently hoped for a solution that would permit Congress to support the war effort against fascism. Other Congress leaders did not share his torment – or his view of the world. They knew little of international affairs and cared even less. Their blinkered vision saw only the road to Indian freedom and to be overmuch concerned about a civil war in remote Europe seemed only a dangerous diversion. Their innocence was profound – and aggressive. What had Nehru's fears to do with them? There were others who welcomed the war, for it could be used to India's advantage. Subhas Bose saw Britain's troubles in Europe as an opportunity for India to snatch independence from the failing grasp of the conqueror.

The need for Congress to define its attitude was demanded on 3 September 1939 when the Viceroy – as was undoubtedly his constitutional right – declared India at war with Germany and promulgated a number of ordinances giving himself special wartime powers. His action underlined the fact that however far India had been taken towards responsible government by the 1935 Act, it was the British who still ruled and that in matters of life and death Indians were not even to be consulted.

The Congress Working Committee met at Wardha in the Central Provinces on 8 September. Two days later Nehru arrived back hurriedly from China. There was no unanimity of opinion about what should be done. Bose, who had been invited to the meeting, called for instant and widespread civil disobedience. But he was alone in his belligerence. Most members wanted the Congress provincial governments to remain in office and this could only be achieved by some sort of compromise with the British. Nehru, who was looking for any reasonable formula that would allow Congress to support the war, found himself on the side of the right-wing leaders. But even they were not thinking of total support. Gandhi was only for India's moral, not active and therefore violent, involvement in the war. Nehru maintained that fascism could not be fought with fine phrases.

But first the British had to be sounded out. Nehru drafted a 'war aims resolution' which demanded that the British should state what they were fighting for. If it was for things as they were, for colonial possessions and privilege, then Congress would not have anything to do with the conflict. On the other hand, should it be for democracy and *democracy for all* then Congress would cooperate. Congress was not alone in wanting guarantees from the British. The Muslim League courteously informed the Government that though it condemned Nazi aggression, it would require an assurance that no decision would be made about India without its approval. 'The Muslim League,' it stated categorically, was 'the only organization that can speak for Muslim India.'

The Government's reply to what was in effect a Congress demand for immediate freedom was bland and unaccommodating. All it was willing to promise was that *at the end of the war* it would 'be prepared to regard the scheme of the Act [of 1935] as open to modification in the light of Indian views'. But the British would make a gesture of goodwill: they would establish some sort of consultative body which would include the Viceroy and representatives of various Indian political groups. This was too feeble to appeal to any of the Congress leaders, even Gandhi. A promise to discuss Dominion status after the war and a consultative body shared with others was quite unacceptable. The Working Committee ordered the Congress provincial governments to resign. With some reluctance the call was obeyed and by 15 November all had given up office. The other ministries remained where they were.

Despite the Congress action, attempts at compromise continued but there was no desire for a solution on the part of the British. The Viceroy, Lord Linlithgow, had an almost Victorian attitude to empire and had no wish to see Indians rule themselves. There also seemed no pressing reason for making concessions. The war in Europe had come to a standstill after the attack upon Poland. Britain remained strong and there was certainly no overt threat in Asia. Nevertheless the Viceroy was not idle. He had a profound dislike of Congress, which he considered a 'movement of Hindu hooliganism'. When Linlithgow heard of a meeting between Nehru and Jinnah that gave the impression a compromise was possible between Congress and the League he set out to cultivate Jinnah. One result was that the League called for a 'day of deliverance and thanksgiving' on 22 December to celebrate the resignation of the Congress governments.

Congress met in session at Ramghur in Bihar in March 1940 in an atmosphere of frustration tempered by a desire for action. Once again it was Gandhi's Congress. Though not officially a member, he was the acknowledged leader behind whom everyone rallied when it came to the point of no return. Though Gandhi stated 'Compromise is in my very being', he called for civil disobedience. But there would have to be a delay as the organization was not yet ready for a non-violent campaign. Congress agreed. Gandhi had their complete approval. It was almost like old times. Any criticism inside Congress was unvoiced. Even Nehru was silent and took no part in the proceedings. Subhas Bose, who had called an 'Anti-Compromise Conference' simultaneously with the Congress session, also demanded action but immediately and with 'no rest or break, nor any sidetracking as happened in 1932'. But the initiative was once again with Gandhi.

The Mahatma did nothing. The Inner Voices were apparently silent. But while Gandhi waited, the war in Europe burst into shattering life. In April Denmark and Norway were invaded, then Holland and Belgium. As the Germans swept into France, the British forces were pushed to the sea, escaping in an armada of small boats from the beaches of Dunkirk in the early days of

June 1940. It seemed to many that the Germans must be irresistible and that Britain would soon be invaded. What then would happen to India? Would the Germans take over? What was to be done? The British Government in London had been aware of the dangers from the start of the German offensive and the Viceroy was instructed to do everything he could to unite Indians behind the war effort. That obviously included Congress. Linlithgow, however, was not prepared to make a move. In May his immobility was encouraged by the appointment as Prime Minister of Winston Churchill, that arch-enemy of freedom for India.

The events in Europe came as a shock to the Congress leadership. Divisions immediately appeared. Nehru was strongly opposed to taking advantage of Britain in its hour of peril. Civil disobedience now would be like becoming allies of the Nazis. Gandhi too did not wish to embarrass the British when they were fighting for their lives. He was also well aware that if the Germans took over India there would be no possibility of a non-violent struggle for India's freedom. The revolutionaries would dominate the nationalist movement and there would be no place for him. Maulana Azad, then Congress president, disagreed with both Gandhi and Nehru. The British by refusing the modest requests of Congress had brought non-cooperation upon themselves. Why should Congress, having denounced the war as imperialist, now change its mind?

The Working Committee met in emergency session. There was a majority for negotiation with the British. The offer was once again of cooperation but this time of *complete* cooperation. There were only two conditions: the declaration of Indian independence to take effect after the war and an all-party national government now as a token of that promise. The armed forces would remain under the British commander-in-chief and the Viceroy's position would be unchanged, though he would be expected not to use his veto except in cases of extreme emergency. The offer was made in all sincerity, a feeling backed by genuine fear. For years Congress had concentrated on its struggle with the British. It was a movement of parochial aims and parochial minds. Only a few like Nehru recognized that India was not isolated from the world outside and that what went on there affected India too. The offer of cooperation was made not to help Britain fight Germany but to help defend India from attack. As Nehru, sensing the mood of Congress, put it in July: 'While India is completely opposed to the idea of the triumph of Nazism, it is no good asking her to come to the rescue of a tottering imperialism.'

The Congress offer also revealed a split with Gandhi. As early as 1938 he had tried to get Congress to agree to the proposition that when India became free it would not have armed forces. There had been some disagreement but the matter had been put aside without decision. Now it was necessary to define the Congress attitude precisely. Under the influence of Nehru, Rajagopalachari and Azad, the Working Committee though accepting non-violent methods as suitable for the struggle *inside* India rejected them as a means of national defence. This resolution was accepted at a meeting of the All-India Congress Committee in July. Four members of the Working Committee abstained from voting and Abdul Ghaffar Khan, the 'Frontier Gandhi', resigned as a protest against the jettisoning of 'non-violence'. Though Nehru tried to soften the blow to Gandhi there was no doubt that Congress had, for the first time since 1920, decisively rejected the Mahatma.

The effect of the resolution upon the left wing of Congress was immediate. Many of its leaders had already been arrested and they looked to Nehru to defend the radical position. One of the leaders of the Congress Socialist Party wrote to Nehru appealing to him to head the opposition against the offer of cooperation with the British. Once again they had mistaken their man. It is possible to see in this episode the hardening of disillusion with Nehru which was to lead finally to the socialists leaving Congress immediately after independence. Many socialists had already come to distrust Nehru and now it seemed that he had finally deserted them for cooperation, however limited, with the British. His reasons did not convince them.

The offer had been made by Congress and it was now up to the British to respond. There were, however, other parties with an interest in the sort of compromise that might be arrived at. Even Congress had recognized that a united front would make some difference. The Congress president had approached Jinnah but had been rejected with the brutal words: 'Cannot you realize that [as Congress president] you are made a Muslim show-boy, to give it colour that it is national . . .? The Congress is a *Hindu* body.' Jinnah particularly resented Azad, a Muslim,, being Congress president because he believed that all Muslims should be members of the League. In March Jinnah had gone further and made what was later to be known as the 'Pakistan Resolution'. 'Muslims,' he had said, 'are a nation according to any definition of a nation, and they must have their homelands, their territory and their State.' Nehru had dismissed this pretension as 'meaningless and absurd'. Why then should Jinnah cooperate with Congress?

The British took some time to answer the Congress offer. The Viceroy consulted Jinnah and was told that there were conditions that had to be satisfied before the Muslim League would agree to join a 'national' government. First, the British must undertake to adopt no constitution, temporary or final, 'without the previous approval of Muslim India'. Secondly, in any wartime administration 'Muslim India must have an equal share in the authority and control of the Governments, central and provincial'. The positions of Congress and the League were obviously incompatible. The British response to Congress came in August. On the matter of independence they would promise no more than that a representative body would be set up after the war to decide on a new constitution. In the meantime they were prepared to invite a number of 'representative' Indians to join the Viceroy's executive council and set up a War Advisory Board, with Indian members.

The British offer differed only in detail from that made in October 1939. But there was one clause which seemed to give to the Muslim League the veto it had asked for. The British would not contemplate any transfer of responsibility to a system of government 'whose authority is directly denied by large and powerful elements in India's national life. *Nor could they be parties to the coercion of such elements into submission to such a Government.*' The offer was unimaginative – and unyielding. When the AICC met in Bombay on 15 September the delegates were in a somewhat chastened mood. The panic which had marked the earlier meeting now seemed exaggerated. Germany had not invaded Britain nor had the British given in under heavy aerial attacks. The inflexibility of the Government's August offer perhaps reflected the optimism of the British. There now seemed no alternative for Congress but to turn back to Gandhi. Nehru and the other members of the Working Committee moved into the background and the Mahatma took the stage again.

Gandhi, as usual, had no plans. In fact he was extremely reluctant to take any serious action. For this there were two important reasons. He still hoped for a compromise with the British and he was not convinced that a civil disobedience campaign would be effective. There was no issue on which to arouse the masses. Congress leaders might be concerned with independence, some of them even with anti-fascism, but these were matters which did not interest ordinary people. Though there had been some shortages of consumer goods after the outbreak of the European war and a rise in the cost of living, this primarily affected the minority middle class. The Indian peasant, constantly at war himself with poverty and starvation, felt very little difference in the texture of the battle for life.

In his endeavour to escape from the trap of ineffectiveness Gandhi approached the Viceroy at the end of September with a demand for freedom of speech to criticize the war, such criticism now being prohibited by ordinance. If this demand was granted, Gandhi wrote, there would be no need for civil disobedience. The Viceroy refused – India was at war and there must be some limitation on opposition to it. The Mahatma now had no alternative but to start civil disobedience. He then chose the most ineffective method. There would be no mass satyagraha, only individuals would defy the law. Nehru found Gandhi's intention feeble, a sign of weakness. He was convinced that Gandhi was wrong but allowed himself to be won over by his devotion to the man.

The first protestor was to be Vinoba Bhave, a disciple of

Gandhi who had tried to make himself into a simulacrum of the master. He made a simple statement which Gandhi had written: 'It is wrong to help the British war effort with men or money. The only worthy effort is to resist all war with non-violent resistance.' On the third occasion of making it in public, Bhave was arrested and sentenced to three months' imprisonment. The event caused no stir at all. No mention of it was made in the censored newspapers. For most Indians it was a non-event.

The next to make this rather futile gesture was to be Nehru, but the Government acted first. There were some, not totally unfounded, fears of agrarian trouble in the United Provinces and Nehru had made a number of speeches which were considered inflammatory. The Government, which still chose to consider Nehru a dangerous revolutionary, had been advised by the Intelligence Department that he should be put in prison. Charged with sedition, Nehru was convicted and sentenced to four years' rigorous imprisonment. This punitive sentence shocked many Indians. The Government made no attempt to prevent the news of this arrest from getting into the papers and obviously hoped that it would act as a warning to others. Instead, Nehru's conviction produced indignation and protest on widely differing levels of Indian opinion. For a time it even seemed to put fire into the civil disobedience campaign. Meetings of protest were held all over the country but no attempt was made by Congress to capitalize on the anger shown there.

Individual satyagraha continued and so did the arrests, though sentences were mild. Then in an endeavour to add a little drama Gandhi informed the Viceroy that members of the Congress Working Committee, the AICC, and members of the legislatures would act in groups. By the end of January 1941 nearly three thousand protestors were in jail. There was little excitement over the arrests, though the Government now extended censorship to the mails. Apart from a truce over Christmas 1940, so the British could celebrate *their* religious festival, said Gandhi, the campaign went on, the clang of the prison gates silenced by censorship. It all seemed rather pointless and there was rising criticism inside Congress and a growing desire to call off the campaign. Gandhi would have none of it. His 'moral protest', he insisted, was 'a token of the yearning of a political association to achieve the freedom of 350 million people'.

By the early summer of 1941 the campaign had all but died out of its own accord. Political India seemed in the doldrums. Yet things were happening. The minority parties were still active. The Muslim League ministries still in power were not being particularly cooperative mainly out of the conviction that the Government would take no action against them. Moderate Indians were still trying to bring about a reconciliation between the conflicting parties, but they held the confidence of no one, not even the British. The Government in London continued to reiterate its promise of full Dominion status after the war – and implied that it could only be granted to a united India. The then Secretary of State for India, L. S. Amery, reminded Indian nationalists that their duty was to 'India first!' This gratuitous advice provoked Gandhi into calling on the British to leave India and let Congress and the Muslim League work out their own problems. 'It may be,' he went on, 'that before we come to that happy state of affairs, *we may have to fight among ourselves.* But if we agree not to invite the assistance of any outside Power, the trouble will perhaps last a fortnight.' By 'fight' Gandhi probably only meant 'argument' but either way it seemed a very naïve proposition. Naturally there was no response from London.

In India there were increasing signs that the Muslim League was being advised on its policies by senior members of the British administration. The terms of the August Offer, which had not been withdrawn, were very slowly implemented and it was not until July 1941 that Indians were appointed to the Viceroy's executive council. When the names were made known they turned out to be those of men of quality and experience but totally unrepresentative of the mainstreams of Indian nationalism. From the nationalist point of view these men, however admirable in themselves, could be no more than puppets. A few weeks later, any confidence in the honesty of British intentions that still remained received a further blow.

The British and American Governments represented by Winston Churchill and President Roosevelt issued a statement on their concept of the post-war world. This 'Atlantic Charter' became part of the war aims of the Allies. When the text of the Charter was released Indians welcomed the clause which claimed that both the signatories respected 'the right of *all peoples* to choose the Government under which they live; and they wish to see sovereign rights and self-government restored to those who have been forcibly deprived of them'. Indians were soon disillusioned, for Churchill hastened to make it clear that this clause only referred to European nations and that India was 'quite a separate problem'.

This qualification reminded some Indians of how the doctrine of self-determination enunciated by President Wilson in the First World War had not applied to colonial peoples either. It seemed as if nothing had changed in the intervening years. An attempt by Amery to equate Britain's offer of an elected constituent assembly after the war with the terms of the Charter was unconvincing. Even those Indians who had never ceased to believe in the sincerity of British promises began to have their doubts.

The pointlessness of Gandhi's satyagraha campaign led to bitterness and confusion in the Congress ranks. What was perhaps more important was that Congress had lost touch with the people. Recruits were flowing in to the British Indian army. Indian factories were working day and night producing war supplies for the Middle East and African fronts. Indian workers were receiving the highest wages they had ever had. Neither labourer nor factory owner, however nationalist he had once been, was prepared to give up this sort of prosperity. One Indian leader, recognizing that Indian freedom could no longer be fought for with any hope of success *inside* India, set off on a search for allies outside. Subhas Bose, gaining release from jail by threatening a fast to the death, escaped from house arrest in January 1941 and after failing to interest the Russians in his plans finally arrived in Berlin in March. But even his voice on the radio calling upon Indians to rise and help those who were willing to help them was heard by only a few, and where was the help he talked of anyway? It was nearer than anyone thought.

On 4 December 1941 the Government unexpectedly released all the Congress prisoners, including Nehru. Three days later the Japanese attacked the American naval base at Pearl Harbor. The same day Japanese aircraft bombed the American island of Guam, military installations in the Philippines and the British naval base at Singapore.

The speed and vigour of the Japanese offensive created a sense of urgency. In Congress the old panic revived, this time with greater intensity. The doctrine of non-violence was again thrown aside. Nehru openly stated his view that bombs could not be resisted by non-violent methods. The demand for some sort of cooperation with the British in the defence of India grew in strength and Gandhi asked to be relieved of the leadership of Congress. This was accepted on 16 January 1942 when the AICC made another offer of conditional support to the British. Not all the members of the Working Committee were in agreement. Prasad and Patel threatened to resign and only Gandhi's influence kept them from doing so. Nehru, though he sponsored the resolution on cooperation, had little faith in its chances of acceptance by the British. Yet, he agreed, an offer must be made.

Rumours were going around that the split between Nehru and Gandhi on policy had hardened into a parting of ways. Nehru denied it and, more significantly, so did Gandhi. The Mahatma went further and publicly stated what most Congressmen had come to expect. 'Jawaharlal will be my successor.' The relationship between them, he said, was a 'union of hearts'. He knew, Gandhi went on, 'that when I am gone he will speak my language' – a highly improbable prophecy which was, perhaps, more a statement of hope. This confirmation of Nehru's position was not welcome to everyone but the opposition was concealed while Gandhi was alive. At the time it did not matter much for should the Japanese invade India, Nehru and Gandhi would probably both be replaced.

Certainly such a possibility was in Gandhi's mind and it

seems unlikely that Nehru had given no thought to the consequences of a successful Japanese invasion. In the middle of
February the 'impregnable' fortress of Singapore fell and in
Burma the British were on the retreat. What was happening
was almost inconceivable. The British empire so unyielding to
Indian nationalism was crumbling before the attacks of the
Japanese. It seemed to many that Subhas Bose had been right,
non-violence had only hindered the march to freedom. Yet in
many ways the imminence of deliverance by the Japanese was
not taken seriously. The Muslim League was more concerned
with fighting Congress. The extreme communalist organization,
the Hindu Mahasabha, defied the Muslims to come out and
fight in the streets. As the Japanese marched on, the politicians
screeched at one another. India, in Nehru's words, was caught
up in the 'mad world of war and politics and fascism and
imperialism'.

Chapter 14
'Do or Die'

On 8 March 1942 Japanese forces occupied Rangoon, the capital of British Burma. Four days later Winston Churchill announced in the House of Commons that a socialist member of the War Cabinet, Sir Stafford Cripps, would go to India to 'satisfy himself upon the spot by personal consultation that the conclusions upon which we are all agreed and which we believe represent a just and final solution, will achieve their purpose'. It was, said Churchill, the desire of the British Government to 'rally all the forces of Indian life to guard their land from the menace of the invader'. There were many, including Churchill and the Government of India, who would have preferred to keep the nationalist leaders locked up for the duration of the war but there were some doubts in Whitehall as to whether the authorities in India, with the Japanese at the gates, would be able to suppress an internal rebellion if such a thing followed the arrests. Undoubtedly there were extremists willing and anxious to act as a fifth column for the Japanese. Churchill saw the attempt at reconciliation as leading to a possible truce, which would leave the British to get on with the task of defending India.

There were also domestic reasons for sending Cripps to India. The British war cabinet was a coalition. The Labour Party, despite its performance when in office, still officially advocated freedom for India. The Labour ministers in the cabinet were, therefore, unwilling to be involved in the suppression of Congress. They also had grounds for believing that Congress would accept a reasonable offer. Churchill was also under considerable pressure from President Roosevelt. In the interests of both cabinet solidarity and the American alliance, a gesture of goodwill was necessary.

The 'Draft Declaration' Cripps took with him to India repeated the terms of the August Offer of 1940 but went further on a number of points. India was conceded the right to leave the British Commonwealth if it wished. This implied that Dominion status now meant the same as independence. Immediately after the war an elected Constituent Assembly would decide on a constitution without interference from the British, who would accept any agreed constitution with only one proviso: that any province had the right to remain outside the Dominion. There were various other clauses concerning such things as a treaty to guarantee 'British obligations'. As for immediate changes, there could be no fundamental ones for the duration of the war. But an interim system of government could be established and the 'leaders of the principal sections of the Indian people' would be invited to join.

The choice of Cripps as negotiator was astute. He was an upper-class socialist and a friend of that other upper-class socialist, Jawaharlal Nehru. He had spoken often and with apparent sincerity on the right of Indians to choose their own form of government. Cripps also had an almost Indian puritanism which, coupled with the fact that he was a vegetarian, endeared him to Gandhi. Cripps believed that he could achieve a solution to the Indian problem but he went hampered both by his brief, which offered pledges only redeemable after the end of the war, and by the taint of association, for he was a member of a cabinet headed by that consistent enemy of India's freedom, Winston Churchill.

Cripps began his talks in New Delhi on 25 March 1942. He met representatives from practically every facet of Indian political life but there was one party not present at the discussions which was always in the minds of those who were – the Japanese army. While Cripps was talking, Japanese aircraft were bombing Indian cities. Though innumerable avenues were explored there was no real desire for agreement. The Muslim League welcomed the implied recognition of Pakistan in the right for provinces to remain outside the new Dominion, but the statement was too vague for Jinnah. The same clause offended not only Congress but the communal Hindu Mahasabha and the Sikhs of the Punjab, who feared that the Muslim majority there would vote for non-accession. The Untouchables saw no guarantee that they would be protected from caste Hindus. Congress also resented the fact that the princes would be allowed representation in the Constituent Assembly. It also turned out that Cripps had exceeded his authority in suggesting that some form of 'national government' would be conceded when all that the British Government in London envisaged was an enlargement of the Viceroy's executive council.

All these, however, were only the formal reasons for the rejection of the offer. Indian nationalists were unwilling to accept promises redeemable only in the distant and rather gloomy future. Faced with the possibility of a successful Japanese invasion there seemed no point in negotiating with the British. Nehru was among the few who did not accept this reasoning. He hoped for a settlement and for a time believed one was possible. Cripps seems to have banked heavily on Nehru carrying Congress with him, but did not realize how isolated from the majority Nehru actually was. The view of that majority was expressed by Gandhi when he was reported, perhaps apocryphally, to have asked: 'Why accept a post-dated cheque on a bank that is obviously failing?' Far better to save energy for negotiations with the Japanese.

Talks did continue but the counter-proposals and arguments put forward were essentially a bluff. The overwhelming majority of Congress – and it was upon Congress that the success or failure of the Cripps mission depended – was quite prepared to gain India's freedom with the help of the first Asian power to strike a blow against western imperialism. Japan's actions in China were undoubtedly unpleasant but this only worried a few sophisticated leaders like Nehru. The rest responded favourably to the Japanese slogan 'Asia for the Asiatics' and put pressure upon their leaders. Under the circumstances there was no possibility whatsoever that the leaders would be allowed to accept less from the British than the majority thought it stood to gain from the Japanese.

Some attempt was made to keep the talks going. President Roosevelt's personal representative, Colonel Johnson, had conversations with Nehru and others. But his interference was resented by both the British and the Indian Governments. Congress put forward the demand that the armed forces should be placed under the authority of an Indian member of the executive council, a proposal that was sure to provoke the unyielding opposition of the Government of India. On receiving the proposal the Viceroy telegraphed his disapproval to London without informing Cripps. On 7 April a secret telegram reached Cripps from London and from that moment his manner changed. So too did that of Congress. After a telephone call from the Mahatma the Working Committee officially rejected the proposals. On 12 April Cripps departed for London, leaving only confusion and bitterness behind him.

Nehru's own feeling throughout the negotiations had been one of continuous frustration. He wanted an agreement and spent a great deal of time trying to persuade his colleagues to concentrate not on those proposals which could only take effect after the war but on arriving at some compromise that would allow Congress to collaborate in the defence of India against the Japanese. But he could not overcome the pessimism and the fear of members of the Working Committee. Gandhi's own role was especially disruptive. His only concern was to prevent any commitment to violence even in the defence of the country. The Mahatma's pacifism paralleled the self-interest of the majority. But Nehru would not give up. He wrote to President Roosevelt that Indians would do their utmost not to submit to Japanese aggression. They could not support the British war effort but they would organize their own. Nehru's solution was guerrilla warfare against the invader. Gandhi dismissed it in his newspaper *Harijan*: 'I am sorry that he [Nehru] has developed a fancy for guerrilla warfare. But I have no doubt that it will be a nine days' wonder.' As usual, Gandhi was right.

After Cripps's departure nationalist leaders anxious to disguise their real reasons for rejecting the British offer turned to virulent attacks both on the offer itself and on Cripps. Jinnah dismissed the 'non-accession' proposals because they did not confirm the right of Muslim self-determination. He also rounded on Congress. If the British had conceded immediate self-government it would have been a 'Fascist Grand Council and the Muslims and other minorities . . . entirely at the mercy of Congress'. Congress chose Cripps as its target. He was, one Congress newspaper alleged, an agent of British reaction and his mission 'the result of American pressure. It was a stage-managed show to buy off world opinion and to foist preconcerted failure on the people of India.' Even Nehru found it 'sad beyond measure that a man like Sir Stafford Cripps should allow himself to beome the Devil's Advocate'.

The All-India Congress Committee met at Allahabad at the end of April. Rajagopalachari, anxious that his colleagues should recognize the dangers presented to India's unity by their treatment of the Muslim League, put forward a resolution accepting the League's demand for Pakistan and called for the immediate formation of a coalition government to prosecute the war. The resolution was decisively rejected as treasonable. Instead the Committee passed a resolution virtually dictated by Gandhi calling for resistance to the Japanese but only in the form of non-violent non-cooperation. 'We may not bend the knee to the aggressor nor obey any of his orders. We may not look to him for favours nor fall to his bribes.' The Government's defence effort was to be neither helped nor hindered. Congress would operate its own scorched-earth policy.

The futility of the resolution is only intensified by the fact that the draft was prepared by Nehru. Once again he had completely surrendered any will of his own to the Mahatma. From conditional cooperation with the British in the defence of India, through the romantic nonsense of carrying on a guerrilla war against the Japanese, Nehru had now arrived at accepting a policy he must have known would never have been carried out. Many of the Congress leaders were preparing to welcome the Japanese. A police raid on the offices of the AICC in Nehru's old home at Allahabad discovered notes by Gandhi himself for a draft resolution assuring the Japanese 'that India bore no enmity' to them and that 'if India were free, her first step would be to negotiate with Japan'. Nehru apparently protested against this but had given in. The authenticity of these documents has been disputed but there is no reason to doubt the sentiments they express.

Rajagopalachari, who had already called upon the people of his own province of Madras to defend themselves should the Japanese, whose warships were off the coast, try to land, resigned from Congress, but only seven colleagues joined him. Nehru was now completely isolated but unable to make the break that might have satisfied his conscience. To settle his misgivings he went early in May for a holiday into the Kulu valley in the foothills of the Himalayas. There, he disclosed later, he thought about the consequences of a Japanese invasion, of the suffering it had already brought to refugees from Burma. He did not approve at all of the Government's scorched-earth policy though he had been quite prepared to accept that of Congress. He had even, it seems, recognized that guerrilla warfare by an unarmed population was absurd. But surprisingly he thought that occupation would do some good, for it would create a national spirit of resistance. Congress had been trying to set up food committees and self-defence units in the towns and villages but he knew that these would not be effective without the co-operation of the Government, which would give no help at all.

These ruminations – for they were nothing more – Nehru revealed in the book he was to write during his next stay in jail, *The Discovery of India*. Much of Nehru is there, for all his works are autobiographical. The innocent wonder, the romantic idealism, the essential naïveté and something more, for there is a note of callousness when he welcomes the war because it might bring a personal experience to millions and 'drag them out of that peace of the grave that Britain had imposed upon us'. With some satisfaction he quotes: 'Only where there are graves are there resurrections.'

While Nehru was away, Gandhi took action. He issued a provocative challenge to the British. Some dramatic gesture was called for. The broadcasts from Germany of Subhas Bose were being heard by more and more Indians. Japanese propaganda was having its effect amongst the intelligentsia. There was an atmosphere of tension and a growing desire among some Indians to seize their own freedom through revolutionary struggle. For the Mahatma the thought that Bose might return in the baggage of the Japanese army was too much to contemplate. Gandhi's challenge was simple: let the British get out and 'leave India in God's hands'. Have no fears about the communal problem, the British created it and it would disappear once they had left.

Anarchy, even internecine warfare, might follow 'for a time' but from it 'a true India will arise in place of the false one we see'.

The slogan Gandhi offered was 'Quit India'. With it once again the Mahatma seemed to have touched a nerve and throughout India thousands rallied to the call. Nehru hurrying back from the quiet of the high hills was appalled. If the British did not respond, and it was highly improbable that they would, Congress would have to follow up with a civil disobedience campaign and that could only help the Japanese. At Gandhi's retreat at Wardha, Nehru and the Mahatma argued over the decision and Nehru gained some concessions. Allied forces, Gandhi allowed, would be permitted to remain in India 'for the sole purpose of repelling a Japanese attack and helping China'. He was even willing to send 'India's ambassadors' to the Axis powers, not to beg for peace, but to show them 'the futility of war'. But Gandhi was immovable on the consequences which must follow the rejection of the call to 'Quit India'.

Nehru tried to persuade the Mahatma not to take his decision to the Working Committee. When the Committee met early in July with no response from the British, Gandhi was adamant. He did not even seem to care about the possibility that non-violence would, as it had always done before, degenerate into violence. 'If in spite of precautions,' he said, 'rioting does take place, it cannot be helped.' In his opposition Nehru was not alone, but Gandhian blackmail worked once more. He would leave Congress and form another organization if his resolution was rejected. Naturally, it was not.

The 'Quit India' call now became the official policy of Congress and was confirmed at a meeting of the All-India Congress Committee in Bombay on 7 August. Until the last moment Nehru resisted but gave in before the meeting so that the Working Committee presented a united front behind the Mahatma. The AICC endorsed the resolution and presented an ultimatum to the British. If it was rejected and if Gandhi approved, the Committee would sanction the 'starting of a mass struggle on non-violent lines on the widest possible scale'. The decision was with Gandhi, and he was quite sure what it would be. He had welcomed the Committee's action in a speech which Nehru admitted privately many years later, saddened and frightened him. 'The voice within me tells me I shall have to fight against the whole world and stand alone! . . . Even if the whole of India tries to persuade me that I am wrong, even then I will go ahead not for India's sake alone but for the sake of the whole world. . . . I cannot wait any longer for Indian freedom. I cannot wait until Mr Jinnah is converted. . . . If I wait any longer, God will punish me. This is the last struggle of my life.'

As the meeting came to an end Gandhi gave his blessing: 'Here is a mantra [a magical formula], a short one, that I give you. You may imprint it in your hearts and let every breath of yours give expression to it. The mantra is: "Do or Die". We shall either free India or die in the attempt.' His meaning was quite unequivocal – 'This is a rebellion' – but his strategy was not very clear. Of course this was typical of his political style. There were no plans and it is possible that he had no intention of starting a campaign immediately. But it seems highly likely that he was once again in the grip of his inner voices. The quiet fury with which Gandhi spoke was obvious to all and not least the police agents who were present. Gandhi may have believed that his words would provoke the Government for he made no real distinction between non-violence and violence. In his exaltation, which one of those present described as 'terrifying', he seemed to be hoping he might be killed and that his death would bring a national uprising.

Whatever Gandhi hoped for, the Government could hardly stand idly by in the face of what was undoubtedly a call not to a few satyagrahis as before but to the Indian people to rise in rebellion. The day after the speech, 9 August 1942, in one swift move the whole of the Working Committee and a number of other Congress leaders were arrested. Gandhi was taken to a palace belonging to the Aga Khan near Poona, Nehru and the others to Ahmadnagar Fort some two hundred miles from Bombay. It was Nehru's ninth stay in prison and his longest, for he was not to be released until June 1945.

For three weeks the prisoners were cut off from the world outside. When finally the Government censors allowed the news to trickle in it was of a nationwide rebellion and its bloody suppression.

The arrest of the Congress leaders sparked an immediate response from the rank and file. There had been no concerted plan of action and all the demonstrations were spontaneous. In the cities life was paralysed by close-downs and strikes. Vast crowds marched through the streets singing nationalist songs and demanding the release of the leaders. At first the demonstrations were peaceful but there were elements, extreme communalists, criminals and professional revolutionaries who saw in the mass outburst of popular anger the chance they had been waiting for. The Government too was edgy and so were the police. Crowds were fired upon and many were injured.

Facing what it believed to be a full-scale rebellion, the Government imposed curfews and banned assemblies of more than five people. Congress was declared an illegal organization and its assets and records were seized. Mass arrests followed and many second-rank Congress leaders went underground. With the destruction of the Congress organization and the arrest of its executive leadership, new men took over the direction of the campaign. Some of these were of Gandhian leanings and tried desperately to keep the campaign non-violent. But in the climate of bloody suppression and with the activities of communalists and criminals, who did not hesitate to stir up religious emotions so that they could loot and rape, there was no chance for moderation.

Into the vacuum of leadership stepped the revolutionaries. Among them were younger leaders of the Congress Socialist Party who turned to underground activity and sabotage. Their activities, though they continued to express loyalty to Congress, was a rejection of the Gandhian way. For years the Congress Socialists had been neutralized by Nehru whose socialism seemed so much more appealing than theirs. The frustrations of the young men were now released and they set about building up an organization that would parallel not only that of the British but also that of Congress. Where before they had been overshadowed by Gandhi, Nehru and the right wing, they now seemed to represent a real alternative leadership with a chance of capturing the masses while the others were in jail.

A wave of sabotage and criminally inspired violence spread across the country. By the middle of September, 250 railway stations had been destroyed or seriously damaged and 550 post offices attacked. A large section of the railway system was put out of action and communications so disrupted that the army on India's north-eastern frontier was deprived of its main channel of supply. Police stations and Government buildings were set on fire and Indian members of the civil administration were threatened with death if they did not join the rebels. A number of those who refused were assassinated. The Government used all the forces at its disposal. British troops were called in and aircraft were used against mobs, machine-gunning and bombing on at least five occasions. In some parts of the country the authorities even revived the terrible spectacle of public hanging.

Though the rebellion was undoubtedly serious there was no mass uprising. Too many elements in the country kept aloof. The peasantry stayed in their fields, businessmen and the professional middle class continued to support the Government. There was no sign of disaffection in the armed forces. The first phase of large-scale sabotage and violence was under control by the end of August. The second phase of isolated but still serious outbreaks was virtually over by the end of the year. The failure of Congress to overthrow the British was welcomed by Conservatives in Britain. It only confirmed what they had been saying all along: Congress did not represent the mass of the Indian people. In the House of Commons in September, Winston Churchill claimed that the rebellion had at least made one thing clear, the 'non-representative character' of Congress and its 'powerlessness to throw into confusion the normal peace of India'. Considering the amount of damage that had been caused and that in certain parts of the country British rule had ceased, and when he spoke had not been reimposed, Churchill's remarks were somewhat less than the truth.

In his jail, while lamenting Government brutality, Nehru denied or excused that of the rebels. But he did not realize then nor did he accept later that Congress had committed a grave error. Apart from the terror and suffering the 'Quit India' resolution had brought to so many while its sponsors sat comfortably in jail, it had left a vacuum in political India which was to be filled by divisive forces. When the time came for Britain actually to quit India, there were no longer just two parties – the British and Congress – who had to agree upon the terms.

Chapter 15
Wars of Succession

For the ageing nationalist leaders confined together in Ahmadnagar Fort, life was not uncomfortable but news of the outside world was scarce. Great changes were taking place in India and elsewhere but their real significance did not penetrate the prison walls. Nehru and his eleven colleagues of the Working Committee shared a series of interconnected rooms in a barrack separated from the main prison and looking on to a neglected garden. There was a private kitchen and convict servants. Patel supervised the kitchen; Nehru and the others worked in the garden. All used to meet at breakfast, Nehru preceding it by yoga exercises. Afterwards Nehru would work on his books and at his writings until about 3 p.m. with a short break for lunch. Then there would be work in the garden and a discussion on politics or culture. In the evening a game of badminton would be followed by more work at his books.

These men who had been together politically for so long represented many points of view. Now that they were living together those differences not only showed more clearly but became more acute. One of the prisoners, Dr Pattabhi Sittaramayya, recalled after his release that in the discussions Patel and Azad were always on the opposite side. Azad was supported by Nehru and the other Muslims, while Patel had the devoted Gandhians, Profullah Ghose and Shankerrao Deo, but also Acharya Kripalani. Ghose and Kripalani were to leave Congress after independence and join the socialists. There were already signs of the tensions and disputes which were to affect both the negotiations for freedom and the pattern of freedom itself.

In the deadening atmosphere of prison life, however, freedom seemed as far away as ever. On 11 February 1943 they saw in their newspaper that Gandhi had begun a twenty-one day fast at Poona. No one seemed to know just why the Mahatma had decided on this form of blackmail for he did not tell anyone. It was assumed by both the Government and the prisoners in Ahmadnagar that it was an attempt to gain his release. The Government did not respond though some Indian members of the Viceroy's executive council resigned as they were unwilling to be a party to something that might lead to Gandhi's death. The Government sent doctors to Poona to see that he was kept alive. To Nehru the fast was another example of the pointless gesture.

The year 1943 was an eventful one for India. In June after a long journey by submarine and aircraft Subhas Bose arrived in Japan. In October he proclaimed in Singapore a 'Provisional Government of Free India' and prepared for the liberation of his country with the aid of the Japanese. The same month a new Viceroy took over. Lord Wavell, a distinguished soldier, had been sent to concentrate the work of the Government of India upon the war with Japan. The British Government was no longer interested in a political settlement in India. All was reasonably quiet and there was every reason not to stir up trouble once again. Wavell did, however, repeat the British offer of 1942. But all the significant events were not confined to politics and war. In 1943 a terrible famine – the worst in India's history – struck Bengal.

The loss to India of rice imports from Thailand and Japanese-occupied Burma and an outbreak of black-spot disease led to serious shortages. Hoarding was commonplace and profiteering its natural complement. Bengal was particularly badly hit. It was then the principal rice-growing area in India and it had to try and supply other areas normally provided for by imports. Consequently there were no Government stocks in Bengal when the crops failed. The famine was made by man. War and administrative inefficiency joined with the greed of Indian merchants and politicians to intensify its effect. The central government would not interfere though it was obvious that the Bengal government – a Muslim League administration – was both corrupt and incompetent. The Viceroy Lord Linlithgow in spite of harrowing reports did not even visit Calcutta to see for himself; it was only after Wavell's arrival that action was taken. The new Viceroy went immediately to the area, British troops were moved in to control the distribution of food and give medical aid. But it was too late to save at least a million and a half lives.

The failure of the Muslim League ministry in Bengal to deal with the famine was a blow to the League's prestige and was followed by a steady decline in support for the League in Bengal. After the arrest of the Congress leaders, Jinnah had immediately set about capturing the Muslim vote and Muslim politicians for the League. In September 1942 the British dismissed the non-League Muslim chief minister of Sind on the grounds that he was anti-British and pro-Congress. The governor allowed a member of the Muslim League to form a government. In Assam, another League ministry was formed on the invitation of the governor. In neither province did the League hold a majority of the elected seats. In April 1943 a League government took office in Bengal and in the next month in the North West Frontier Province. All these had been made possible by the arrest of Congress supporters in the provincial legislatures. Only in the Punjab, where Muslims participated in a coalition government, was Jinnah unsuccessful in capturing the administration.

Jinnah's achievement was demonstrative rather than real. He could not prove that he had captured the Muslim vote without an election and many Muslim politicians still refused to join the League. Jinnah's public meetings, which in spite of the wartime regulations were permitted by the British showed a decline in attendances. Jinnah retired to Kashmir to think out his next moves. While he was there the British and Gandhi came to his aid.

In May 1944 the Government released Gandhi on the grounds of ill health. The Government was now convinced that Gandhi would no longer call for revolt and in any case it had no intention of releasing the other Congress leaders. Rajagopalachari, who because he had resigned from Congress had not been included in the round-up of its leaders, had been permitted to see Gandhi in Poona during his fast. There he had persuaded the Mahatma to endorse an approach to the Muslim League. The formula suggested was that Congress and the League should cooperate in working for independence and a provisional national government. After the war plebiscites could be held in the Muslim majority areas to see whether they wanted some form of separation from the rest of India. If the answer was 'yes' then autonomous Muslim states would be formed and become part of a loose all-India federation with a central government responsible for such things as defence, foreign affairs, commerce and communications.

On Gandhi's release Rajagopalachari persuaded him that he should meet Jinnah to discuss the formula. This delighted Jinnah for not only did the formula recognize the principle of Pakistan but a meeting with Gandhi was an acknowledgement of Jinnah's equality of status. Before the meeting took place Jinnah denounced the Rajagopalachari formula. It offered, he said, 'a shadow and a husk, a maimed, mutilated and moth-eaten Pakistan'. After this it is surprising that Gandhi was still prepared to meet Jinnah but the meeting did take place at the latter's house in Bombay in September. There was no possibility of agreement. Jinnah wanted an unequivocal acceptance of the principle of Pakistan. Gandhi was not prepared to give it. The meeting was a blunder because Congress now seemed committed to some form of partition and when the more intransigent leaders were released from prison they could constantly be reminded of it. Gandhi's foolishness in meeting Jinnah also alarmed the Hindu extremists. The leader of the Hindu Mahasabha protested that 'the Indian provinces were not the private property of Gandhiji or Rajaji so that they could make a gift of them to anyone they liked'.

As 1944 came to an end it was becoming increasingly obvious that the war in Europe would not last much longer. The Allied landing in Europe had been followed by a victorious sweep into Germany itself and, though there was still heavy fighting to come, the result was no longer in doubt. The end of the war in Europe would mean a transfer of emphasis to the campaign against Japan already in slow retreat in Burma and elsewhere. In India most nationalists were resigned to the fact that Britain would probably emerge from the war even stronger than before and less likely to be generous in its treatment of demands for freedom. Of the nationalist leaders only Jinnah believed that the British would keep their word. That belief supplied the motive for his rejection of the offer made by Gandhi.

The imminent end of the war in Europe and the general consensus of military opinion that it would take at least a year to defeat Japan convinced Wavell that the time was ripe for a new approach to the Indian political problem. The country appeared quiet but only on the surface. Below lay potentially explosive forces which would undoubtedly emerge as soon as the campaign against Japan was over. The war, for all its physical remoteness from the lives of most Indians, had had profound social and economic effects. One element had, of course, been affected directly – the volunteer soldiers of the Indian Army. Nearly two million recruits had been taken, mainly from the villages. They had been taught modern trades and military discipline and in some measure had been jerked out of the traditional into the modern world. At the end of the war most of them would have to be demobilized and they would return to their villages with at least some feelings of frustration.

The war too had given opportunities to the Indian middle classes which had previously been denied them. Indians were allowed into the officer corps and into the higher posts of the civil service in substantial numbers. Unprecedented industrial expansion created openings for Indians at technical and managerial levels. Status and responsibility were two of the fundamental nationalist demands and because of the war they had to some extent been satisfied. An important sector of the population began to feel not only a sense of national identity but of self-respect and confidence that they were perfectly capable of doing things for themeslves. Throughout the war years the nationalist claim for independence ceased to be the ideal of professional politicians and instead became the conviction of those who, when it came, would have to work it.

The expansion of a war economy had had both social and economic effects. The demand for labour brought men out of the villages and into the cities. Even women, traditionally excluded from independent activity, got themselves jobs in offices and in the woman's army corps. From the beginning of 1943 there had been a rapid rise in prices which by 1945 had resulted in dangerous inflation. Food prices spiralled and all levels of the population – despite the opportunities for employment – found themselves with decreasing purchasing power even in a situation of rising incomes.

All these factors were known to the Government and they formed part of the case presented by Wavell to the British Cabinet in London when he arrived there in March 1945. That the time was ripe for concessions was accepted by the coalition government. But before action could be taken Germany surrendered and the coalition government resigned. A general election was announced but in the meantime a caretaker government of Conservatives headed by the wartime Prime Minister, Winston Churchill, held office. Churchill agreed that Wavell should return to India and sound out nationalist opinion. In order to assist him the members of the Congress Working Committee would be released.

On 14 June 1945 Wavell returned to India and disclosed the new proposals. They were basically those offered in 1942 with the addition that the Viceroy's executive council would consist entirely of Indians except for the Viceroy himself and the commander-in-chief. The Viceroy would not exercise his reserve powers unreasonably. For the Muslim League there was a special attraction – there would be equal representation for caste Hindus and Muslims on the council. This was not a division of seats between two *political* groups, Congress and Muslim League, but between two *religious* entities. It was, in essence, a recognition that there were 'two nations' in India, as Jinnah maintained. After outlining the proposals, Wavell invited representative political leaders to meet him at a conference to be held in the hill-station of Simla on 25 June.

Preparatory to their release the members of the Working Committee had been sent to jails in their home provinces. Nehru was released on 15 June at Almora, the rather remote hill-station in the United Provinces. He hurried to Allahabad for a family reunion and then to Bombay for a meeting of the Working Committee at which it would be decided whether to accept the Viceroy's invitation or not. It was already clear that Jinnah would claim the right to appoint all the Muslim members of the executive council and this was rejected in advance. Congress would, however, attend the conference. There was only one problem, the invitation when it arrived was to Gandhi who was still not formally a member of Congress. The Muslim president of Congress, Maulana Azad, had been pointedly ignored. Gandhi informed the Viceroy that personally he could not officially represent Congress but would attend as an observer at the Viceroy's insistence. The invitation must go to Azad. The invitation, which seems to have been deliberately withheld, was duly sent.

Though the twenty-one delegates at the conference represented every conceivable interest group from the Europeans who as a minority held reserved seats in the central assembly, to the Untouchables who made up 15 per cent of the population, the real protagonists were Congress and the League. Jinnah was insistent that the League represented *all* Muslims and must therefore nominate *all* the Muslim seats. Congress claiming that it was not a Hindu organization but a secular one demanded the right to put up Muslims itself. Jinnah would not even speak to Azad whom he dubbed a 'symbolic affront' and attempts to persuade him to change his attitude were unsuccessful. Wavell tried to mediate and asked both parties to submit lists of potential candidates. Jinnah demanded an assurance that the five Muslims nominated by the League would all be accepted but Wavell refused to commit himself. By 7 July all the parties except the League had presented their nominations. For a week the Viceroy tried to get Jinnah's cooperation but the League leader was immovable. Wavell therefore ended the conference on 14 July. Jinnah had made perhaps the most important point – he was now in a position to veto changes by refusing to cooperate.

Was Jinnah's intransigence merely bloody-mindedness as many Congress leaders including Nehru thought? Certainly the claim that the Muslim League represented *all* Muslims would have been difficult to prove at the time. Though the League had succeeded in seizing control of some of the provincial governments after the arrest of the Congress legislators, its positions had been steadily eroded. During the early months of 1945 the Government had released many of the Congress members of

the legislatures. This had led to the defeat of the League ministries in Assam, Bengal, Sind and the North West Frontier
Province. Jinnah hoped by forcing the Government of India to
recognize the League as the sole representative body of Indian
Muslims to reinstate its position at least in the minds of the
voters. There is evidence that Jinnah was encouraged in his
action by the Churchill Government in London and by at least
one British member of Wavell's executive council.

Nehru attended the conference but played no important part
in it. After the meeting was over he went to Kashmir for a
holiday. While he was there recuperating in the hills he loved
so much, a Labour Government was swept to power in Britain.
Would Labour now fulfil its often repeated pledge to give India
freedom? At least the reactionary Churchill had been decisively
rejected by the British electorate. The new Government wasted
no time in making its attitude plain. On 15 August, as the war
with Japan came to an end after the dropping of two atomic
bombs, the new British Parliament opened with the speech from
the throne outlining the Government's future policy. The speech
contained these words: 'In accordance with the promises already
made to my Indian peoples, my Government will do their
utmost to promote, in conjunction with the leaders of Indian
opinion, the early realization of full self-government in India.'
The words were welcome but not altogether reassuring. 'Full
self-government' did not sound like 'independence'. A few days
later Wavell was called to London for consultations and as an
earnest of the new Government's good faith it was announced
that elections both for the central and provincial assemblies
would be held in the winter.

When Wavell returned to India a month later it became clear
that the Labour Government, though it had acted quickly in
making a declaration of intent, had not given any real thought
to the problem. Naturally it was more concerned with the wishes
of its own electorate who by their vote had shown that they had
had enough of war. One thing at least was clear in the minds of
the Labour leaders. They could not expect to hold down India
by force. The British people wanted their husbands and sons
demobilized and sent home, not fighting colonial wars.

On his return Wavell made another statement. It was also not very reassuring. The Labour Government still seemed to think that the Simla proposals were an adequate basis for discussion. After the elections a constitution-making body would be convened and the Viceroy's executive council reorganized. In his statement the Viceroy did not use the word 'independence' but only once again 'full self-government' and it was obvious that Dominion status was still the British Government's aim. With some justification Congress considered the announcement 'vague, inadequate and unsatisfactory'. Perhaps the most disappointing thing of all was that there was no mention of *immediate* concessions. Why should not the old provincial governments which had resigned in 1939 resume office in the interim period before the elections? And surely the franchise could be extended to more than the 10 per cent of the population who had been enfranchised by the 1935 Act? It looked as if the Labour Government was not only offering the same old solutions but the same old reasons for rejecting them.

All parties were nevertheless determined to contest the elections and in doing so prove their popularity in the country. The last elections for the central assembly had been held in 1934 and for the provincial legislatures in 1937. The representation in these bodies did not reflect the views of the voters. Jinnah was convinced that he had captured the Muslim voter for the League and was anxious to show that this was true. Congress conversely was determined to demonstrate that it was an all-community party. Many Congress leaders felt that the elections would prove no more than that and were really only a device to gain time for the British.

The Congress election manifesto was the usual collection of appeals to a wide spectrum of interests, their conflict suitably disguised by ambiguous language. But it did contain a residue of the Rajagopalachari formula in the promise of a federal structure with autonomy for its constituent parts. Finally Congress reaffirmed its belief in the principles of the 'Quit India' resolution of 1942. But, Congress assured its potential supporters, the real issue was not the promises in the manifesto. Congress was contesting the election only 'to show that the inevitable result . . . must be to demonstrate the overwhelming solidarity of opinion of the voters on the issue of independence'. The claims of any other party were brushed aside as the statement continued. 'Therefore in this election, petty issues do not count nor do individuals nor sectarian cries – only one thing counts: the freedom and independence of our motherland from which all other freedoms will flow to our people.'

These sentiments did not worry Jinnah who was preparing to fight on quite different issues: that a united India would be dominated by a Hindu majority and that Muslims could only be protected in their own homeland, i.e. Pakistan. The Congress statement also only partly concealed real divisions inside the Congress leadership. Ironically, though not unexpectedly, those divisions were on communal lines. The president, Azad, a Muslim, said that Congress did accept the principle of self-determination 'even to the extent of separation under certain circumstances' though he personally did not consider that the partitioning of India would be to the ultimate advantage of the Muslim community. Despite his apparent reasonableness Azad was constantly under attack from Muslim League newspapers. Hindu-minded Congressmen like Patel would have none of Azad's softness to Muslims. Patel was not going to allow India to be divided on religious grounds and said so publicly. Nehru remained outside the controversy but indicated that he was not in favour of any compromise with the Muslim League. Anyone interested in finding out exactly what Congress did think would have found no help from the confusing statements that came from Congress spokesmen. Freedom must come to a united India, they said, though, naturally Congress 'cannot think in terms of compelling people'!

Neither Congress nor the League seemed capable of jolting the mass of the Indian people out of their indifference to politics. Another of those regular periodic torpors had descended and there were no really inspiring and dramatic issues at hand to break it. As so often before the Government came to the rescue. The British had become increasingly worried about the effect upon Indian soldiers of the propaganda that was being spread by returning members of Subhas Bose's Indian National Army.

The INA had not fought well against the British but there was a romantic aura about its activities and those of its leader. Bose had died on 18 August 1945 from the effects of an air crash in Formosa while making for Japan. His last words had been: 'Tell my countrymen, India will be free before long.' The death of Bose was now public knowledge and his exploits were taking on the high gloss of heroism and martyrdom.

Most of the members of the INA had been recruited from Indian prisoners of war in Malaya. The Government felt that it must take some action against them if only to bolster the morale of the British Indian Army. In August 1945 Nehru had suggested that the INA could not be treated as ordinary rebels. Any punishment given them, he said 'would in effect be a punishment on all India and all Indians, and a deep wound would be created in millions of hearts'. Despite this the Congress attitude both to Bose and the INA was lukewarm. It was not anxious to publicize their exploits. After all, Bose and the INA had actually fought for India's freedom while the Congress leaders had merely gone to jail.

The Government took the decision that the rank and file of the INA 'who yielded to pressure and were so misguided as to join forces raised by the enemy' would be leniently treated. But the leaders and those guilty of atrocities must be court-martialled. The initial reaction of Congress was favourable but when reports from Congress members all over the country revealed the immense interest people were taking in the saga of the INA, the All-India Congress Committee decided to use the impending trials for its own ends. In mid-September the AICC resolved 'that it would be a tragedy if these officers ... were punished for the offence of having laboured, *however mistakenly*, for the freedom of India' and called for their release. Two days later Congress set up a Defence Committee to help the accused.

The Government's determination to have a show trial was undiminished. In November 1945 in the Red Fort at Delhi, which had once been the palace of the Mughal emperors, three former Indian army officers who had held high rank in the INA were charged with waging war against the king-emperor, that is, rebellion, and in one case of ordering executions.

Though there seems to have been no particular intention behind the choice of defendants, one was a Muslim, another a Sikh and the third a Hindu. It was as if the Government was prepared to antagonize all three communities. Seventeen lawyers including some of the ablest legal minds in the country appeared for the defence. Among them was Nehru.

Nehru's motives in donning his barrister's gown after nearly thirty years seems to have been primarily dictated by political necessity. To have kept aloof would have cut him away from a great popular issue and would certainly have reduced his popular image. He could not condone atrocities but he preferred to consider the prosecution not as a question of law but as a 'trial of strength between the will of the Indian people and the will of those who held power in India'. The proceedings in the Red Fort 'dramatized the old contest . . . England versus India'.

Despite complicated legal arguments, the prisoners were found guilty and sentenced to be cashiered and transported for life to the penal islands. Under heavy pressure, however, the commander-in-chief remitted the sentences of transportation but confirmed the other penalties. The remission was considered by many to be an acquittal under duress. A few days before the commander-in-chief's decision was made known it had been announced that there would be no more trials except for atrocities. Congress was jubilant. The INA officers toured the country like returning heroes. The old anti-British feelings of the great days of the civil disobedience movement had been successfully aroused. During the trial there were violent demonstrations of sympathy for the accused in Madras, Bombay and Calcutta. Police were compelled to fire on the crowds and in Calcutta the disturbances lasted for three days before they were brought under control.

There were however even more sinister effects. The Government had hoped through the trials to reinforce the morale of the Indian army. It succeeded only in lowering it. If Subhas Bose and the men of the INA had been in the right – and the whole country seemed to think so – then the soldiers of the Indian army had betrayed their country by supporting the

British. It began to dawn on the Government that the Indian army which had always been above politics might now not be trustworthy. The Indian army had not only been the backbone of British rule, it was also the ultimate guarantee of civil peace. With the rapid demobilization of British troops the Government's ability to hold the ring and enforce the rules diminished. Conciliation not force would soon be the only course open to the British.

Congress propaganda and its success in arousing the masses also frightened Jinnah and the League. The threat of Hindu rule now seemed greater and more immediate than ever. The election campaign was therefore fought not on the issue of independence but on whether India should be divided or not. The I N A trials were used by Congress to glorify the right to rebel against foreign rule and Nehru himself called on the people to prepare for 'a mass battle for freedom'. This and many other incendiary speeches convinced Muslims that Congress was in a belligerent mood. In particular the direct references to the communal problem were especially provocative. Congress leaders once again called on the British to get out and leave the problem to them. 'Civil war if necessary' was the theme of many public statements. The general implication was that if Jinnah wanted Pakistan he would have to fight for it.

It was in this atmosphere of growing incitement to violence that the elections took place. They revealed the polarization that many hoped for and many feared. The League won all the seats reserved for Muslims in the central assembly with 86 per cent of the Muslim vote. In the provinces, where in 1937 it had won only 108 seats out of the 492 reserved for Muslims, the League now won 428 with 76 per cent of the Muslim vote, though in two of the provinces – Assam and the North West Frontier Provinces – which were claimed by Jinnah as part of the proposed Pakistan, Congress and the Congress-supported 'Redshirts' respectively won absolute majorities. In the remaining three provinces that would make up the new Muslim state, though the League was the largest single party it did not have an absolute majority. Congress was able to form ministries in eight of the eleven provinces, the League, in Bengal and Sind, and the coalition Unionist Party with the support of Congress in the Punjab. Superficially it might appear that the League had failed in the heartland of its chosen territory but this was not so. The number of seats allotted to Muslims under the 1935 Act no longer represented the size of the Muslim population which had grown considerably in the intervening years. In any case it was the *size* of the vote for the League which counted. That showed that Jinnah's claim to be the sole voice of Muslim India was firmly grounded and that the fight for succession to British power was between Congress and the League.

The general tension had, not unnaturally, increased during the election campaign. The Labour Government, now concerned over the possible breakdown of law and order, sent out a low-powered parliamentary delegation to assure Indians of the Government's sincerity. The announcement was received with almost unanimous indifference. An imaginative gesture was required and all the Labour Government could think of doing was to send a second-rate mission of goodwill. The reason for this feeble response was the Cabinet's unwillingness to believe what it was being told by the Government of India whose members it did not trust. Ideological blindness prevented Labour ministers from realizing that though indeed there were partisan elements in the administration in India the reports from India were relatively unbiased. Soon, however, the real dangers of the situation were brought home to the Labour leaders in the most dramatic way.

Early in 1946 there were a number of mutinies in the armed forces. The first was all the more shattering as it took place among British troops. In the middle of January, ground and maintenance units at Dum Dum airfield near Calcutta and at other RAF stations in India mutinied over delays in repatriation and demobilization. On being given assurances by a visiting member of the British Parliament the men went back to duty. There had been no violence but the local army commander had moved troops and artillery to the area. The mutiny at least brought home to the Government that it would be unwise to rely on conscript soldiers for such unpleasant tasks as riot control.

The RAF mutiny was followed by one in the Royal Indian Air Force. This too was peaceful but when units of the Royal Indian Navy went on strike in Bombay and other ports in February their demands were backed by guns. Some three thousand Indian sailors took to the streets of Bombay in vehicles flying Congress and League flags and there were armed clashes between the mutineers and troops. The sailors had been incited to mutiny by communist and left-wing agitators. Though Congress sympathized with the men this was a challenge to Congress authority. Patel hurried to Bombay and managed to persuade the sailors to surrender with a promise that there would be no victimization. Patel had the full support of Nehru who had begun to realize that with the imminence of some sort of responsible government at the centre such things could not be tolerated in the armed forces. He also began to fear – and not without reason – that the inflammatory speeches of himself and his colleagues were encouraging lawlessness. Further proof was offered when after the end of the mutiny in Bombay the city continued to be racked by civil rioting for another four days. The mutiny at Bombay was followed by others at Calcutta, Madras and, rather more seriously, at Karachi, where the army commander opened fire on the ships with artillery causing considerable casualties.

The Bombay mutiny undoubtedly had its effect in London for a day after the outbreak Clement Attlee, the British Prime Minister, announced that a delegation of senior British cabinet ministers would go to India to meet political leaders there and attempt to arrive at a solution to the problems of India's future. The mission would consist of Lord Pethick-Lawrence, Secretary of State for India, Sir Stafford Cripps, President of the Board of Trade, and A. V. Alexander, First Lord of the Admiralty. To reinforce the impression that these men meant business, as did the Government that sent them, Attlee announced that the mission's purpose was to set up a constitution-making body and a representative Viceroy's executive council. It would take to India no British proposals on the form of the constitution – that was for the Indians themselves to decide without interference. There was no mention of Dominion status. If Indians wanted to remain in the Commonwealth, that was to be their choice and theirs alone.

Before it left England, however, the mission decided to do all it could to bypass the Pakistan issue. Attlee's words, in fact, contained what appeared to be a snub to the Muslim League. 'We are mindful,' he said, 'of the rights of minorities and minorities should be able to live free from fear. *On the other hand, we cannot allow a minority to place a veto on the advance of the majority.*' Jinnah responded by remarking: 'The issue is, to give a simile, "Walk into my parlour" said the spider to the fly, and if the fly refuses it is said that a veto is being exercised and the fly is being intransigent.' It was hardly the best of omens for the mission's success. Congress, of course, was delighted.

The mission was very soon aware of the naïveté of its assumptions. Its members had many talks with Indian leaders, and all confirmed that there was very little chance of bypassing the issue of Pakistan. Jinnah was unmoving. He would negotiate nothing which did not satisfy Muslim claims. Congress, on the other hand, was not willing to agree to anything that opened the way to partition. Congress leaders advised the mission once again that the best solution was for Britain to withdraw and leave India to settle her own problems.

It was now becoming clear to the mission that Jinnah and the Muslim League held the key to any sort of progress. Did they really insist on every area they had previously claimed for Pakistan? Such concessions would mean that the new state would include large areas where Muslims were, in fact, a minority. The alternative – to slice off the Muslim-majority areas in, for example, Bengal and the Punjab – would only create other problems, for in both provinces there was a common language and a common cultural tradition shared by Muslims and Hindus alike. To divide the Punjab would also entail cutting in two the homeland of about four million Sikhs, who would be unlikely to take it lying down. Furthermore, the new state would itself be divided into two different sectors, with dangerous frontiers and 800 miles of India in between. On any reasonable assessment it was madness. Congress was demanding that Britain should 'Quit India', while the Muslim League insisted that it should 'divide and quit', that the British should not leave until they had imposed partition, by force if necessary.

In these unhelpful circumstances, it was left to the mission to search for some workable compromise. One was suggested by Maulana Azad, still Congress president. The formula he offered was the same as that put forward by Gandhi in 1944. There should be full autonomy for the provinces within a loose federation, with a central government responsible only for defence, foreign affairs and communications, although the provinces should be able to cede powers to the central government in order to allow overall economic and administrative planning. The view of the mission – or, more specifically, the view of Cripps – was that the last part of the suggestion, the ceding of powers to the central government, would not work for purely functional reasons.

At this stage the mission departed for a short holiday in Kashmir, expressing the hope that while they were away the two parties might arrive at a settlement for themselves. When the mission returned and found that no such settlement had been achieved, it began once again the round of talks with Congress and League leaders.

The result was a new scheme, very little different from that suggested by Azad; there would be a central government responsible for defence, foreign affairs and communications, and the provinces should be divided into two groups, one predominantly Hindu and the other Muslim. The mission invited Congress and the League to send four negotiators each to explore the possibility of an agreement on this basis. They did so, and the conference met at Simla on 5 May 1946. The delegates Nehru, Patel, Azad and Abdul Ghaffar Khan for Congress, Jinnah, Liaquat Ali Khan and two others for the League were supplied by the mission with a mass of data outlining the details of how such an arrangement might work.

Surprisingly enough, it seemed as if both Congress and the League were approaching the proposals with unprecedented seriousness. In reality they had no interest in understanding each other. Any suggestion of a strong central government was anathema to the League and axiomatic for Congress. Later, the mission tried to claim that both parties had been 'prepared to make considerable concessions' but it was deluding itself and everyone else by saying so. Congress did apparently agree to provincial groupings, but only if there was to be a strong centre. The League was prepared to submit to a central government, but only if it was weak. No concessions were actually made at all. Reluctantly, the mission was compelled to announce the failure of the Simla conference.

The mission, however, had not reached the end of its resources. With the approval of the British Government it proposed its own immediate solution. The statement contained one paragraph which read: 'We are unable to advise the British Government that the power which at present resides in British hands should be handed over to two entirely separate sovereign states.' Instead it proposed an Indian Union, very much as before, with autonomy for the provinces which were to be 'free to form groups'. A new suggestion was that there could be fresh consideration of the arrangements every ten years, but the main virtue of the proposals lay in their outline of a way in which the constitution-making body might be set up. The mission also advocated the immediate formation of an interim government. Fundamentally, what they now offered was not a solution but the machinery for arriving at one. The statement ended with a claim that the plan offered a way for India to attain independence 'in the shortest time and with the least danger of internal disturbance and conflict'. The alternative, it said, was 'a grave danger of violence, chaos and even civil war'.

The mission's attempt to substitute action for talk was – to its surprised satisfaction – received favourably by both Congress and League. Gandhi, with inapposite rhetoric, hailed the plan as containing 'a seed to convert this land of sorrow into one without sorrow and suffering'.

Both sides, inevitably, interpreted the proposals to suit themselves. Congress said that the clause on grouping meant that each province could choose either to join the appropriate group or stay out. The League, on the other hand, believed the clause meant that grouping would be compulsory. The analysing of words was an example of the different ways in which British and Indians treated the English language – the British with characteristic looseness and the Indians with dictionary precision. 'Free to form groups', said the lawyers of Congress, implied freedom not to form groups. The mission said this was not what it meant; it was the mission's intention that grouping should be compulsory.

Nevertheless the mission seemed to have achieved a major breakthrough. The Muslim League accepted the proposals on the understanding that grouping would be compulsory, and Congress announced that it was prepared to cooperate in setting up a constituent assembly. Both parties tentatively agreed to join an interim government. Unfortunately this happy suitation was not to last.

The arguments now moved to the matter of the composition of the interim government. The point of contention was the continuing one of the allotment of seats between the various parties. Wavell had tried to get agreement on the basis of an equal number of seats for Muslims and Hindus and representation for the minorities. He suggested five representatives from Congress and five from the League and two from the minorities. Congress was not prepared to accept parity. Wavell next put forward an ingenious compromise – thirteen seats, six going to Congress on the understanding that one would be filled by a representative of the Untouchables, five to the League and two from the minorities. Parity would be maintained but Congress would have one extra seat. Jinnah replied that he understood the offer of a ratio of five:five:two was final. Wavell denied this and Jinnah offered to put the new formula to his own leadership but only *after* Congress had accepted it. This Congress would not do.

The mission and the Viceroy now published their own proposals which differed in no substantial way from Wavell's previous offer: six Hindu members of Congress including one Untouchable, five from the League, one Sikh, one Indian Christian and one Parsee. The reaction of both Congress and the League followed the now familiar lines but when it became known that Congress proposed appointing a *Muslim* to one of its seats even though they were reserved for Hindus the League exploded in fury. Jinnah immediately insisted that the only Muslims must be those nominated by the League.

During these events Nehru had been away from Delhi. He had left for Kashmir in an attempt to assist at the trial of an old friend Sheikh Abdullah, who had been arrested by the state government on a charge of treason. The Maharaja of Kashmir had prohibited his entry and when Nehru defied the order he was detained. Nehru was criticized at the time and later for deciding that Sheikh Abdullah was more important than the discussions in Delhi. He was even unwilling to return and only did so after assurances from Gandhi that if necessary the Mahatma himself would go to Kashmir.

Between 20 and 25 June the Congress Working Committee was in almost permanent session. Gandhi was for the total rejection of the new plan and threatened to leave if his colleagues did not agree. The Working Committee rejected the proposals for an interim government but stated that it was still willing to go ahead with the plans for a constituent assembly.

On the same day as the Working Committee informed the Viceroy of its decision, Jinnah was called to meet Wavell and members of the mission. He was told of the Congress decision and informed that because of it the whole scheme has broken down but that the Viceroy would be willing to reopen negotiations after a short interval. In the meantime new elections would take place for the constituent assembly and it would probably be better to get them over first. Jinnah went straight from the interview to a meeting of the League's highest executive body. In his view, he told its members, the Viceroy was obliged to form an interim government even it if excluded Congress. Jinnah now accused the Viceroy and the mission of a breach of faith and demanded the postponement of the elections for the constituent assembly. The Viceroy replied, briefly, 'We do not propose to postpone them'. He also appointed a caretaker government to function until such time as the nationalist leaders could agree on the composition of a new one.

The cabinet mission left India on 29 June under the impression that, despite everything, a constituent assembly at least would come into being. It took back with it to Westminster the atmosphere of unreality in which it had operated in India, for both Cripps and Pethick-Lawrence claimed in Parliament that the mission had been a success. Yet, apart from the very doubtful acceptance of a constituent assembly, the mission had produced no change in the attitude of the two major parties. Whatever Azad might say Congress was not prepared to move an inch from its position that power must only be transferred to a united India, and the League was still determined that this should never happen.

At least one thing, however, now seemed indisputable. The British really meant to leave India. Even this created new problems, for there was now no incentive which might lead Congress and the League towards a compromise. There was to be no need for a war of independence against Britain, only for wars of succession, a fight over the inheritance.

The slide towards anarchy now began, and it was to be an anarchy in which most of the victims were the innocent. While politicians made inflammatory speeches and threatened violence, others put the violence into practice. All over India, ordinary people were looking anxiously over their shoulders, eyeing neighbours of a different religious persuasion, and wondering who would strike first. All kinds of people were preparing for the worst; some were even planning it. Extremist Muslims and Hindus consumed with religious arrogance; Sikhs remembering the time, a century before, when they had had their own state; the Indian princes, wondering if at last they might shake off the impotence that British rule had forced upon them; left-wing agitators fresh from Moscow; and criminals with an eye to loot – all were waiting for some great opportunity they were convinced was near at hand. It was to come sooner than anyone had expected.

Elections for the constituent assembly took place and Congress and the Muslim League surpassed even their triumphant showing at the previous election. The League won 73 seats – all but five of those which had been reserved for Muslims – and Congress won 205. Ironically, the results delighted both parties. Neither, however, was prepared to breathe life into the assembly itself. Nehru had already said on 10 July 'We [Congress] will remain in that assembly as long as we think it is good for India. . . . *We are not bound by a single thing.*' He had gone on to outline ideas for a much more powerful central government than the one which had been suggested by the mission, and he also added that it was his belief that there would probably be no groupings of provinces at all. In effect, he was rejecting the whole basis of the mission's plan, so hopefully devised to placate Jinnah and the League. Nehru was, of course, under considerable pressure from the representatives of such provinces as Assam, which had a Hindu majority but which would probably be forced to join a Muslim-majority group. He was also under attack from the left wing of Congress, which seemed to think that nothing had changed since 1942 and that the real enemy was still Britain. Nehru was simply restating the belief that the British were soon to leave and that Congress would then be able to brush the Muslim League aside.

With Nehru's words echoing in every ear, Jinnah met the council of the League. He had already demanded an assurance from the British Government that the constituent assembly would be forced to follow the mission's plans for it, and had received some mild assurances in the House of Commons. Jinnah, however, was now ready for a showdown – no more talk of compromises, no more trust in the words of the 'treacherous' British. 'I feel we have exhausted all reason,' he said. 'It is no use looking to any other source for help or assistance. There is no other tribunal to which we can go. The only tribunal is the Muslim nation.'

The League withdrew its acceptance of the cabinet mission's plan for the constituent assembly. Jinnah spoke with feeling of his attempts to reach a compromise. The British had deceived him; they had backed down in face of Congress threats of another violent struggle; Congress was planning to dominate the assembly with its 'brute majority'. Henceforth, Muslims must fight their own battles. 'Are we,' he declaimed, 'alone to be guided by reason, justice, honesty and fair play, when, on the other hand, there are perfidious dealings by Congress? . . . Today Muslim India is stirred as never before; and has never felt so bitterly. . . . Now there is no room left for compromise. Let us march on.' Jinnah claimed that the League had never in its history ' done anything except by constitutional methods.... But now we are forced into this position. This day we bid goodbye to constitutional methods.'

The Muslim League declared 16 August as Direct Action Day. According to League spokesmen, it was to be a silent statement of the League's attitude. The British, Jinnah argued, were preparing to suppress the nationalist movements. 'I also,' he said, 'am going to make trouble.' The threat impressed Congress, but not enough to stimulate it into constructive action. Under pressure from the Viceroy, Nehru did go to Bombay to confer with Jinnah but their prejudices were effective insulation against any possibility of contact. They met on Direct Action Day, although in Bombay – with its very small Muslim population – Direct Action meant little more than the flying of black flags.

In Bengal the situation was very different. The Muslim League administration there was headed by the flamboyant figure of H. S. Suhrawardy, who was believed at the time to be planning to make Bengal an independent state after the British had gone. Nobody took him very seriously. Suhrawardy decided to use Direct Action Day in Calcutta to make a display of his own popularity and power. His private army of strong-arm men organized a demonstration which got out of hand. Bloody riots broke out. Muslims attacked Hindus and Hindus attacked Muslims. For four days this great city of over two and a half million people was given over to torture and murder. Criminal elements took advantage of the tensions to loot shops and warehouses. Official sources later gave the very conservative figures of four thousand dead and ten thousand injured. The British Governor, an ex-railwayman appointed by the Labour Government in London, proved unequal to the crisis, and it was not until the second day that he called in British troops.

Towards the end of that bitter August, Attlee instructed the Viceroy, Lord Wavell, to go ahead and form an interim government. On 2 September it took office. There were twelve members of whom eight belonged to Congress. Three members were

Muslims, but none of them represented the Muslim League. The League ordered every Muslim in India, from Jinnah himself to the 'smallest and most frightened little man in his hut, to fly a black flag from his housetop in silent contempt for the Hindu government'. The one thing that Jinnah had been fighting to avoid had now happened. There *was* a Congress-dominated central government and it was headed by that most outspoken opponent of the League, Jawaharlal Nehru.

This had come about by another of the Mahatma's manoeuvres in favour of his protégé. During the negotiations with the cabinet mission Congress had elected a new president for the first time since 1940. On previous occasions the office of president had conferred status but not power, for the real decisions inside Congress rested partly with the right wing which dominated the organization and ultimately with Gandhi whose position whether he was officially in or out of Congress was that of a super-president. In 1946, however, the situation had been changed with the imminence of an interim government. The president of Congress would undoubtedly expect to be the leader of the Congress representatives and as Congress was the majority party would probably be the head of the interim administration, Prime Minister in effect if not in name. The election, therefore, was of considerable importance to the various groups inside Congress.

In 1946 there were three candidates, Patel, Kripalani and Nehru. The principal support was for Patel who had already been denied the office twice in favour of Nehru. Gandhi, however, was determined once again to have Nehru elected. He seems to have been convinced that Nehru would be more acceptable than Patel to the Labour Government in London. Gandhi therefore persuaded Patel and Kripalani to withdraw from the contest leaving Nehru as the only candidate. Though Patel accepted the Mahatma's decision he did so with great reluctance and his displacement intensified his dislike of Nehru. The conflict between the two men was to take on a sharper edge as freedom approached. Both men joined the interim government, Nehru as vice-president of the Viceroy's executive council, as it was still called, and member for external affairs and commonwealth relations. Patel was appointed to take charge of the portfolio of home affairs.

The Muslim League, fearing that the new Government would take decisions affecting its own position, reversed its previous stand: it would now be prepared to join the interim administration. On 13 October 1946 Jinnah wrote to the Viceroy that the League had decided to nominate five members. Only one of these, Liaquat Ali Khan, was an important figure in the League. Another was not a Muslim at all but a representative of the Scheduled Castes Federation, the organization representing the Untouchables.

The League's decision to join the interim government took place against a background of continuing communal violence which may well have contributed to it, for it seemed that some kind of civil war was actually in progress and it was a civil war that the League could not control. Calcutta had remained uneasy after the great killing and there had been numerous outbreaks of violence in the city. In Dacca, a city in East Bengal infamous for its communal troubles, there had been numerous clashes between Hindus and Muslims. From about 10 October there had been reports that, in the districts of Noakhali and Tippera, also in East Bengal, the Muslim majority was carrying out an organized war against Hindus. Refugees escaping from these two districts brought with them lurid tales of murder, rape and arson. Hindu women, they said, were being kidnapped and forcibly married; conversions were taking place under threat of death. Panic spread to the surrounding districts and many Hindus in places far away from the trouble-spots fled from their homes, fearing that their Muslim neighbours were about to attack them. Hindu newspapers were full of atrocity stories and the Muslim press retaliated with accusations that they were exaggerating and creating panic with the sole intention of discrediting the Muslim League government of Bengal.

This time the British acted swiftly, though Noakhali and Tippera were remote and communications difficult. Troops and armed police quickly moved in. The R A F dropped leaflets, food and medical supplies, and refugee camps were established. By the end of the month the trouble had died down. Though Gandhi and a number of League and Congress leaders, including Nehru, visited the area where there had been communal disturbances and helped to calm some of the people, others whose intentions were rather different were also active. Once again, extremist agitators were at work, and so were criminal elements. The killings, which reached their peak in the first week of November, resulted in the deaths of about six thousand Hindus. Many thousands more had been forced to leave their homes.

Communal conflict was just as strong within the reconstituted interim government. The League had not entered the Government to cooperate with Congress but to prove that cooperation was impossible. Nor was this all. Owing to the haste with which the League had joined the Government, there had been no discussion over the other League decision to boycott the constituent assembly. This was supposed to meet on 9 December, but when the date was announced Jinnah made a statement declaring it to be a blunder and that no League representative would attend the opening session. The only way to break the deadlock, the Viceroy believed, was to call the nationalist leaders to London for discussions with the Prime Minister. When the invitation was issued, Congress leaders were reluctant to accept, as it was now 27 November and the talks might be used as an excuse to postpone the first meeting of the constituent assembly. Nehru made known these doubts in London and suggested a meeting in Delhi instead. The Secretary of State replied with an assurance that the purpose of the conference was to *ensure* that the constituent assembly opened on time and that the British had no intention of modifying the mission's plan.

Jinnah, who had been following these exchanges with growing anger, cabled Attlee: 'Unless it is open to us to discuss the whole situation [i.e. the basis of the mission plan] it will be no use my going to London.' In reply he was assured by Attlee that his refusal must have been 'based on a misunderstanding of my telegram to Nehru. There is nothing to prejudice full consideration of all points of view.' Again there is the imprecise language so typical of the British side and two mutually exclusive promises seem to have been made. Jinnah was satisfied with the one made to him and on 1 December, Wavell, Nehru, Jinnah, Liaquat Ali and Baldev Singh (representing the Sikh community) left for London by air.

The discussions lasted only four days and on 6 December the British Government issued a statement which made it quite clear that no settlement had been arrived at. It explained the absence of results by claiming that it had not expected any, 'since the Indian representatives must consult their colleagues before any final decision is reached'. The discussions had centred mainly on the interpretation of the mission's plan, and, in particular, the clause concerning grouping. The mission, though it had not actually said so, had intended that the constituent assembly would decide on groupings by a simple majority decision of the assembly, but that any province which might find itself forced by the majority vote into a group to which it did not wish to belong would be safeguarded by being allowed, after the first general election held under the new consitution, to withdraw from the group on the basis of a simple vote in the province's own legislature. This interpretation had not been acceptable to Congress, which wanted each province to decide independently whether to join a group. But Congress modified its view and said it would be prepared to abide by an Indian Federal Court ruling on its interpretation of the grouping clause. The British Government, however, made it clear that as far as it was concerned the British Government's interpretation was the official interpretation, and that it must be accepted 'by all parties in the constituent assembly'. The Government urged Congress to acknowledge this ruling in order to open the way for the League's reconsideration of its boycott. If it would not, then the matter would be referred to the Federal Court as soon as possible.

The League was naturally jubilant over the vindication of its views, but it was quick to condemn any suggestion of reference to the Federal Court. However, the League's main satisfaction was to be derived from the last paragraph in the British Government's statement.

There has never been any prospect of success for the constituent assembly, except upon the basis of an agreed procedure. Should a constitution come to be framed by a constituent assembly in which a large section of the Indian population had not been represented, His Majesty's Government could not of course contemplate – as the Congress have stated that they would not contemplate – *forcing such a Constitution upon any unwilling parts of the country.*

It is in the last sentence that the significance lies, for it seemed to imply that the British Government now considered it might have to implement the Pakistan solution in one form or another. The statement did not suggest that a constitution arrived at without League participation would be void; it said that it would not be forced upon 'unwilling parts of the country' by the British *nor would the British allow it to be imposed by Congress.* This implication was bluntly put into words by Sir Stafford Cripps in the House of Commons when he said: 'If the Muslim League cannot be persuaded to come into the constituent assembly then the parts of the country where they are in a majority cannot be held to be bound by the results.' The statement, however, also implied that any 'unwilling' parts of provinces claimed for Pakistan would not be forced into accepting a Pakistan constitution either.

The League claimed that the statement meant that a second constituent assembly should now be set up. This was not acceptable to the British Government for though it had implied the *possibility* of some sort of Pakistan solution it still hoped to be able to transfer power to a united India. In this it was supported by the Conservative opposition but with some reservations as not all the Conservative leaders were in agreement.

The visit to London of the Indian leaders had not been without its fringe benefits. Nehru made a deep impression upon the Labour leaders while Jinnah, cold and inflexible, had merely confirmed their dislike for all he stood for. On the other hand, Jinnah had made some headway with Conservative politicians, and he remained in Britain after the conference was over to spread propaganda for Pakistan. In his conversations with members of the party of big business, he had emphasized the probability of civil war (and its effect on British business interests in India) if power was transferred to a Congress-dominated Government. Winston Churchill still maintained in Parliament that power should be handed over only to a united India and that Britain should stay in India until such time as agreement was reached between the two main parties, but he also suggested that there were in fact three choices before the British Government. The first was 'Quit India regardless of what may happen there'; the second, 'Partition India between the two different races'; and the third, set up an 'impartial administration responsible to Parliament . . . to maintain the fundamental guarantees of life, liberty and the pursuit of happiness'. Just how these 'fundamental guarantees' could be sustained Churchill did not say, though he must have been aware of the real situation in India.

The British administration in India was even thinner on the ground than it had been in 1945. There had been no civil service recruitment during the war, and a scheme launched soon after it ended had been abandoned in the face of Indian opposition to any further recruitment of Europeans. Britain's control of the Indian army was weakening rapidly as Indianization of the officer corps increased, and British army troops in India were decreasing at a considerable rate as demobilization proceeded. Very soon there would be practically no one to withdraw. The only alternative to departure open to the British Government would be, in the case of the civil service and the Indian army, to reopen recruitment to Europeans, which would be unacceptable to Indians and not particularly appealing to British subjects looking for a secure career. As far as the British army was concerned, the Labour Government could certainly not extend the service of wartime conscripts. If it did, it would be faced with mutinous behaviour from the civilian-soldiers and heavy pressure from their relatives at home, most of whom had voted the Labour Government into office.

The only sensible solution was to do something which should have been done long before – fix a definite date for the British withdrawal from India and invite Indian leaders to work out some agreement for the transfer of power. Indeed though the Indian leaders were not aware of it, Attlee was considering such a step almost immediately after their departure from London.

The constituent assembly met in Delhi on 9 December 1946 – without the Muslim League but with the Sikhs who though initially opposed had been persuaded by the combined efforts of Nehru and Patel to attend. Congress had an overwhelming majority of the seats – 205 out of the 296 allotted to British India. The rulers of the princely states had still to make up their minds whether they would join the assembly. It was, however, much more than a collection of politicians, for Congress had nominated a number of men from outside its ranks who were distinguished in the law, scholarship and public affairs.

One Congress leader was conspicuous by his absence. Gandhi – the 'architect of this assembly', as Nehru put it – was still tramping through Bengal on his outstandingly successful mission of peace and reconciliation. Some of the members of the assembly, in particular the Liberal party leader and a representative of the Anglo-Indians, warned the assembly not to hurry decisions that might be resented by 'absent friends who might later decide to join the assembly', and the Indian princes also publicly regretted the 'raising of any fundamental issues' in their absence. But the Congress majority was anxious to get on.

Nehru informed the assembly that the London declaration of 6 December had come as an unexpected blow. It was quite obvious that the Attlee Government had 'no imagination in the understanding of the Indian problem'. He had gone to London only in the hope that the League could be persuaded to join the assembly. Congress, he went on, had considered withdrawing from the assembly itself but had decided that it might look like a rejection of the British plan. Nehru was apologetic, as he should have been, for it was obvious to many that Congress had been outmanoeuvred. Nehru however was still defiant. 'India as she is constituted today wants no one's advice and no one's imposition upon her. . . . Any attempt at imposition, the slightest trace of patronage, is resented and will be resented.

There was no defiance of the Muslim League or of the princes for Nehru pledged the right of the people of the states to keep their form of government. An Objectives Resolution called for the declaration of a sovereign independent republic, a union between old British India and the princely states. There was no mention of socialism and Nehru explained that the omission was merely to keep the Resolution non-controversial. In fact the absence of any radical ideas represented a victory for Patel and the right wing of the party. The conflict between Nehru and Patel was soon to come into the open as was that between Nehru and the Congress socialists.

Despite what had been said by Nehru in the assembly, neither the League nor Congress had officially announced its views on the British Government's statement of 6 December, but when Jinnah returned to India with Liaquat Ali on 21 December he held a press conference in Karachi. Jinnah declared that unless Congress accepted the declaration the League saw no good reason why it should change its attitude to the assembly. The next day the Congress Working Committee issued a long statement the gist of which was a recapitulation of its old point of view. The meeting had been stormy. Nehru threatened to resign from the interim government, Patel was strongly opposed. He condemned Nehru's willingness to make public statements *threatening* to resign so often that no one now believed him. In any case it would be the height of foolishness to leave the interim government to the League. Patel had also been against the London conference, and though he had been initially included in the British Government's invitation, refused to go. The responsibility for its failure was Nehru's, Patel implied.

Gandhi, who was still in Bengal, was visited by Nehru because the Mahatma refused to come to Delhi. It was partly a journey for advice, partly to persuade Gandhi to use his influence with members of the Working Committee and in particular with Patel. Nehru was also near to despair and as so often before he needed the physical presence of Gandhi to re-assure him. Gandhi wrote to Patel who replied that he was opposed to Nehru's threats that never came to anything because they made Congress look weak and hesitant. As for the differences in the Working Committee, 'they are not of today's growth. They have been there for a long time.'

The rift between Nehru and the Congress Socialists was funda-mentally ideological. The CSP leaders did not believe that Britain intended to give up power. According to traditional

Marxist theory, power could not and would not be transferred by the will of the British and in negotiating the British were only stalling. Under the circumstances the socialists considered it necessary for the Indian people to prepare for a mass struggle. The socialists refused to join the constituent assembly and opposed official Congress policy whether expressed by Nehru or Patel. As for Nehru he had finally shown his true colours and instead of standing firm for the revolutionary struggle now seemed willing to cooperate with the British. The socialists contended – and not without reason – that the Congress leaders were more interested in personal power than in winning freedom for a united India.

Because of the disagreements in the Working Committee no decisions were taken. These were left for the next meeting of the All-India Congress Committee early in January 1947. Partisans of such provinces as Assam who thought that it would be forced to join a Muslim-majority group were lobbying for some bold action by Congress leaders. Certainly Congress could not delay its decision much longer. Gandhi privately advised the representatives of Assam and of the Sikhs not to cooperate in the British Government's plan. To Nehru Gandhi proposed that Congress nominally accept the plan but that the parties affected by it – Assam, the Sikhs and the NWFP – should be allowed freedom of action. A resolution embodying this highly ambivalent decision was carried but against considerable opposition and a large number of abstentions.

When the constituent assembly met for its second session on 20 January 1947 the League had still not reacted officially to this Congress resolution and it was not until eleven days later that the executive of the League met in Karachi. It issued a 3,000-word analysis of the constitutional problem, the gravamen of which was that the constituent assembly was illegal and should be dissolved, and that Congress's acceptance of the British Government's plan was merely a trick.

The constituent assembly went on with its business, dividing itself into committees and declaring that a chair would always be kept warm for representatives of the League. But the League had no intention of joining. It had seen a weakening in the

British Government's determination to hand over to a united India and Jinnah hoped to capitalize on it. The League, if it had wanted to make the constituent assembly work, could have entered it and waited to see whether or not Congress had been genuine in its acceptance of the mission plan. It could, too, have shown some public understanding of the fears that plagued Assam and the Sikhs of the Punjab, by giving them some assurance of fair treatment, but in all the words of the League's statement there was no glimmer of any such assurance.

Congress now demanded that the League should resign from the interim government and, on 15 February, Patel asked that the British Government should force the League to either join the assembly or leave the 'cabinet'. The League claimed it had as much right to remain in the interim government as Congress had. Congress retaliated by itself threatening to resign if the British Government did not act.

The Government did and with promptness, for Attlee had already made up his mind that a bold stroke was necessary to get things moving. On 20 February he announced in the House of Commons that despite the lack of agreement on the mission plan he wished to make it clear that it was the Government's 'definite intention to take the necessary steps to effect the transfer of power into responsible Indian hands by a date not later than June 1948'. As to whose those 'responsible' hands might be, Attlee could not say but, he went on: 'His Majesty's Government will have to consider to whom the powers of the Central Government of British India should be handed over, on the due date, *whether to some form of Central Government for British India or in some areas to the existing Provincial Governments, or in such other way as may be most reasonable and in the best interests of the Indian people.*'

At the same time, as if to dramatize the beginning of a new era, the Prime Minister announced that Lord Wavell's 'wartime appointment' as Viceroy would be ended and that he would be succeeded by Admiral Viscount Mountbatten of Burma.

Chapter 16
The Pledge Redeemed

Attlee's statement was received in India with a variety of predictable reactions. Nehru welcomed the declaration because it brought 'reality and a certain dynamic quality to the present situation'. In private he was not quite so enthusiastic and expressed to Gandhi his fear that there might be trouble because the statement was so imprecise. On the other hand there were Congress leaders who thought it was far too precise in offering an open invitation to the Muslim League to continue its boycott of the constituent assembly. The League also complained that the statement was too vague about the manner of the transfer of power. Nevertheless its leaders were convinced that the principle of Pakistan had been accepted by the British Government. The League had now only to intensify its efforts to ensure that the British handed over power not to a united India but a divided one. Gandhi was perhaps the only Congress leader who clearly saw this. 'This may lead to Pakistan for those provinces or portions which may want it,' he warned Nehru. 'No one will be forced one way or the other.' Essentially the statement of 20 February 1947 was the same as that of 6 December 1946. The British Government would indeed not force an all-India constitution on any unwilling parts of the country.

In Britain the Prime Minister's statement was hotly debated. The Conservative opposition which had, generally speaking, supported the Labour Government's policy in broad principle attacked the statement as far too radical. It was significant, however, that Conservatives with some recent experiences of India spoke in support of the Government. Lord Irwin – now Earl of Halifax – declared that he was not prepared to oppose the Government's policy because he could not honestly recommend a better solution. The main criticism from other speakers was concerned with the shortness of the time allowed for framing a constitution either for a united India or a divided one. Churchill, Sir John Anderson and R. A. Butler – the principal

Conservative spokesmen in the Commons debate – pointed out that the Prime Minister's statement did not envisage protection of the minorities or of the rights of the princes, and was in essence a complete departure from the original Cabinet mission offer. Anderson called it 'an unjustified gamble', and Churchill declared that 'in handing over the Government of India to these so-called political elements we are handing over to men of straw, of whom, in a few years, no trace will remain'. He claimed that the nationalist leaders did not represent the mass of the Indian people and although this argument was not unfounded it was hardly helpful. Who else could the British negotiate with? Churchill was so infuriated by Labour's 'treason' that he even went so far as to suggest that the Government should resort to the aid and advice of the United Nations. Butler was rather more in touch with reality, and he made it clear that he believed there would be more than one heir to the state when the time came for Britain to hand over power. When it came to the vote, however, the opposition was helpless.

In India the Congress Working Committee asked the British to give the interim government the immediate status of a real cabinet with full executive control of the armed services and the administration. It also issued an invitation to the Muslim League to join in discussions. This invitation was ignored; the League had other matters claiming prior attention. According to the new timetable it had fifteen months to establish its claim to take delivery of Pakistan. To do this the League must first establish itself in those provinces which would make up the new state. There was a League provincial government in only two – Bengal and Sind – of the six 'Pakistan provinces'. Baluchistan had no elected government, being administered by a British chief commissioner. In the North West Frontier Province (NWFP) and in Assam there were Congress administrations, while the Punjab was governed by a coalition ministry of the Unionist Party (a party including Muslims, Hindus and Sikhs), Congress, and the Sikhs' own political party.

The main League target was the Punjab. Not only was it the largest and most fertile and prosperous of the north-western provinces of India, but it held a strategic position and, if the

League could gain control, would cut the N W F P off completely from the rest of Congress India. In the Punjab, 56 per cent of the population was Muslim and the largest single party in the legislature was the Muslim League. The provincial League party believed it had hitherto been kept out of office by the British governor, who had encouraged a hastily formed coalition to take office. But in fact the very existence of a government representing the principal communities had helped to maintain communal peace in the Punjab. The government alliance, however, was an uneasy one and the legislative assembly was called only when absolutely necessary in order to pass the provincial budget. Well before the 20 February statement the Muslim League executive had instructed the provincial League organization to launch, at the end of January 1947, an 'all-out non-violent mass struggle against the reactionary Punjab regime' using as a pretext the special powers which the coalition government had assumed in order to reduce the risk of communal disorder. The provincial League had adopted Gandhian tactics, announced that it was fighting for civil liberties, and invited Hindus and Sikhs to join it in the struggle. It soon became clear that the League did have the support of the Muslim masses, for thousands of demonstrators throughout the Punjab began to defy the government's ban on public meetings and processions. The authorities acted swiftly and with the minimum of fuss. They arrested only the ringleaders and removed the remainder in lorries to a considerable distance and left them to walk home! The All-India Muslim League had now opened its own attack on what it called 'persistent and widespread persecution', and League members of the interim government had become vocal in their support of what was nothing other than a campaign to overthrow a legally elected government.

Peaceful demonstrations had soon degenerated into violence, and after the British Prime Minister's declaration of 20 February it became obvious that the coalition government in the Punjab no longer served any purpose. It had been formed in the belief that there was a distinction between problems of provincial administration and those affecting India's constitutional future, and that the negotiations with the British referred only to the central government. Now the whole business seemed to have been thrown open for discussion once again. The Punjab's chief minister decided it was necessary for all parties to confer upon the attitude the Punjab should take towards future events. His first step was to reach a settlement with the provincial League party, which, in return for the release of prisoners and the removal of the ban on public meetings, agreed to call off its civil disobedience campaign. On 2 March the Unionist ministry resigned, and the following day the governor called upon the Muslim League leader in the legislative assembly to attempt to form a ministry.

The various communities of the Punjab were now in a belligerent mood. For months they had been collecting arms and drilling their private armies. This had been done quite openly although the Unionist ministry had chosen to shut its eyes to it. On the same evening as the Muslim League was invited to form a ministry, the Master Tara Singh – the political leader of the Sikh community – addressed a mass rally. Waving a large sword he declaimed 'O Hindus and Sikhs! Be ready for self-destruction. . . . If we can snatch the government from the Britishers no one can stop us from snatching the government from the Muslims. . . . Disperse from here on the solemn affirmation that we shall not allow the League to exist. . . . We shall rule over them and will get the government, fighting. I have sounded the bugle. Finish the Muslim League.'

The provincial League was unable to convince the governor that it could form a stable ministry and on 5 March, under the constitutional authority vested in him, the governor himself took over the administration of the province. Communal disorder now began to spread with the aid of inflammatory speeches from so-called responsible leaders. Fierce battles took place between rival gangs, and whole streets were set ablaze by fire-raisers in the principal towns of the Punjab. By the end of March strong measures had restored some order to the towns but in the villages the terror continued. Official figures gave two thousand as the number of lives lost but there were probably many more. The casualties in the wars of succession were beginning to mount up. Under the circumstances then reigning in the Punjab, there was no likelihood of any return to ministerial government. The Muslim League, in its endeavour to gain power, had not only ensured that power would be denied it but had also brought the Punjab to the edge of civil war. Civil disobedience had once again inevitably led to bloodshed.

The Congress leaders now began to realize that the wars of succession were being fought with more than words and that the background to their arguments was dark and bloody. Nehru returned from a visit to the Punjab, sickened by what he had witnessed. 'I have seen ghastly sights,' he said, 'and I have heard of behaviour by human beings which would degrade brutes. All that has happened in the Punjab is intimately connected with political affairs. If there is a grain of intelligence in any person he must realize that whatever political objective he may aim at, this is not the way to attain it. Any such objective must bring, as it has in a measure brought, ruin and destruction.'

As the Punjab smouldered, the Congress Working Committee met to discuss the British Government's declaration and to decide upon future strategy. In one of its resolutions passed on 8 March, it recommended partition of the Punjab into predominantly Muslim and predominantly Hindu and Sikh areas, a principle already suggested by the Hindus and Sikhs of the eastern part of the Punjab. This did not mean that Congress envisaged the possibility of dividing India itself; it simply meant that, whatever happened in the future, one thing was now sure – there would be some sort of provincial autonomy, and it was obviously a good idea to set about creating new provinces which would not suffer from the basic communal problem. Even if the division of India actually came, any Hindu areas which had already been cut away from the Muslim area of the Punjab and Bengal would naturally opt for India. But this was only the long-term purpose of the resolution. Congress still believed that Jinnah was an ordinary politician, out – as they themselves were – for what he could get, and although he persisted in his demand for the six 'Pakistan provinces', they thought he would finally back down when faced with the certainty that two of these provinces – the Punjab and Bengal – would be divided. Since it also seemed very unlikely that either Assam or the NWFP would join a Pakistan grouping, Congress believed Jinnah would realize that Pakistan could not work, either administratively or economically. It is obvious that the Congress leaders still did not understand Jinnah's determination to prevent Congress from ruling an undivided India even if it were the loosest of federations. He had also no intention of allowing Congress to strike the first blow and the League was already at work organizing civil disobedience campaigns in the NWFP and Assam.

The situation in the North West Frontier Province was unique. Of all the provinces of India it had the largest Muslim majority – 92 per cent of the population. Because of this it was virtually free from communal rivalries. The odds against non-Muslims were indisputable even in the streets. Early in nationalist history when the Muslim League was of little consequence, Congress had claimed the allegiance of Muslim nationalists in the NWFP who had been organized into the 'Redshirt' movement by Abdul Ghaffar Khan and his brother, Dr Khan Sahib. The latter was now chief minister of the province. The population of the provinces was mainly Pathan by race. Between the NWFP and the frontier of Afghanistan there were tribal areas, not directly administered by the NWFP government, whose tribes were also Pathan by race and semi-independent. Relations between the tribes and the British were handled by officers of the central department of external affairs. Muslim League propagandists had been active among the tribes, so that when Nehru visited tribal areas in October 1946, in his capacity as member for external affairs, he was received with hostility and even open violence wherever he went. The League used Nehru's visit for all it was worth as a symbol of that Hindu domination it claimed was threatening the Pathans, and then, in the second half of February 1947, launched a civil disobedience campaign in the NWFP which soon followed the same pattern as that in the Punjab. The League called for the resignation of Dr Khan Sahib, but he refused to be stampeded.

The situation in Assam differed both from that in the Punjab and from that in the NWFP. In Assam the Muslims were in a minority, making up only about one third of the population, and the League's claim to Assam as one of the six 'Pakistan provinces' was based solely on its geographical position. Because of their comparatively small numbers, the Muslims in the province could not hope to achieve much success with a civil disobedience campaign, but this did not prevent them from trying. Conveniently for them, they could make use of an issue which had almost become traditional. Assam, fearing immigrants into its fertile lands from Bengal's poverty-stricken Muslim majority, had a history of evicting Muslim squatters. The British had done it, a coalition government headed by a Muslim League chief minister had done it, the current Congress ministry merely carried on the tradition. The League, however, nothing daunted, proceeded to organize mass invasions by Muslims from Bengal, and encouraged them to squat upon government-owned grazing land. As usual, the invasion began peacefully enough but soon degenerated into indiscriminate and bloody violence.

Assam and the NWFP were not the only places in India menaced by violence. Only the south seemed reasonably quiet. The 20 February declaration had confirmed that the British intended to leave and there were many who saw advantage in it. The extremist communal parties were active in the slums of the great cities, meeting on their missions of incitement communist agitators intent on spreading unease among the workers. There were also signs that communist influence was growing among the peasants in certain districts. Nine out of eleven provinces of British India were now subject to security ordinances which gave the governments wide powers of arrest and control over demonstrations. The police and the army still seemed immune from virus of the communalism but no one could guarantee how long that immunity would last.

It was to this scene of blood, conspiracy and fear that the new Viceroy came, landing at Delhi in the hot afternoon of 22 March 1947.

The day after Lord Mountbatten's arrival, Nehru emerged on the stage for which he felt himself especially qualified – that of international politics. It was another example of the

escape from the parochial to the universal which had on previous occasions been an antidote for despair and which was later
to serve as a surrogate for achievement in domestic affairs. On
23 March in an immense marquee erected inside the walls of the
Purana Qila, an old fort built by one of the Muslim rulers of
Delhi in the sixteenth century, the first Asian Relations Conference met in an atmosphere of enthusiasm and suspicion.

Though the inspiration for such a meeting had come from
others, the reality was very much of Nehru's making. In the
spring and early summer of 1945 the idea of an Asian conference seems to have grown up among a number of the Asian
delegates to the United Nations Conference on International
Organization then meeting at San Francisco. One of the unofficial delegates was Nehru's sister, Vijaya Lakshmi Pandit.
Mrs Pandit was approached with the suggestion that her brother
'should take the lead in summoning such a conference in Asia'.
When this was conveyed to Nehru it was picked up, amplified
and given a special gloss in a series of public speeches in the
latter half of 1945. In December of the same year Nehru gave
an interview which was published in *The Hindu* of Madras and
in the *Manchester Guardian*.

Nehru began by stating that in his opinion an Asian Federation was 'a possibility in the near future'. All really depended
upon whether the United Nations was an effective body. If not
then large groups would form in Asia for 'their own protection
against outside aggression' for unity against war and also
against 'economic penetration'. For these reasons and because
of old cultural ties, Nehru predicted with confidence that 'a
closer union of the countries bordering on the Indian Ocean
both for defence and trade purposes is almost certain to emerge'.
There would also be 'cooperation on foreign policy'. Nehru
also mentioned that he hoped an Asian conference would be
called to meet in India. If it did there would be no racialist bias
among the delegates 'nor will it be opposed in any way to
America or the Soviet Union or any other power or group of
powers'.

After this interview Nehru had begun to work actively for the
conference and had collected money for it as well as sounding

out other Asian leaders during his tour of south-east Asia in March 1946. In the following month planning was begun in earnest by an unofficial body known as the Indian Council of World Affairs. It is significant that during a period of bloody rioting in India and tortuous negotiations which would lead to Indian freedom, Nehru could find time to help in the preparation for the conference. When he took charge of external affairs in the interim government in September, Nehru saw that official assistance was given to the ICWA, though the fiction was maintained that the Council was merely arranging an unofficial gathering of scholars to discuss Asian culture!

Nehru's anxiety to get a conference in Delhi was made plain in January 1947 when he ordered a British official of the external affairs department to attend executive meetings of an organizing committee set up by the Council. The diplomatic missions of the British Government were also asked to cooperate in delivering invitations, a piece of naïveté which was responded to with non-cooperation. The organizing of such a conference with all the difficulties of communications with potential delegates was a heavy task for an unofficial council which had only been established for three years and which had small resources in manpower and finance. Nehru, however, was particularly active. While the future of India lay in the balance and innocent people were being killed in communal riots, while he had become the chief executive in an interim government faced with manifold problems for dealing with which he had neither training nor experience, Nehru diverted energies that might well have been expended on more worthwhile matters to attending committee meetings and prodding others into getting the Asian conference off the ground. If his interest and activity was not an escape from more pressing reality then he must have expected something of great importance to emerge from the conference.

What this could have been is rather obscure and has never been properly clarified. When speaking in 1946 of the objectives of such a conference he talked only about promoting good relations and the pooling of ideas. There is no mention of cooperation in the anti-colonial struggle. A clue lies in Nehru's main preoccupation throughout the conference. This was to persuade delegates to create a permanent organization to carry on the conference's work – which would, he expected, lead to the establishment of an Asian Federation. It is an interesting indication of the sort of thoughts that occupied Nehru's mind at this, the most crucial, period in the history of modern India.

When the conference met there were twenty-eight delegations, a great deal of innocent enthusiasm and considerable political ambivalence. The Muslim League judged it a gambit by 'the Indian Hindu Congress' to spread its influence abroad and boycotted the meeting. There were other conflicts too, but for Nehru the symbolism of a meeting in Delhi of Asians emerging out of the dark night of colonial subjection overrode everything. Nehru dominated the proceedings. Indeed the other Congress Leaders were more concerned with India's problems and did not attend. As in the past Nehru was encouraged to have 'foreign affairs' all to himself. Patel was sure that the conference was a waste of time but at least it kept Nehru occupied. In fact no concrete results emerged from the conference. Its principal effect was to convince Nehru that he had a significant role to play in international affairs.

For the time being, however, there were domestic demands that could not be ignored. After Mountbatten's official installation on 24 March, he began a round of talks with the principal Indian leaders: Nehru, Patel, Gandhi, Jinnah and Liaquat Ali Khan. From the beginning Nehru and Mountbatten were drawn to each other and established a close relationship which was not shared by anyone else. Where Nehru had distrusted the bluff, honest Wavell, he found Mountbatten very much to his liking. This was not surprising as the two men had much in common. Both had considerable charm, a not totally dissimilar upper-class background and large reserves of personal vanity. But Mountbatten had for Nehru even more attractions. He was dynamic and decisive and radiated self-confidence. Nehru's life had been a series of dependences on stronger characters than his own. First there was his father, then Gandhi, now it was to be Mountbatten.

Mountbatten tried to exercise his charm on the other leaders but failed. Jinnah was as self-confident as Mountbatten and infinitely more rigid. Patel was indifferent and maintained contact with the Viceroy mainly through Mountbatten's constitutional adviser, V. P. Menon. As for Gandhi there was no possible point of contact. He and the Viceroy might have been of different species. At their meeting Gandhi put forward the old Rajagopalachari formula that called for the handing over of the interim government to Jinnah. But neither the Viceroy nor, more importantly, Congress was impressed. In fact Gandhi no longer spoke for Congress and it is very doubtful whether he could have reimposed his authority even if he had wanted to. Gandhi had never yearned for political power and that was what the negotiations were about. Nor did the Congress leaders need him any more. The Mahatma returned to Bengal and took no further part in the negotiations.

Mountbatten very quickly realized that it was not possible to hand over power to an undivided India. For the first time the actual strength of Jinnah seems to have been properly appreciated by someone in authority and Mountbatten, unlike previous negotiators, had plenipotentiary powers. The security situation was deteriorating and swift decisions were necessary. The politicians, too, were at each other's throats.

The interim government was divided into two blocs who were scarcely on speaking terms, each pursuing policies designed to antagonize and humiliate the other. Nehru, in making diplomatic appointments abroad, for example, sent a Muslim member of Congress as ambassador to the United States, while the commerce minister – a member of the Muslim League – dispatched trade representatives abroad who were more concerned with spreading propaganda for Pakistan than with doing business for India. The finance minister, Liaquat Ali, primed with advice from a Muslim finance-department civil servant who was pro-League, put forward a practical budget imposing a 25 per cent tax on business profits over £7,500 per annum. Since it was Congress which proclaimed a policy of socialism, the tax should have been welcomed by Congress, but the one snag was that most of its funds came from Hindu big business. Liaquat's proposal was in fact a deliberate attempt to create a division between the business and socialist wings of Congress, but it caused so much trouble that the Viceroy was compelled to intervene and the amount of tax was reduced.

The charade of the interim government was essentially a side-show. The real decisions were taking place outside and, in particular, in the attitudes of the Congress leaders. Nehru was appalled by the chaos and confusion that surrounded him. He knew that freedom was near and it seemed to be evading everyone's grasp. There appeared to be only one way out of the deadlock. 'By cutting off the head,' he was to say later, 'we shall get rid of the headache.' By the end of April he had made up his mind. 'The Muslim League can have Pakistan', was now his opinion. 'But on condition that they do not take away other parts of India which do not wish to join . . . .'.

Nehru was not the only one who had come to accept the inevitable. Sardar Patel had reported that the Congress machine was falling apart under the strain of communal disorder and the failure of its leaders to achieve independence quickly. Inside Congress, various groups were jockeying for power. There was a growing feeling that even a divided India was preferable to no India at all. Business was declining, factories had been made idle by strikes; landlords were threatened by uprisings of their tenants. Powerful capitalist interests in Congress were now preparing for the possibility of disowning Nehru, just as they had disposed of Gandhi, and Patel was their spokesman. It was he who had first persuaded them to put up their money – now they were beginning to demand their dividends. It was Patel who had put forward the resolution calling for the partition of the Punjab and Bengal. Now he was to put forward the partition of India, not to satisfy Jinnah but to save Congress from collapse. However, the public had to be kept in the dark; Congress must seem to yield to the logic of the situation, to accept the Pakistan solution reluctantly but in the interests of *the Indian people*.

Patel's new position was soon made known to Mountbatten through V. P. Menon, who informed the Viceroy that though Patel was reluctant to accept a divided India he might be persuaded. As Mountbatten was himself totally convinced that partition was inevitable, this news was received with some satisfaction. Mountbatten, however, was still considering taking Gandhi's old advice to the British – get out and leave India to do the dividing itself. This opinion he had not disclosed to the nationalist leaders. In fact on 11 April Mountbatten handed to Menon 'the bare bones of a plan for the transfer of power' which at least implied that the British might do the dividing. Menon was asked for his comments on how, for example, to partition the Punjab, Bengal and Assam. Menon's reply which was cleared with Patel, though not with Nehru, included a number of suggestions for dealing with this and other problems.

While the Viceroy was keeping his own views to himself and sounding out a number of options, the Muslim League was continuing its campaign for partition by the British before they left. The division of British India was not just a question of drawing lines on the map. The assets of the empire must also be divided. The most important of these assets was the Indian army. On 8 April Liaquat Ali Khan put forward to Mount-batten a suggestion that the armed forces should be reorganized so that they could easily be divided when the time came for partition. This of course prejudged the outcome of the political settlement and Mountbatten was not prepared to consider it. But Liaquat was not going to give up the initiative. Instead, he produced a remarkably detailed plan, remarking that the preparation for such a plan would take time, but 'if taken in hand immediately it should be ready about the time that a decision on the main constitutional issue is reached'. He also pointed out that the British Government's deadline for the transfer of power was so near that the Viceroy ought to have some plan ready just in case it became necessary. This was obviously an occasion when Congress – if it had really been prepared to fight partition – should have resisted any suggestion of dividing the armed forces, for it was clear to everybody that Liaquat's proposal was loaded. If the army should be divided, the greatest obstacle to political partition would have been overcome.

The only real resistance to Liaquat's plan however came from General Auchinleck, the commander-in-chief, who bluntly replied that 'the armed forces of India, as they now stand, cannot be split up into two parts each of which will form a self-contained armed force', and he buttressed his opinion with facts and cogent argument, the gist of which was that there was not enough time for reorganization before June 1948. Auchinleck further warned that rumours of a plan to divide the army should not be allowed to reach the general public. 'I wish to stress,' he wrote, 'that in the present state of communal unrest in India any publication of such discussions might well be disastrous to the continued morale and efficiency of the armed forces.' For the time being the matter was put aside, at least until there was some definite commitment to partition.

It was now time for Gandhi to emerge from his self-imposed silence. He did so to condemn any suggestion of partitioning the Punjab and Bengal. After a brief talk with Jinnah arranged by the Viceroy, the Mahatma declared that he could not 'accept the principle of division' and immediately began to preach the gospel of unity – though without much of his old conviction. Jinnah, too, was against the division of the two provinces. He denounced any proposal to divide them as a 'sinister move' and asked why, if such a division was logical for the Punjab and Bengal, it should not be applied to other provinces? Perhaps, he suggested, the problem of Hindu minorities in the new Pakistan, and Muslim minorities in Hindu India could best be solved by an exchange of population.

While partition was still being argued, the chances of fragmentation seemed to be increasing. Some of the larger princely states pointed out that when the British left they would be legally independent as their treaty relations were not with the Government of India but with the British Crown. Though it might be expected that they would join one or other of the new Dominions they would not rule out the possibility that they would choose complete independence for themselves. In the Punjab, the Sikhs were demanding a state of their own. In the NWFP the Pathans were suggesting a 'Pathanistan' as the answer for their own claim to nationhood. In Bengal the Muslim League chief minister Suhrawardy declared that rather than submit to partition he would create a 'sovereign, independent and undivided Bengal in a divided India'. Jinnah naturally denounced this but certain provincial Congress leaders, after being assured that there would be a place for them in the government of independent Bengal, gave Suhrawardy their support.

With all these rival claims in the air, violence was growing just when the administration was becoming progressively weaker. Calcutta had a daily toll of dead and was always on the edge of new massacres: in the Punjab, fire-raising and assassination continued; 'Redshirts', the pro-Congress movement in the NWFP, abandoned non-violence and began arming volunteers. In retaliation the League was smuggling arms, many of them of Russian origin, from Afghanistan.

Large-scale migration from 'unsafe' areas was already taking place, and many refugees flooded into Delhi and the surrounding countryside. The administration's grasp was obviously weakening. Rumours of division *had* reached the army. The police were not above suspicion, as everyone had thought; in fact they were riddled by communal divisions. One thing became apparent – even June 1948 was too far away, and it was more than possible that the existing machinery of government would not last that long.

Events now began to move with great rapidity. On 2 May Lord Ismay, one of Mountbatten's staff, flew to London with the Viceroy's appreciation of the situation and his proposals for action. Among them was a draft plan which Ismay was instructed to 'hammer out clause by clause with the Government and officials concerned'. Before Ismay left there had been a continuous round of discussion and argument over one question of considerable importance, or so it appeared to Mountbatten. This was whether, after independence, India would remain within the British Commonwealth. If past speeches by Congress leaders were anything to go on, they did not want to remain in the Commonwealth, because membership would imply the Dominion status which they had rejected long before. But at the meeting before Ismay left for London, a member of the Viceroy's staff casually disclosed that V. P.

Menon had told him Patel *might* be willing to accept Dominion status, at least for some period after independence. Menon had in fact managed to convince Patel that, as the situation now stood, Britain favoured the Muslim League, but partition, 'with both India and Pakistan as Dominions, would eliminate the League's preferred status with the British' and 'facilitate the parliamentary approval of the transfer of power'. Patel had yielded to this argument. But Nehru was not told of it; it was now becoming fairly obvious that Patel was the most important figure among Congress leaders.

Menon was soon, with the Viceroy's approval, to put a Dominion status plan to Nehru, and the time was approaching when Congress leaders would jettison all the beliefs to which they had stuck so tenaciously before it became obvious that the British were leaving. Menon was 'asked to prepare a paper setting out the procedure whereby a form of Dominion status under the alternative plans of Partition and Demission' might be agreed, a simple-sounding request, but one of considerable future importance for India and the Commonwealth. Its final effect was to change the form of the Commonwealth and even allow a republic to remain inside it.

The plan Ismay took to London on 2 May was highly ingenious. Before he had left for India, Mountbatten had received from Attlee a number of skeleton plans, prepared by the Prime Minister's advisers, for settling the Indian problem. But no Indian had been involved in putting the flesh around this one, and the comments which V. P. Menon attached to a draft given him by Ismay were ignored; Menon later insisted that he told Ismay the plan would not function. It had in fact been yet another draft that had been sent to Menon, in the hope that he would leak the gist of it to Patel, and the plan Ismay actually took to London was an altered and amended version.

The plan was deceptively simple – to transfer power to the provinces, leaving only a weak federal administration at the centre. Any polarization into groups would then be a matter for the individual provinces to decide, *after the British had left*. Mountbatten thought that the only likely resistance to this plan would come from Jinnah. As no one other than Mountbatten and his staff had actually seen the plan in its final form – only a few highlights had been disclosed verbally – the Viceroy should have had every reason for feeling uneasy. But it was not from Jinnah that Mountbatten was to receive the first signs of criticism. This came first from V. P. Menon, who had accompanied the Viceroy to Simla on 7 May and was at last able to put forward his – and Patel's – view on the subject.

On 8 May, at the invitation of the Viceroy, Nehru arrived at Viceregal Lodge, Simla. On his arrival, Mountbatten gave V. P. Menon permission to talk to him about Dominion status – to which Patel had already agreed – but not about the plan which Ismay had taken to London. The next day, 9 May, there was a general discussion at which the Viceroy encouraged Menon to outline to Nehru his own scheme for the transfer of power to two central governments, one for Pakistan and one for Hindustan, each with an interim constitution based upon the old India Act of 1935. Nehru found the scheme appealing, though he made a show of not altogether liking the idea of Dominion status on the grounds that it still retained overtones of dependence. But he was by now determined that even Dominion status should not stand in the way of India's freedom, and in any case, after independence, a free India could easily decide to leave the Commonwealth if it wanted to. Such questions, though important perhaps to the British Government, did not carry the same weight with Nehru or Patel. Having swallowed partition it was highly unlikely that they would choke on Dominion status.

On 10 May, however, Mountbatten suddenly decided to see what effect the draft plan would have on Nehru. Within half an hour Mountbatten was forced to face the fact that he had completely misjudged the reaction his plan might bring from Indian leaders. Nehru was blunt – the draft was totally unacceptable. It would, he wrote next morning in a memorandum to the Viceroy, 'invite the Balkanization of India' and 'provoke certain civil conflict'. He also condemned the plan as likely to 'endanger relations between Britain and India'. This was undoubtedly serious – for the Viceroy. Ismay in London had convinced Attlee that the plan he had brought with him was workable because it would be acceptable to the Indian leaders. Now one of them had shown that it was not.

Fortunately, there was at least one thing on the credit side – the plan had not yet been made public. It was even more fortunate that an alternative scheme was already in existence – Mountbatten had encouraged V. P. Menon to explain his own plan only the day before. Nehru was asked if Congress would accept a new draft plan based on the Menon scheme and incorporating Nehru's own criticisms. Nehru replied – rightly, for he was not in any position to do so – that he could not speak for Congress. Not, he added, without first seeing a revised draft. Since Nehru was leaving that evening for Delhi, it did not seem possible to produce anything for him before he left; but with only a few days to go before the much publicized meeting at which the Viceroy was supposed to present a new plan to the Indian leaders, the utmost speed was necessary. Menon was instructed to get his scheme in writing before Nehru left Simla.

Menon produced his draft on time, and has since been praised for taking 'exactly four hours to draw up a plan which was to change the face of India and the world'. This is by no means the case for Menon had had his plan ready to produce ever since he received from Ismay the draft of what was later to form the basis of Mountbatten's scheme, and he had even discussed it in outline with Patel. He already knew that his scheme was acceptable to Patel and if there were to be any opposition from Nehru, Patel could soon overcome it.

Mountbatten now had to tell London what had happened. There was also the imminent meeting between the Viceroy and the nationalist leaders. The first thing to be done was to postpone that meeting. An announcement was made that because of the parliamentary recess in London the conference had had to be put off until 2 June. This naturally caught the British Government unawares.

Mountbatten was now faced with a mystified and angry Attlee. Cables came from London demanding explanations. Ismay, too, who had used all his powers of persuasion to get the original plan accepted, complained that he had not the remotest idea what was going on. One cable from Attlee demanded the Viceroy's immediate presence in London so that he could explain his behaviour in person. For a while Mountbatten was not sure whether to go or whether to stand on his dignity and threaten to resign if he did not receive what would be in effect a vote of confidence. On reflection he cabled Attlee that he could fly to London on the 18th. When he left Delhi, Mountbatten took Menon with him. It was a wise move. His sober and intelligent approach was just what was needed to convince Attlee. It succeeded, though Attlee's confidence in Mountbatten's judgement was somewhat tarnished. But Mountbatten was able to convince the Prime Minister that the new plan represented, reasonably accurately, the view of the nationalist leaders and that it actually could be carried out despite the shortness of time. On Mountbatten's instruction, Ismay had already suggested that the date for the transfer of power should be moved forward, and Attlee had also been advised by other sources that the June 1948 date was unsatisfactory on purely administrative grounds.

During the discussions in London, one date now seemed to meet with general if somewhat dismayed agreement – 15 August, barely two and a half months ahead.

Between the Viceroy's return from London on 31 May and his meeting with the Indian leaders two days later the atmosphere was clouded by a number of contradictory and ominous statements. Jinnah declared that he was immovably opposed to the partition of the Punjab and Bengal though in fact the League leaders were now prepared to accept it. Jinnah's purpose was to sustain the pressure just in case Mountbatten returned with yet another 'solution'. To keep matters as tense as possible Jinnah even demanded that there be a corridor 800 miles long through 'Hindu' India connecting the western and eastern parts of Pakistan! Nehru called the demand 'fantastic and absurd', which indeed it was.

Gandhi too was giving the impression that he would try to persuade Congress to resist partition even at the risk of violence. 'Even if the whole of India burns,' he said at his prayer meeting on 31 May, 'we shall not concede Pakistan, even if the Muslims demand it at the point of the sword.' Why Gandhi made this peculiarly violent threat has never been adequately explained. At a meeting of the Working Committee held while Mountbatten was in London, Gandhi had accepted the fact that both Nehru and Patel now favoured partition as the only way to achieve freedom. He did complain that no one had told him of the changed attitude of the Congress leadership. Nehru replied that Gandhi had been constantly kept in the picture. Gandhi denied this and Nehru then remarked that East Bengal where the Mahatma had been trying to reduce violence was far away from Delhi and that though he may not have sent Gandhi full details, at least he had kept him informed of the broad outlines. No minutes of this meeting were kept and the story rests on the selective memory of the survivors. Nevertheless it does seem that Gandhi either by omission or design had not been kept fully informed in case he might try to throw his weight against the decision of the other Congress leaders.

The Mahatma was, however, not prepared for a show-down and contented himself with saying that Congress must honour the decisions of its leaders. This being so – and none of the evidence denies it – why should he have made his inflammatory statement of 31 May? The answer seems to lie in Gandhi's new attitude to Congress and to the future. Gandhi was angry at his rejection by the Congress leaders and he was considering the possibility of dissociating himself from the movement which had been so much his own creation. His aim had always been to reform Hinduism and it seems probable that he had come to recognize that Congress was no longer the ideal instrument for his plans. He did not wish to jeopardize his own future by being associated with a decision to divide the sacred land of India. Whatever Gandhi's motives, they no longer counted in the discussions that were now to start though his words did contribute to the communal violence which was to follow them. Mountbatten seems to have thought that Gandhi might still be in a position to influence Congress but there was really nothing to worry about.

The nationalist leaders met the Viceroy on 2 June. Those present were Nehru, Patel and Kripalani, now president, for

Congress, Jinnah, Liaquat Ali and Sardar Nishtar for the Muslim League, and Baldev Singh for the Sikhs. For all the significance of the meeting there was little sense of the drama of the occasion. Mountbatten made a formal appeal to the leaders to accept the old mission plan but this was only a gesture. Everyone present was in agreement with the new proposals.

Next day the plan was published. It was mainly concerned with the way in which inhabitants of the 'Pakistan provinces' could express their opinion on whether they wanted a new constituent assembly or were content with the present one. This was a roundabout way of saying that the provinces were to be asked whether they wished to join Pakistan or not. The method of tapping opinion was to vary in the different provinces. In Sind, Bengal and the Punjab the choice was to be made by members of the provincial legislative assemblies, but in the two latter provinces the assemblies were to meet in separate parts – one representing the Muslim-majority districts and the other the rest of the province – and to vote separately. If each part then decided that it wished to remain united with the other, the assembly as a whole was to be asked to vote upon whether it wished to join Pakistan or India. If, however, either part voted in favour of division from the other, then it would be assumed that division should for the time being be drawn between the Muslim and non Muslim-majority districts. The Viceroy would thereafter appoint a boundary commission to arrive at a final decision.

If Bengal decided in favour of dividing itself, a referendum would then have to be held in the Sylhet district of the province of Assam – the only Muslim-majority district in that province – to find out whether its inhabitants wanted to join their Muslim brethren in what would be East Bengal. A method also had to be devised for voting in British Baluchistan, which had never had an elected government, and in which there were no electoral registers.

The North West Frontier Province, where the 'Redshirt'. government still held office, presented a different problem. There, a legislative assembly would be unlikely to reflect the real views of the electorate, and it was therefore decided that there should be a referendum.

The plan concluded with a statement that the British Government was prepared to hand over power before June 1948, and that it intended to introduce legislation during the current session of the British Parliament to transfer power to one or two successor states at some date in 1947. At a press conference on 4 June, the Viceroy indicated – though not officially – that the date the Government had in mind was 15 August.

On the evening of 3 June the nationalist leaders announced their agreement to the Indian people. In a hot, crowded studio of All-India Radio the Viceroy, Nehru, Jinnah and Baldev Singh went to the microphone. Jinnah called upon the League in the NWFP and Assam to abandon its 'civil disobedience' campaign. Baldev Singh in a colourless speech managed to disguise the dissatisfaction of his community. Only Nehru tried to rise to the grandeur of the occasion. 'We are little men,' he said, 'serving great causes but because that cause is great something of that greatness falls upon us.'

A week later the council of the Muslim League, by a vote of 400 to 8, gave Jinnah authority to 'accept the fundamental principles of the plan as a compromise'. The All-India Congress Committee met a few days afterwards and also passed a resolution of acceptance – by 137 votes to 29 with 32 abstentions mainly by orthodox Hindus. The principal opposition came from the communalists, the Muslims and the socialists. Nehru spoke only briefly and it was left to Patel to make the main speech of the meeting. Patel was, as always, precise and blunt. Freedom without partition was impossible. Cut off the diseased limb and save the main body. Gandhi also spoke but no one was really listening. All that concerned them was that he did not disapprove.

Now that the plan had been accepted by Congress and the League there were only two months in which to set up the machinery for partition; demarcate, at least in general terms, the new frontiers after decisions had been made in the legislatures of the affected provinces; and to embody the constitutional procedures in a Bill to be presented to the British Parliament.

The machinery set up to prepare for partition was basically simple. At the apex there was a Partition Committee with Lord Mountbatten as chairman, Patel and Rajendra Prasad representing Congress, and Liaquat Ali and Sardar Nishtar, the League. Baldev Singh was excluded after Jinnah had objected that he would be too pro-Congress. The committee's function was to coordinate the work of a large number of expert committees and sub-committees dealing with everything from the division of the armed forces, through railways and telegraphs to the duplication of files.

The Armed Forces Committee included a British chairman and a number of British officers. Their task was both dangerous and difficult, for there was no easy way to divide army units. Until shortly after the Mutiny of 1857, entire regiments had been either Hindu or Muslim, but units were then mixed to strike a balance between the two religions, so that each might act as a restraint upon the other. Because of this, units would now have to be broken up completely and then reassembled, although while this was being done it was arranged that some central administrative control would remain. At the same time, commanders-in-chief of the two new Dominions' armies were to be appointed so that they and their headquarters administration would be ready to take over. In the interim, the supreme commander was to be the then commander-in-chief of undivided India, who was to be subordinate to a Joint Defence Council. He was to have no operational control over the new armies, except in the case of units in transit between the two Dominions, and his only function was to oversee the proper division of men and materials. It was hoped that joint control would come to an end after 1 April 1948.

The division of the armed forces was to take place in two stages. The first was to consist of a rather rough-and-ready separation on a purely communal basis, followed by the immediate concentration of Muslim-majority units in what was to be Pakistan and of other units in the rest of the country. The second stage was to cover the voluntary transfer of individuals who wished to join units in either Pakistan or India. The first stage was carried through with unexpected smoothness. Before the end of June 1947, final decisions had been reached on the navy and on some units of the army.

The civil services also had to be divided, and both European and Indian members were asked to stay on and help with necessary reconstruction after the transfer of power.

By the end of June both Bengal and the Punjab had decided in favour of internal partition. In Bengal the decision was reached in an atmosphere comparatively free from communal disorder, though tension was only just below the surface. In the Punjab, however, there was a daily quota of bomb explosions, fire-raising and murders in Lahore, the provincial capital, and Amritsar, the sacred city of the Sikhs. The Muslim-majority areas had voted against the division of the Punjab, as was to be expected, but the non-Muslim areas voted in favour. The consequence of these votes was that the central Partition Committee was replaced by a Partition Council, the only change being that Jinnah took over from Sardar Nishtar. Partition Councils were also set up in the Punjab and Bengal and, in the latter, the Muslim League government was enlarged to include Hindu ministers from the western districts. In Sind the legislative assembly voted to join Pakistan and in Baluchistan a council of tribal chiefs unanimously voted to do the same. In the Sylhet district of Assam, the referendum resulted in a majority vote in favour of Pakistan. From an organizational point of view, everything seemed to be running smoothly.

But there still remained the North West Frontier Province. The choice before the electors was to join either Pakistan or India; but actually there was no choice. For simple geographical reasons, the province could not join Congress India, and for religious reasons, the people would not join Hindu India. The verdict was a foregone conclusion, and the population would obviously vote for Pakistan. Nevertheless, the Redshirt movement was still angling for the alternatives to be changed to Pakistan or Pathanistan. Even Gandhi thought this a good idea. Abdul Ghaffar Khan had asked Jinnah to agree to the NWFP declaring itself independent on the understanding that it would join Pakistan if the new Pakistani constitution was acceptable; he told Jinnah that he and his followers would even be prepared

to send delegates to a Pakistan constituent assembly, on condition that they would be able to withdraw if they wanted to.
To this 'insidious and spurious' demand, Jinnah would not
listen, especially as he knew that Muslim League influence had
grown immensely in the NWFP after the partition plan had
been announced. The referendum passed off peacefully in the
presence of some 15,000 troops moved in for the occasion. The
result was 289,224 votes in favour of joining Pakistan and
7,874 in favour of India.

While all this was going on, the Indian Independence Bill was
being piloted through the British Parliament. The Bill's twenty
clauses were given a third reading on 15 July. Three days later it
received the royal assent.

The new Act provided for the handing over of power to two
new Dominions on 15 August 1947. The territories of the two
states were defined though not precisely as the results of a
boundary commission would have to be awaited. Each Dominion was to be headed by a governor-general though the Act
stipulated that one person could hold both appointments.
Until the new states worked out their constitution that of the
1935 Act would remain in force without the special powers
granted by it to the governor-general. All laws would stand
until amended by the successor governments. These clauses
ensured that the continuity of fundamental institutions was
preserved. As for the princely states, all treaties with the British
Crown would lapse on 15 August. The states now had freedom
of action to join one of the new Dominions or, so it implied,
declare themselves independent.

Two of the provisions were to cause trouble. The question of
the joint governor-generalship, which the British Government
assumed would be held by Mountbatten, generated long-lasting
suspicion. Congress was very willing to accept Mountbatten.
Nehru particularly liked the idea of keeping his new guru
during the coming months. But Jinnah, who neither liked nor
trusted Mountbatten, would have nothing to do with the suggestion and informed the Viceroy that he would himself be the
first governor-general of Pakistan. Congress under pressure
from Nehru repeated their invitation to Mountbatten to

become governor-general of the new India. After some misgivings Mountbatten accepted, a decision which only intensified
Jinnah's suspicion that Mountbatten was pro-Congress.

Of more immediate consequence was the position of the
princely states. The British Government had preferred to abandon the treaties rather than transfer them to the governments
of the two new Dominions. From a purely legalistic point of
view this was perfectly correct. The British had some obligations
towards the states having preserved them as part of their
imperial system. By abandoning them they thought that the
states would actually be strengthened in their negotiations with
their successors. The Congress attitude to the princes had
never been friendly though on occasion soft words had been
spoken. With the imminence of independence both attitudes
were maintained. Nehru had made clear in a speech to the
meeting of the AICC on 15 June that he believed that the states
must transfer their dependent relationship to the new governments. He went further and warned foreign governments that
the recognition of any princely state as independent 'will be
considered an unfriendly act'.

Mountbatten, too, recognized the possibilities of Balkanization if the states were not encouraged to accede to either
Pakistan or India. The problem in Pakistan was comparatively
minor as very few of the 562 princely states were within its
proposed borders but for India the situation was fraught with
danger, especially as there were British members of the department responsible for dealings with the princes who were encouraging their friends to consider independence for the larger
states and federation for some of the others. These intrigues were
revealed to Nehru who exploded in anger at a meeting between
nationalist leaders and the Viceroy. One consequence was the
setting up of a States Department with Sardar Patel as its head
and V. P. Menon as its secretary. 'I am glad,' Mountbatten wrote
to Attlee, 'that Nehru has not been put in charge of the new
States Department, which would have wrecked everything.
Patel who is essentially a realist and very sensible, is going to
take it over . . .'

Patel indeed acted with discretion rather than useless anger. He publicly assured the princes that all that had to be agreed upon were the three subjects of defence, external affairs and communications. Patel seemed to be offering a partnership in the new India. All that was needed was a push from the representative of the king-emperor. Mountbatten obliged on 25 July when he addressed the princes in an attempt to persuade them to accede to one or the other of the Dominions.

Mountbatten outlined his case to the apprehensive rulers. Technically and legally, he said, they would all be independent after the British had gone, but in fact they had always been a part of India, economically and administratively. If they tried to break away altogether, the structure would dissolve in chaos, and they, he reminded them, would be the first victims. He then produced a draft instrument of accession which had been circulated prior to the meeting. This document called for cession only in the three fields of defence, external affairs and communications. There would be no financial liabilities and no encroachments upon the individual autonomy or the sovereignty of the states. He pointed out that, of course, this document applied only to India, in which most of the states would lie. Jinnah had already agreed to negotiate separately with those few states which would lie within the borders of Pakistan. 'My scheme,' said the Viceroy, 'leaves you with all practical independence you can probably use, and makes you free of all those subjects which you cannot possibly manage on your own. You cannot run away from the Dominion Government which is your neighbour any more than you can run away from subjects for whose welfare you are responsible.' The princes had now been apprised of the Crown's opinion as to what they should do. For years they had looked to the British for advice – and here was the last they were likely to get.

Under Patel's guidance, Congress organizations in the states made it clear that they would raise the people against the rulers if they did not accede. Emissaries advised the princes that if they wanted to save their wealth they must make up their minds quickly. For most, the mixture of Congress threat and viceregal persuasion was enough. By the time of the actual transfer of power all but three of the states had made up their minds. But the three who had not, Kashmir, Hyderabad and Junagadh, were to cause trouble between the two Dominions within a few weeks of independence and one, Kashmir, was to lead, eighteen years later, to open war.

Friction between Congress and the League remained underground until independence. So too did conflict over the decision of the boundary commissions. Though the commissions under the chairmanship of Sir Cyril Radcliffe, a distinguished British lawyer, produced their decisions by 9 August, the Viceroy delayed the announcement until after independence day, in case they should mar the euphoria of the occasion.

The day came in an atmosphere of unreality in New Delhi. The men who gathered in the assembly building to welcome the end of the long struggle for freedom did so in what appeared to be an anarchy of blood and violence.

As independence day approached the signs of chaos had risen to the surface. The public services slowly collapsed as the engine-drivers, the engineers, the soldiers and the civil servants began to move from one part of the country to the other. To add to man-made troubles, the overdue monsoon threatened a shortage of food. This would have been bad enough in normal times, but when transport was dislocated by the division of rolling-stock, serious famine was far from improbable. The transfer of police officers – Muslims to Pakistan, Hindus to India – had demoralized a service which was not particularly trustworthy at the best of times. The Sikhs, whose homeland was to be arbitrarily divided between Pakistan and India, whose holy places would be on both sides of the border, and of whose people nearly a million were about to be left to the mercy of the Muslims of Pakistan, had already begun to battle for their faith and their possessions. Extremists on both sides were inciting the mobs to revenge. Criminals who hoped to benefit from the breakdown of public order were patiently at work.

Mountbatten and his advisers, however, were more worried about the effects of partition in Bengal than in the Punjab. Everyone, despite evidence to the contrary, had expected the Sikhs to accept the division of the Punjab quietly. But at last the Viceroy began to realize that the Punjab was potentially even more explosive than Bengal. On 15 July he called a meeting of his immediate advisers to discuss the Punjab situation, and four days later he himself visited Lahore for talks with the governor. Mountbatten saw enough to convince him that something had to be done. At a meeting of the Partition Council held soon after his return to Delhi, it was decided to establish a Punjab Boundary Force to maintain law and order in the province under the direct control of the supreme commander and the Joint Defence Council.

It was also decided that the force must be operational by 1 August. The commander was to be Major-General Rees, a veteran of the Burma campaign against the Japanese. The force was composed of both Muslims and non-Muslims and Rees was to have as advisers Brigadier Ayub Khan (later to become President of Pakistan) and a Sikh, Brigadier Brar. Later, two additional advisers were appointed. Altogether, the force numbered about 50,000 men and there was a high proportion of British officers to command them. This super police force was to operate in an area of some 37,500 square miles, where the population consisted of over fourteen million Hindus, Muslims and, above all, Sikhs. Everybody was confident that such a force would easily preserve the peace. Rees was sure that his force could handle a few ill-armed peasants, which was all he and everyone else expected he would be up against.

In this expectation everyone was to be proved tragically wrong. By 14 August, the edge of independence, thousands of innocent people had already been killed in the streets of Lahore and Amritsar and in the villages of the Punjab. Refugees were beginning their sad journeys out of the Punjab, Muslims to Pakistan, Hindus to India. Many were attacked and butchered on the way. About 80,000 Hindus and Sikhs had collected in Delhi alone. Hindu extremists, too, were at work in the border regions, inciting the people to murder and arson.

Calcutta, however, confounded the pessimists by remaining reasonably quiet. Much of this was owed to Gandhi who though he had visited the Punjab to see what his presence might do had not been well received by the Sikhs. In Calcutta he was outstandingly successful. When the politicians in Delhi and Karachi were hailing independence the Mahatma sat in a Calcutta slum, fasting, spinning and praying.

But if Gandhi was not present at the celebrations, Hindu India was. There had been some difficulties over the exact day on which independence should fall. 15 August had been decided upon for no special reason but when it became known there was occult opposition. Leading astrologers insisted that 14 August was a more auspicious day. Nehru hit upon a compromise. The constituent assembly was called in the afternoon of 14 August and continued in permanent session until midnight when according to the western calendar the 15th dawned, well within the propitious period by the Hindu calendar.

It was Nehru's occasion, though the hour was to be ushered in with the sound of conch shells and the chiming of an English clock. In the last minutes of British rule Nehru, referring to the time in January 1930 when he and other nationalist leaders had raised the Congress flag and taken a pledge to win freedom for India, spoke those moving words: 'Long years ago we made a tryst with destiny, and now the time comes when we shall redeem our pledge, not wholly or in full measure, but very substantially. At the stroke of the midnight hour, when the world sleeps, India will awake to life and freedom. A moment comes, which comes but rarely in history, when we step out from the old to the new, when an age ends, and when the soul of a nation, long suppressed, finds utterance.' He ended with an appeal. 'This is no time for petty and destructive criticism, no time for ill will or blaming others. We have to build the noble mansion of free India where all her children may dwell.'

Chapter 17
Successions in Dispute

The period from 1947 to 1951 was one of challenges both to the state and to Nehru himself. The threat to the stability of the new India posed by partition and the problem of the princely states was settled by January 1950 when the republican constitution came into force. The threat to Nehru's position from the conservative and Hindu-minded elements inside Congress ended in September 1951 when Nehru became president of Congress as well as Prime Minister of India. The violence of the times, a violence which included the assassination of Mahatma Gandhi, helped to consolidate conservative forces which despite the personal triumph of Nehru dominated the actual performance of his Government and institutionalized that characteristic feature of Congress rule – the permanent non-revolution.

The violence in the Punjab burst out strongly once again when the terms of the Boundary Commission's report was released on 16 August. Radcliffe had had great difficulty in drawing his lines on the map. Indeed he had found it almost impossible to get hold of large-scale maps on which to draw them. Interested parties had supplied him with maps which had been specially prepared to make their own case and Radcliffe had been forced to work with inadequate data. His problem in the Punjab was not just that of dividing areas of community as it had mainly been in Bengal. In the Punjab it was a matter of water.

The Punjab had been the showplace of British India. There the British had built up a vast and complicated irrigation scheme, based upon the five rivers which give the Punjab its name. Because of these canals, the Punjab had become the garden and the granary of India. The irrigation system must necessarily be disrupted by partition since the rivers that fed the canals and ditches that watered the fields were in the eastern part of the area, which was destined to go to India. Radcliffe suggested that, before he announced his award, some agreement should be reached between the two sides for joint control of the waters. He was brusquely told to mind his own business and get back to drawing lines on the map.

Nevertheless in arriving at his recommendations Radcliffe had to take into consideration these essentially economic factors. In applying them to the district of Gurdaspur and awarding it to India, Radcliffe created a political conflict between the two new states. Gurdaspur was the only land link between India and the princely state of Kashmir and it was assumed by Pakistan that it had been deliberately given to India to facilitate communications with the state. As the conflict over Kashmir came to a head this accusation took on a particularly barbed significance. But Gurdaspur was merely one of many complaints – on both sides. The boundary recommendations were most strongly attacked by Pakistan. Ministers described them as 'disgusting', 'abominable' and 'one-sided' in statements diplomatically mild. The true feeling in Pakistan was expressed by the official Muslim League newspaper *Dawn* which threatened that 'even if the Government accepts the territorial murder of Pakistan, the people will not'.

Such statements only inflamed a situation which was already serious. On 16 August the Joint Defence Council met to consider conditions in the Punjab. It does not appear that the real seriousness of the situation was fully appreciated. The next day a meeting took place at Ambala in the East Punjab between Nehru, Liaquat Ali, and the governors and ministers of the two Punjabs. The meeting issued a joint statement calling for peace and the Boundary Force was considerably enlarged. But the situation had deteriorated so much that by 20 August the Punjab was completely cut off from outside except by air. Really drastic measures were now necessary.

On 29 August the Joint Defence Council, presided over by Lord Mountbatten and attended by Jinnah, met at Lahore. The Boundary Force was now almost helpless against well organized Sikh opposition and its commander was being attacked in the Pakistani and, much more virulently, in the Indian press. The Council now decided that the Boundary Force must be disbanded and that the task of keeping order in the frontier areas should be taken over by the armed forces of the two Dominions. This was undoubtedly the best move, for it transferred responsibility from a joint force, harassed by the suspicions of both sides, to the two Governments and their armies where it should have lain all along. It was decided that the two separate army headquarters intended to control the boundary areas should both be situated in Lahore. After the meeting, Nehru with Liaquat Ali, and Baldev Singh with Sardar Nishtar, toured the troubled areas. On 1 September the Boundary Force ceased to exist and Mountbatten hastily called its commander to Delhi to which the communal war was now spreading.

The main problem which faced the governors of the two Punjabs was not so much the violence within the territory – for there were now signs of a slight improvement in the situation – as the vast numbers of refugees fleeing from their homes to the protection of their co-religionists in India or Pakistan. At first, both Governments had tried to persuade minorities to stay where they were, but this was hardly the sort of advice that people in deadly peril of their lives could be expected to take. Gathering up their belongings, they left their homes, blocking the roads or congregating together in vast camps without shelter, food or sanitation. To make their situation worse, the monsoon broke and torrential rain added to the refugees' misery. Unfortunately they carried with them tales of horror which were retold in the press of both countries and given official sanction by the information services of the two Punjabs. Jinnah, even while he appealed for calm and peace, still bitterly attacked the Radcliffe awards as 'unjust, incomprehensible, and even perverse'. The Sikh leader Master Tara Singh continued to thunder his denunciations. Nothing was being done to reduce tension.

When news from the Punjab reached Calcutta, the harmony that had been so carefully built up between Muslims and Hindus fell to pieces on 1 September when rioting broke out again and bombs were thrown in the streets. The authorities acted swiftly and the trouble was not allowed to get out of hand. Vast demonstrations of Hindu-Muslim solidarity continued to take place.

But the situation remained fraught with danger and Gandhi, who was still in the city, decided that he would begin a fast to the death which he would 'end only if and when sanity returns to Calcutta'. The entire police force of north Calcutta, Europeans included, undertook a 24-hour fast in sympathy, while continuing with their duties. After four days, Gandhi received a pledge from Hindu, Muslim and Sikh leaders to keep the peace in their own areas, and broke his fast. The city became quiet almost overnight.

In Delhi tension was growing as increasing numbers of refugees from the Punjab flooded into the city and the surrounding countryside. By 5 September some 200,000 had arrived and the recital of their sufferings was stirring up feelings against those Muslims who still remained in the city. In the narrow streets of old Delhi the pattern of stabbings, hackings and rape began to form. Sikhs and Hindus attacked Muslims who were fleeing along the road to the airport in the hope of escape to Pakistan: others were attacked in the railway station. There, after one particularly terrible affray, the platform actually *did* run with blood, and bodies littered the tracks. Mobs – many made up of refugees who had lost everything in the Punjab – screaming with frenzy, hurled great stones into flimsy Muslim shops, and women and children looted everything within sight. In the early stages, the police – Hindus and Sikhs themselves – looked the other way and occasionally even helped the rioters. But soon a military force of five thousand men including British and Gurkha troops, with no communal sympathies whatsoever, began to impose some sort of order. The streets were patrolled day and night and the men had orders to shoot to kill. The Muslims of Delhi were collected into large camps protected by troops, though nothing was done for some time to provide them with food or shelter from the monsoon rains. After four days of bloodshed during which all communications out of the city were suspended and nearly a thousand people lost their lives, British and Gurkha troops finally managed to restore order.

During this terrible period Delhi and, in effect, the nation was being ruled by an emergency committee consisting of

Mountbatten, Patel and Nehru. The administration the British had left behind them staggered but did not fall. Nehru was particularly shocked at the bloodshed in Delhi. It was a denial of maturity and seemed to confirm the forebodings of those like Winston Churchill who had maintained until the last that Indians were not ready for freedom. But the greatest shock was to his belief that communal passions would disappear at partition because their purpose – the creation of Pakistan – had been achieved. It had been a sad misreading of mass psychology and of the evidence of five months of communal violence in the Punjab. Unfortunately Nehru was not alone in his myopia. Both Mountbatten and Patel had also expected a smooth and peaceful transfer of power in which isolated outbreaks of violence could easily be controlled. For Mountbatten there was some excuse. He knew nothing about India and was too preoccupied with the mechanics of the transfer to listen too closely to those who did. For the others the only explanation seems to be that they were so concerned with the problems of power that they were out of touch with reality.

When the terror of that reality was actually brought home to them, all acted with vigour. Mountbatten was responsible for the strategy, Patel put it into practice with that ruthlessness which he had always shown. Nehru involved himself personally by touring the streets and rushing unarmed into rioting mobs. Patel did not approve of Nehru's single-handed attempt to bring back sanity. There would be more police available for riot duty, he complained, if they 'did not carry the additional burden of looking after Jawaharlal'.

The improvement in the situation in Delhi was not unfortunately paralleled in the Punjab. Streams of refugees still crossed the borders between the two new Dominions. In the first fortnight of independence it was estimated that 500,000 had crossed. By September some two million people were on the move. They travelled in bullock carts, in lorries and in trains. Some of the convoys stretched for fifty miles. Both trains and convoys were attacked by armed bands of Muslims or Sikhs. In the end the situation was so bad that rail traffic between Delhi and Lahore had to be suspended. Torrential rains had added to the terror and the confusion. Refugee camps on both sides of the border were flooded and cholera followed. The rains too had breached the roads and destroyed food stocks.

Both sides carried on a barrage of propaganda. The newspapers, completely uncontrolled, bristled with atrocity stories and calls for revenge. Extremist leaders demanded that troops should be sent across the borders to rescue their co-religionists. The Pakistan Government alleged that India was deliberately driving Muslim refugees into Pakistan in order to bring about administrative and economic collapse. It was, Jinnah trumpeted, a deep-laid and well-planned conspiracy to bring Pakistan to her knees before she had even properly stood up. Counter-accusations flared back from India, and even Gandhi gave way and joined in the general bitterness by attacking Pakistan.

The atmosphere of almost incendiary suspicion between India and Pakistan was further inflamed by the behaviour of the three princely states which by independence day had not committed themselves to accession: Junagadh, Hyderabad and Kashmir.

Junagadh, a comparatively small state of four thousand square miles, lay on the south-western coast of the Kathiawar peninsula north of Bombay, an area of great beauty and scenic grandeur. Its chief seaport was some 350 miles away from Karachi, the new capital of Pakistan, and it was surrounded on all sides except the sea by states which had acceded to India. The complex of states in Kathiawar was like some demented jigsaw. Most were tiny fragments scattered over the peninsula. There were even bits of Junagadh embedded as enclaves inside other states, and enclaves of other states' territories remained inside Junagadh. The Nawab of Junagadh had given the impression that, though he himself was a Muslim, he would accede to India as most of the other states in Kathiawar had already decided to do. It was a most sensible decision, since over 80 per cent of the 816,000 inhabitants of Junagadh were Hindu. But the Nawab postponed the actual signing of the instrument of accession until after 15 August and then plumped for Pakistan. He even went further and occupied two tiny states, Mangrol and Babariawad, which had decided to accede to India in an attempt to assert their independence of him and the overlordship he claimed over them.

The other Kathiawar states, led by Nawanagar, regarding this as a threat to peace, appealed to the new Government of India and began to mass their own state troops on the Junagadh borders. The Indian Government had not been officially informed of the Nawab's accession to Pakistan – in fact, they only learned of it from the newspapers. The Government complained to Pakistan but got no reply. Apart from sending a few men to help the Nawab's depleted police force, the Pakistanis did nothing except sit back and enjoy the situation. The Indian Government was reluctant to walk into what was so obviously a trap. Soft words had been issuing from Sardar Patel's lips. The princes, though still slightly uneasy, had been on the verge of breathing again, and a delicate relationship might very easily be upset if one of their number was 'coerced'. There was also a possibility that Pakistan might object. A request to Liaquat Ali Khan to allow the people of Junagadh to decide for themselves received no reply.

While continually repeating its desire for an amicable solution, the Indian Government was finally forced to act. If it had not done so, the rest of the Kathiawar states might have gained the impression that India was unable or unwilling to protect them. Indian army troops were sent to the Junagadh borders and all communications with the state, as well as supplies of coal and petrol, were cut off. A body of Congress supporters from Junagadh itself was encouraged to set up a government-in-exile, in accordance with the best European precedent.

The Pakistan Government did not react officially until 7 October 1947, when it claimed that, since Junagadh had legally acceded to Pakistan, no one else had any right to intervene. It said it was obvious nonsense to suggest that Junagadh was a threat to the other Kathiawar states. The Pakistanis, however, were willing 'to discuss conditions and circumstances wherein a plebiscite should be taken by any state or states'; but India should first withdraw her troops from the borders of Junagadh. The phrasing of this Pakistani offer was deliberate. The sting was in the word 'any'. The Pakistanis really hoped for a plebiscite in Kashmir, a Muslim state, with a Hindu ruler who was still dithering over which Dominion he should accede to, but the Government of India refused the idea of a plebiscite unless they received firm assurance that Pakistan would agree to deal with the case of Junagadh and Junagadh alone.

Indian troops in Kathiawar were now reinforced to a strength of 1,400 men, a troop of light tanks, and a squadron of aircraft. In addition to these, there were 2,000 states' troops. On 26 October, seeing the red light, the Nawab left Junagadh in his private aircraft for the safety of Karachi. The chief minister, faced with disorders organized by Congress workers, soon appealed to the Government to take over the administration of the state. The Government agreed and Indian troops crossed the state frontier. Nehru, in telegrams to Liaquat Ali, explained that the occupation of Junagadh was merely temporary and would only last until such time as a plebiscite could be held. He invited the Pakistan Government to send representatives to discuss the procedure. Pakistan, however, preferred to stick to the letter of the law; Junagadh's ruler had acceded the state to Pakistan as he had every right to do; the Indian occupation was therefore a violation of Pakistani territory, and until India withdrew there was no purpose in holding discussions. There the matter rested until February 1948 when a plebiscite resulted in the decision to join India.

The situation in Hyderabad had one thing in common with that in Junagadh. Over 80 per cent of the population was Hindu but the ruler, known as the Nizam, was a Muslim. The army, the police and the government were all in the hands of the Muslims, who formed a ruling minority. There the similarity ended. Hyderabad was considerably larger in area – some 82,000 square miles – and had a population of sixteen millions. The state, positioned roughly in the centre of the Indian peninsula, had no outlet to the sea and after partition would be completely surrounded by Indian territory. Consequently, it was not practicable for the Nizam to accede to Pakistan with which his only communication would be by air. The only choice other than state independence was that he should accede to Congress-dominated India, but such a choice was abhorrent to the Nizam, who had always considered himself superior to all the other princes, and had been allowed by the British to act with considerable independence. If he were to accede to India, he would be giving in to his Hindu subjects, who, under Congress instigation, were now becoming vocal. In addition to his natural dislike of Congress, the Nizam was influenced by the fact that his own personal position was largely dependent on Hyderabad's ruling Muslim minority. This minority was backed by a kind of political party, called the Ittehad-ul-Muslimin, which was fanatically pro-Islam. Without their support, the Nizam could not have continued to rule. Since they demanded independence, so must he. Despite pressure from the Ittehad, however, the Nizam was not prepared to act foolishly. He realized that it would be wise not to antagonize India, so he dispatched to Delhi a negotiating committee whose principal members were the chief minister of the state, the Nawab of Chhatari, and Sir Walter Monckton, his constitutional adviser.

It seemed from this negotiating committee's attitude that the Nizam was willing to give up most of the powers demanded by the instrument of accession, but that he wanted to do so by treaty, as if he were an equal. Also, he insisted on the right to remain neutral if there should be a quarrel between India and Pakistan, and he reserved the right to send his own representatives to Britain and elsewhere. Earlier, the Nizam had asked the British Government for Dominion status for Hyderabad, and this had naturally been rejected. But the Nizam still wanted to retain some sort of relationship with the British Crown, although what he hoped to gain from it is not clear. Mountbatten's advice to the Nizam, however, was direct – forget about the past, sign the instrument of accession, *then* negotiate with Congress. The advice was sound; India could hardly grant concessions to Hyderabad without inviting the risk of demands from other states. Even the biggest of the states would have to agree to the same terms as everyone else. It seems very likely that the Nizam would have accepted Mountbatten's advice if it had not been for the pressure put upon him. By 15 August no accession had been made. The Muslim press in Hyderabad was referring to the Nizam as 'His Majesty' (before, he had merely been His Exalted

Highness), and Muslim mobs were celebrating Hyderabad's independence.

A standstill agreement had been arrived at to fill the vacuum so that the various services could continue, but the life of the agreement was only two months. During these months, the Hyderabad army was enlarged to about 25,000 men, and armament purchases were made abroad and flown in by air, some in aircraft loaned by Pakistan. The Ittehad was arming a force of terrorists known as the Razakhars. At the same time, however, the Nawab of Chhatari and Monckton were spending most of their time in fruitless journeys back and forth to Delhi. The Indian Government, with the massacre in the Punjab to demonstrate what could happen when communal violence got completely out of hand, was unwilling to make concessions to the Nizam. Meanwhile, the Hyderabad state Congress, with powerful support from outside, began a civil disobedience campaign demanding accession to India and popular government in Hyderabad. It did not suggest deposing the Nizam, for it was obviously hopeful of driving a wedge between him and his more fanatical Muslim supporters. By the end of September, however, more than 1,300 local Congress leaders had been arrested. Under the circumstances both Chhatari and Monckton tendered their resignations to the Nizam, but he refused to let them go, partly because he was not a free agent and wanted to keep the negotiations going in the hope that some agreement might merge which he could reasonably accept.

At Mountbatten's suggestion, Patel, as head of the States' ministry, allowed the governor-general to see whether he might succeed by personal negotiation. It was possible that as a cousin of the former king-emperor he might have more influence with the Nizam than the Congress leaders. By 21 October, Mountbatten had managed to extend the standstill agreement by one year, during which time it was hoped that some wider agreement might be arrived at. When Chhatari and Monckton returned to Hyderabad to obtain the Nizam's ratification of the agreement, however, news had reached there that Kashmir had acceded to India. Muslim mobs demonstrated outside Chhatari's house demanding that Hyderabad should make no concessions to

India, and the Ittehad threatened 'direct action' against the Nizam, if he should give in to India. Under this pressure, he refused to ratify the agreement and publicly announced that he did not contemplate acceding to India. Chhatari and Monckton again offered their resignations and this time they were accepted. A new negotiating committee was appointed which included a representative of the Ittehad.

Congress was now becoming impatient, and Sardar Patel made a number of speeches pointing out that what had happened to Junagadh might well happen elsewhere. Despite everything, negotiations continued, and the standstill agreement was finally ratified in November. The situation in Hyderabad, however, did not improve. The Razakhars took control of the government and began to raid villages in Indian territory. Patel waited until Mountbatten had departed for home at the end of his period in office in June 1948 and then began a propaganda campaign alleging that Hyderabad was in a state of internal disorder. In September 1948 Indian troops entered the state and the Nizam formally acceded to India. The Indian army remained in direct control of the state for a year and was then replaced by a civil administration.

Though Pakistan was not unwilling to interfere in the matter of Junagadh and to make friendly gestures towards Hyderabad neither affected Pakistan directly. The case of Kashmir was very different and remains so to this day. Unlike Junagadh and Hyderabad, Kashmir had frontiers with both Pakistan and India. The frontier with Pakistan was long and the only all-weather roads into Kashmir ran from Pakistan. To India there was only a fair-weather highway, running through the Gurdaspur district, which was closed by snow in winter. In Kashmir also were the headwaters of Pakistan's most important rivers, the Indus, the Jhelum and the Chenab. The situation of the Maharaja of Kashmir was the opposite to that of the rulers of Junagadh and Hyderabad for he was a Hindu ruling a state in which 77 per cent of the population were Muslim.

As independence approached it did not seem unreasonable that the Maharaja would consider acceding to Pakistan, but the political situation in Kashmir, like that of the North West

Frontier Province, was by no means simple. There was a
Muslim party in the state, closely tied to the All-India Muslim
League, but the most important figure in state politics was
Sheikh Abdullah who, though a Muslim, was president of the
National Conference party, which was equally closely tied to
Congress. In June 1946 the Sheikh had been imprisoned for
demanding the Maharaja's abdication, and in August 1947 he
was still in jail. As in Hyderabad, only in reverse, the mainly
Muslim state was governed by a Hindu Maharaja with Hindu
officials and mainly Hindu troops.

The choice before the Maharaja was by no means an easy
one to make. If he acceded to Pakistan it would probably mean
that he himself would have to abdicate. If he joined India he
would be going against Kashmir's geographic, religious and
economic affinities, which all lay with Pakistan. Complete
independence was out of the question, because the state could
not exist without supplies from outside. He was under considerable pressure from Congress not to make a hasty decision, for
haste would probably have meant accession to Pakistan.
Kashmir held considerable personal interest for Nehru, whose
ancestors had come from there. But, more realistically, because
Nehru hated the thought of an India divided by religion, the
state's accession to India was important. If Kashmir went to
Pakistan for religious reasons alone, it might result in public
demonstrations which would imperil the lives of Muslims still
left in India. As a result, the Maharaja was advised not to make
up his mind at least until he had been able to talk to Nehru.
Gandhi said the same thing, and even offered to go to Kashmir
to talk to the Maharaja. Mountbatten, however, decided he
must go himself. He did not succeed in persuading the Maharaja to accede to India – or to Pakistan. By 15 August all that
had been achieved was a standstill agreement between Kashmir
and Pakistan, and negotiations were in progress for a similar
agreement with India.

Congress had hoped that the Maharaja would release Sheikh
Abdullah and that he and his followers could arrange popular
pressure in favour of accession to India. But the decision was
taken out of the Maharaja's hands. The Muslim inhabitants of

the district of Poonch were a martial people who had supplied thousands of hardy soldiers to the old British Indian army. After partition, former soldiers in Poonch demonstrated in favour of Kashmir acceding to Pakistan. When these demonstrations were fired upon by the Maharaja's Hindu troops, the demonstrators rose in rebellion and put the state forces to flight. The rebellion sparked off further disorder, for the rule of the Maharaja had not been pleasant.

Strictly speaking, the state was known as Kashmir and Jammu, the latter being a Hindu-majority area. Into Jammu, which bordered the Punjab, had fled many Hindu and Sikh refugees from the massacres in the Punjab, lusting for revenge against Muslims. They attacked the Muslim minority in Jammu with fire and sword.

While all this was taking place, the tribes of the Frontier areas were responding to the cry of 'Islam in danger!' And on 22 October thousands of tribesmen invaded Kashmir. Though the Pakistan Government denied any responsibility for the tribal invasion, it undoubtedly supplied the tribes with transport, machine-guns, mortars and light artillery, while Pakistani army officers, ostensibly on leave, led the contingents. The tribes swept across Kashmir killing and burning as they went. When they were only twenty-five miles from the state capital, Srinagar, they paused. On 24 October the Maharaja decided to accede to India and appealed for India's help against the tribes. He also informed Mountbatten that he was about to set up an interim government under Sheikh Abdullah, who had recently been released from detention. Indian troops were flown in and after a fortnight beat back the invaders. The fighting gave way to a military stalemate. The United Nations appealed to for help was unable to enforce a solution and the Kashmir 'problem' remains to this day a source of enmity between India and Pakistan.

The civil war in the Punjab, the Kashmir affair and the problems of the princely states had a profound effect both on the relations between Congress leaders in the Government and on those between Congress and the Government. There was dissension on a wide range of vital issues particularly on economic policy and the treatment of minorities. The Congress leaders in the Government were fundamentally men of inexperience, even if some of them had held office in the provinces during the operation of the Act of 1935. Congress itself continued to behave like a rally of national liberation rather than a ruling political party. The principal figures of the struggle for freedom remained the principal figures in the fight for national survival and roughly in the same position of authority they had occupied on the eve of independence. The most important figure in the cabinet was not Nehru, the Prime Minister, but Sardar Patel, in charge of home affairs and the states. The Mahatma, still outside Congress, was without direct influence on the decisions of Government. Yet Gandhi's position as the supporter of Nehru and the mediator between him and Patel was unimpaired. It was Gandhi's all-powerful *moral* authority which conditioned the conflicts between Nehru and Patel and limited them to an extent which precluded a final showdown that would have led to either leaving the Government. The challenge represented by Patel and the right wing to Nehru therefore was not to his position as Prime Minister but only to the extent of his authority in the making of policy.

The division of labour between Nehru and Patel, though it was not altogether a rigid one, had already been demarcated during the life of the interim government. Nehru was Prime Minister and Minister of External Affairs and on matters of foreign policy, Kashmir and commonwealth relations his decisions were seldom, if ever, queried. Nehru's views on Kashmir were violent enough to satisfy the most communal-minded though they sprang from very different motives. On domestic matters Patel was virtually supreme though it seems that he took no major decision without informing Nehru and receiving at least his acquiescence. The levers of *domestic* power were totally controlled by Patel for not only was he responsible for home affairs but also for information and broadcasting. In addition Patel retained his dominant position in the Congress organization.

It is in these two important roles that Patel was the true founder of the Indian state. Under his guidance the States

Ministry and in particular its secretary, V. P. Menon, changed
the structure of the country. Despite the promise both overt and
implied that the princely states would be partners in the new
India, all were finally integrated. Apart from Junagadh, Hyderabad and Kashmir it was a bloodless exercise in national
consolidation which made possible the construction of a new
political framework for the country as a whole. The hundreds
of principalities were merged into twelve viable units adding
almost half a million square miles of territory – as much as had
been lost by partition – and some ninety million people to the
Indian Union. The princes were treated generously, primarily
because it was considered essential to achieve stability and order
with the least friction and controversy.

Nehru played little part in this immense enterprise though the
policy was fully in agreement with his often stated views. There
was certainly no clash or conflict here. Nor was there much
over Patel's creation of the institutional framework in which
Nehru operated. Before independence Nehru had been a strong
critic of the army and the bureaucracy. Though over the years
he modified his opinions about the civil service he did not
change his attitude significantly about the military which contributed to some extent to the débâcle of Indian forces during
the Sino-Indian imbroglio of 1962. Patel, however, had a much
more refined sense of the needs of the modern state. The new
India had inherited from the British an administrative structure
which, though it had been drained of some of its best men by
partition and the retirement of British members of the civil
service, remained an efficient instrument of power. Indianization
of the services had gone a long way before the transfer of power
and there was a legacy of competent and experienced officials
who could take the higher places vacated by the British. For
years Indian members of the civil and military services had been
vilified as traitors by Congress. Nehru in particular had been
outspoken in his criticism and had promised fundamental
reforms and drastic changes in personnel after independence.

As Home Minister, Patel took steps to protect the members of
the civil service, guaranteeing salaries and privileges. In effect
the new state took over the whole structure of the public

services almost intact and most of the personnel as well. Patel's argument was that the need to stabilize the new political order as soon as possible in face of external and internal threat was against radical reform. The preservation of this inherited structure of administration not only kept essential services running but permitted the effective establishment of government authority in the first years of independence. As the establishment of law, order and authority was the most urgent task facing the new India, this was Patel's second vital contribution to the nation. Though there is no evidence that Patel wished to do more than preserve functional continuity, the retention of what was in effect a colonial civil service designed almost exclusively for the maintenance of law and order contributed to the conservatism of India's political development. The traditions of the service, its hierarchical, in fact caste, structure, its administrative procedures, were not tuned to the demands of rapid social and economic change.

Patel's preservation of an essentially conservative administrative system was paralleled by his transformation of Congress from a nationalist movement with limited aims into a conservative modernizing political party. In this Patel was assisted not only by the past but also by the violence and terror of the first years of independence. The past had given to Congress a legacy of progressive economic and social policy commitments which owed much to Nehru's pioneering. The conservative supporters of Congress among the business and professional classes had no deep antagonism to the reformist programmes put foward by Congress radicals. Before independence the Indian business community identified with Congress had already accepted the principle of government economic planning. It had also accepted Gandhi's demands for greater social and economic equality because of his opposition to the use of violence or even legislation to bring them about. Indian capitalists did not believe that they had anything to fear from radical programmes because the reforms they advocated would never be implemented, at least not fully and certainly not as long as Gandhi and Patel were alive.

Patel knew that he – and the government – had nothing to

fear from the moderate conservative majority in Congress but there were still the socialists and Hindu communalists to contend with. Patel was helped in the case of the socialists by the consequences of partition which reinforced a general desire for order rather than revolutionary change. The Hindu communalists with whom Patel had considerable sympathy demanded that Congress should become a more militant Hindu organization. The assassination of Gandhi by a Hindu fanatic changed Patel's attitude and turned him against the overt Hinduization of Congress.

The transformation of Congress took time. One of Patel's first moves was to reduce the image of the party in favour of intensifying that of the Government, which now held most of the principal party leaders. This had already begun in 1946 when the party secretary, Kripalani, was made president rather than one of the nationally known leaders. After independence the party president was excluded from the decision-making process and on the whole ignored by the Government. This was resented by many, including Gandhi, and in September 1947 Kripalani resigned on the issue.

Discontent in the party coincided with friction in the cabinet. Patel seemed to be less than impartial in his treatment of Indian Muslims. In public speeches he demanded that they give practical proof of their loyalty. This offended not only Nehru, who was determined that religion must play no part in the definition of citizenship, but also the Mahatma. On economic matters, however, Gandhi supported Patel and the business community.

There is no doubt that at this time Nehru began to feel increasingly isolated. Proof of this is provided by the revival of his close relationship with Gandhi which had been somewhat tarnished by the coming of Mountbatten and the conflict between Nehru and the Mahatma over the acceptance of partition. During the last months of 1947 Nehru paid a daily visit to Gandhi returning visibly refreshed. This in itself was surprising because Gandhi was going through an intense period of despair himself and believed, not without reason, that he was responsible for communal violence – a shattering revelation which seemed to be tearing him to pieces. He was also worried by the behaviour of many Congressmen who, it was reported to him, were taking bribes from businessmen to get them licences, profiting from black market activities, and putting pressure on top civil servants to arrange appointments and transfers for their friends. Gandhi put forward the startling suggestion that Congress should dissolve itself and form a Lok Seva Sangh or Servants of the People Society instead.

Gandhi who had consulted his inner voices with increasing frequency since independence, received instructions to fast. His main purpose was to create communal harmony in what was once again a rapidly deteriorating situation. On 12 January he announced his decision. It is an interesting comment on Nehru's own mental state that in spite of his well-known attitude to fasting as a political weapon he not only supported the Mahatma but began a fast himself and only gave up on Gandhi's insistence. At a public meeting Nehru told the crowd that 'the loss of Mahatma Gandhi's life would mean the loss of India's soul'. Once again the blackmail worked. The Mahatma's fast was successful in bringing peace to Delhi. It also affected an important cabinet decision.

Before the fast had begun the cabinet had decided to postpone payment of 550 million rupees due to Pakistan under the partition agreements as its share of the cash balances. Patel had argued that the money should not be paid until other outstanding agreements particularly on Kashmir had been honoured by Pakistan. There are conflicting reports on Nehru's attitude. Some sources say that he was indifferent and followed Patel's lead without argument, others that Nehru believed that the agreement should be honoured. Rumours were put around that the Mahatma was fasting against the cabinet decision and Patel's strong line with the Muslim community. There is no doubt that relations between the Mahatma and Patel were strained partly over these two issues but mainly over the growing hostility between Patel and Nehru.

The weight of the evidence supports the view that the whole cabinet was in agreement over the delay in the payment of the cash balances to Pakistan. Nehru, Patel and Azad visited Gandhi on 13 January in an attempt to convince him that it was the right decision. Gandhi was firm in his attitude, the payment must be made whatever Pakistan had or had not done. There were arguments in which both Nehru and Azad changed sides and supported the Mahatma against Patel. In the face of such opposition Patel yielded but not without rancour. After an emergency cabinet meeting it was announced that the funds would be transferred immediately.

Patel was both wounded and angered by Gandhi's stand. 'The old man has gone senile', he was reported to have said. After this episode cabinet meetings revolved around the friction between Nehru and Patel, ending with an outburst from Nehru which seemed to herald an open break. Patel went on a tour on 15 January and left behind him a letter for Gandhi submitting his resignation from the Government – in itself an index of Gandhi's importance to the Congress leadership. On Patel's return Gandhi made no reference to the letter. Gandhi had in fact been too ill to give the matter thought and it was not until after the breaking of his fast on 18 January, made possible by the assurances of communal leaders that there would be peace in Delhi, that he was able to consider what should be done. His decision was simple, the country needed both Nehru and Patel.

On 20 January Gandhi's prayer meeting was disturbed by the explosion of a small bomb. No one was injured but both Nehru and Patel pleaded with the Mahatma to accept police protection. The Mahatma's reply was a blunt refusal: 'God is my protector. If he cannot protect me, nobody can.' For some reason no attempt was made to infiltrate plain clothes men into the mansion of the cotton magnate, G. D. Birla, where the Mahatma was staying.

About four o'clock in the afternoon of 30 January Patel arrived to see the Mahatma at the latter's request. By all accounts Gandhi bluntly ordered Patel to make his peace with Nehru and to promise not to leave the Government. Patel appears to have spoken equally bluntly. Just after five o'clock Patel left. Nehru was due in the evening and Gandhi would make the relations between the two men the subject of his prayer meeting on the following day when he also proposed to put forward his ideas for the reorganization of Congress. After Patel's departure Gandhi walked slowly across the grass to the site of that day's prayer meeting. Half way there a young man approached and bowed holding his hands palms together in the traditional salutation. Gandhi replied in the same way. The young man then pulled out a revolver and fired three shots hitting Gandhi in the chest and the abdomen. The Mahatma fell to the ground crying: 'Hai Rama Hai Rama' (Oh God, Oh God). In a few moments he was dead.

Nehru and Patel rushed to the scene followed by Mountbatten. The governor-general was received with the shout that the assassin had been a Muslim but had the great presence of mind to reply loudly: 'You fool. Don't you know it was a Hindu.' Fortunately it turned out to be true – if a Muslim had been the culprit there would undoubtedly have been a holocaust throughout India. Mountbatten also took the opportunity of heightened emotions to approach Nehru and Patel who were sitting together in shocked silence in a corner of the garden. Mountbatten told the two men that Gandhi had spoken to him about the conflict between them and his hopes for reconciliation. Surely if nothing else the Mahatma's death would bring them together. Nehru and Patel agreed and embraced each other, tears streaming down their faces.

A few moments later Nehru went to talk to the crowd. He climbed a lamp-post and told them: 'Mahatmaji is gone.' Later that evening he spoke over the radio. His speech was unprepared but eloquent with his sense of grief and loss:

Friends and comrades, the light has gone out of our lives and there is darkness everywhere. I do not know what to tell you or how to say it. Our beloved leader, Bapu as we called him, Father of the Nation, is no more. Perhaps I am wrong to say that. Nevertheless we will not see him again as we have seen him for these many years. We will not run to him for advice and seek solace from him, and that is a terrible blow, not to me only, but to millions and millions in this country. And it is a little difficult to soften the blow by any other advice I or anyone else can give you.

The light has gone out, I said, and yet I was wrong. For the light that shone in this country was no ordinary light. The light that has illumined this country for these many many years will illumine this country for many more years, and a thousand years later that light will still be seen in this country and the world will see it and it will give solace to innumerable hearts. For that light represented something more than the immediate present; it represented the living, the eternal truths, reminding us of the right path, drawing us from error, taking this ancient country to freedom. All this has happened when there was so much for him to do. We could never think that he was unnecessary or that he had done his task. But now, particularly, when we are faced with so many difficulties, his not being with us is a blow most terrible to bear . . .

The assassination of Gandhi could not have been more timely if it had been arranged by the Government. In one sense it had been, for it was a permissive murder encouraged by the laxity of the security services and of the police. After the bomb explosion of 20 January the elements of a conspiracy were known to exist by the special branch of the police in Bombay where the murder plot was hatched. An inquiry held in 1967 revealed that police documents were missing from files and the inescapable conclusion from the evidence at that time is that nothing was done to warn Patel or Nehru, whose assassination was probably also planned, because there were people who did not want anything done. The true story is still unknown and will probably remain so.

Gandhi's death was timely because, though it did not bring any real reconciliation between Patel and Nehru – the emotional display engineered by Mountbatten over the dead body of the Mahatma was only another incident in a momentary tragedy – it did have its effect both on the health of Patel, who was then over seventy, and on his overt attitude towards Hindu communalism. The fact that the murderer of Gandhi was a Hindu extremist turned Patel at least publicly against Hindu extremism. His attachment to the Mahatma was as profound and rather less emotional than that of Nehru, yet Patel's immediate reaction was to turn against those whom he had in the past supported. He did not hesitate to take a strong line on Pakistan when there was a further flow of Hindu refugees from East Bengal but he also warned Hindus not to give way to communal hatred. He moved against extremist organizations such as the Hindu Mahasabha and the Rashtriya Swayamsevak Sangh (RSS), a para-military body with which the murderer of Gandhi had been associated. But Patel did not move against the communalists inside Congress and there is some basis for the criticism that his acceptance of the banning of the RSS and the arrest of many of its members was primarily designed to destroy a potentially dangerous opposition to Congress.

The manner of Gandhi's death however quietened the Hindu communalists and prevented their open opposition to the adoption of a secular constitution. The communal violence of the months following independence and the openly communal character of Pakistan prepared the country for a constitution which eschewed religion while expressing what was taken to be Gandhian tolerance to all religions. Nevertheless the Hindu-minded took what was essentially a communal stand when they tried to get constitutional approval to make Hindi, the language of the Hindu heartland, India's national language. Though Patel was sympathetic to the Hindi lobby he was significantly more concerned in preserving English for some time in case its replacement upset the civil service and administrative procedures. There was also strong opposition from non-Hindi speakers and their reaction was the beginning of a new conflict which was to replace the communalism of the pre-independence period with that of linguistic nationalism. The decision was a compromise. English would remain the official language for fifteen years.

The constitution which was adopted on 26 November 1949 is too complex a subject to be discussed in any detail within the scope of the present book.[1] It is almost purely western in character drawing upon not only the 1935 Government of India Act but upon various European and American constitutions including that of the Soviet Union. The parliamentary form of government was accepted by all without much discussion, as were the

1. The making of the constitution and its provisions are dealt with in Granville Austin, *The Indian Constitution: Cornerstone of a Nation*, Oxford University Press, 1966.

secular provisions. Neither Nehru nor Patel played a continuously active role in the discussions of the Constituent Assembly – their primary concern was with ensuring the stability of the state. The foremost figure was that of B. R. Ambedkar, the Untouchable leader and Law Minister in the central cabinet until 1951. Both Nehru and Patel, however, often addressed the Assembly and spent much time in privately persuading those who disagreed with their fundamental views. When the two men were divided on some issue, as in the case of the clauses relating to property, factions would line up behind them and debate would be long but when they agreed, as they did more often than not, everyone accepted the situation and took unanimous decisions. It is not claiming too much to say that the constitution represents the individual character of the two men and the differences between them for it is a mixture of idealistic social and economic provisions with articles of a practical, administrative and technical nature.

The influence of Gandhi's death both on the country and on the two principal personalities in the Government began to wear thin towards the end of 1949. Relations with Pakistan, which had been eased by a cease-fire in Kashmir, sponsored by the United Nations, became tense again after the refusal of Pakistan to devalue its currency following India's devaluation in September 1949. Difficulties over negotiating a new exchange rate brought a complete cessation of trade between the two countries in December. India then stopped coal supplies to Pakistan on the grounds that the latter was holding up supplies of raw jute. East Bengal, which before partition had produced over 75 per cent of India's jute, was left with unsold stocks while the mills which were in West Bengal had no material to process. The unemployed factory workers of Calcutta found an outlet for their fears and frustrations by joining with others suffering the economic effects of partition in anti-Muslim riots. These were further inflamed when a new migration of Hindus from East Bengal (East Pakistan) began.

Extremist politicians and newspapers began to retail atrocity stories and one went so far as to take a poll of its readers as to whether India should go to war with Pakistan. A natural consequence of this threatening atmosphere was a migration of Muslims from West Bengal to Pakistan. By March this two-way flow of refugees had become a flood on a scale resembling that in the Punjab in 1947. The cabinet in Delhi was divided on what should be done. Patel was for a strong line – the expulsion of ten Muslims from India for every Hindu forced to leave Pakistan. In this he was supported by communal-minded members of the cabinet and in particular by S. P. Mookerjee. Nehru advocated negotiation with Pakistan and was able for the time being to carry the rest of the cabinet with him. On 17 March 1950, after several visits to Calcutta and the border areas, Nehru announced in parliament that he was not prepared to consider either war or an exchange of populations as the solution. Instead he suggested that he and the Prime Minister of Pakistan, Liaquat Ali Khan, should make a joint statement assuring minorities in both countries of protection and fair treatment. He also issued an invitation to Liaquat Ali to come to Delhi.

The meeting between the two Prime Ministers did not take place until 2 April and led to an agreement six days later. But before the meeting the cabinet had again been split, S. P. Mookerjee demanding that any agreement should contain a clause providing for sanctions against whichever country failed to honour the agreement. This Nehru pointed out would sabotage the talks before they even started. Most of the cabinet agreed with him and Mookerjee submitted his resignation as did another non-Congress member of the cabinet the day before the talks opened. Mookerjee, who until the end of 1948 had been a member of the Hindu Mahasabha, now began, with other like-minded Hindu communalists, to organize opposition to the Government and in particular to Nehru and his agreement with Liaquat Ali.

An obvious base could be found for opposition among the various refugee organizations. A conference of such organizations was held in Delhi in July 1950 and Mookerjee was welcomed by banners proclaiming 'We Do Not Want Nehru's Anti-Hindu and Cowardly Government' and 'Death to the

Nehru-Liaquat Pact'. Significantly, among the three leading political figures at the conference, Mookerjee himself, N. B. Khare, president of Hindu Mahasabha and Purushottamdas Tandon, the latter was president of the U.P. Congress Committee and a close associate of Patel.

By the summer of 1950 Nehru's position was extremely insecure. Without the presence of his political father, Gandhi, he was dependent only upon those progressive elements in Congress who had not abandoned him. The Congress Socialists had already left Congress in 1948 and formed their own party though their going had made little difference to Nehru's position because the socialists no longer trusted him. Congress was completely controlled by the right wing. The cabinet seemed to be breaking up with resignations and Nehru's handling of affairs was continually being questioned within Congress itself though not publicly.

Patel had already succeeded in defeating Nehru on the important issue of who was to be the first president of the Indian republic. Nehru had wanted C. Rajagopalachari, who before the constitution came into force in January 1950 had been governor-general in succession to Mountbatten. However Rajendra Prasad, then president of the Constituent Assembly, had assumed that he would naturally be preferred. A meeting of Congress was called by Nehru formally to approve his choice of Rajagopalachari. After Nehru had finished speaking in support of his candidate, member after member, none of them of the top rank, began to attack Rajagopalachari for resigning from Congress in 1942 and for his plan to placate Jinnah which had been taken up by Gandhi. In order not to embarrass Nehru publicly by a vote, the decision was left to him and Patel, but in the light of the overwhelming body of Congress opinion Nehru was forced to accept Prasad.

From this time onwards Nehru began to suspect a real intent on the part of Patel and the right wing to undermine his political position. The issue of Pakistan and refugees was not pressed by Patel. On the contrary, the decision having been made he supported it in public speeches in Calcutta and elsewhere demanding that the pact between the two Prime Ministers should be given a fair trial. This was the act of some physical as well as political courage because the crowds, particularly in Calcutta, were large and hostile and in March 1950 Patel had suffered a heart attack. But when Nehru announced his determination to see the passage of the Hindu Code Bill through parliament Patel was strongly opposed. The Bill which would largely have invalidated Hindu personal law had been subjected to a determined filibuster ever since its first introduction into the Constituent Assembly in 1948. Patel's opposition now kept it in limbo for a further period. There was also conflict over the setting up early in 1950 of a National Planning Commission, which the Indian business community feared would be the beginning of socialism. Patel's hostility did not decrease even when it turned out to be nothing of the sort. But it was assumed that Patel had had something to do with what was in effect a retreat from socialism.

The summer of 1950 saw Congress split though not openly and the factions lining up behind their respective leaders. Up until then the conflict had been kept out of the public gaze though it was well known that it existed. Both Nehru and Patel had their courtiers and rumours were constantly being circulated. But there was no longer any need for dissimulation when in September 1950 Congress met in annual session at Nasik. The occasion was the election of party president. Nehru and Patel were each identified with one of the candidates and it seemed obvious to all that this was the beginning of an open struggle between the two men.

Patel's candidate was Purushottamdas Tandon, an orthodox Hindu who represented the extreme communal wing of the party. His views were well known. He hated industrialization and advocated a harsh line towards Pakistan. The ideal of the state was Hindu raj epitomizing all the old Hindu values. Most significant of all Tandon demanded that the Government should be the creature of the party. His rival was Kripalani, no friend of Nehru but a firm supporter of the secular ideal. Nehru did not endorse Kripalani's candidature but it was assumed by all that he was Nehru's choice. When the AICC announced on 2 September that Tandon had been elected though only by a small majority it was taken as a victory for Patel and a setback for Nehru. Commenting, Nehru warned Congress members gathering for the full session that 'communal and reactionary forces have openly expressed their joy at the result'. He then went on to reaffirm his belief in secularism and demanded that the meeting should 'declare its policy in this matter in the clearest and most unambiguous terms'.

On this demand and on resolutions concerning foreign policy and other matters Congress satisfied Nehru, for the simple reason that they had no immediate effect on anybody's welfare or profits. Patel and the right wing only opposed Nehru's concept of a regulated economy. A resolution in favour of abolishing existing controls was defeated but by so narrow a margin that it only dramatized the split in the party and its leadership. This split was given further definition when Tandon refused to appoint to the Working Committee one of Nehru's closest supporters, Rafi Ahmed Kidwai, an opponent of Tandon in the U.P. and Minister of Communications in the central government. Kidwai had tried to persuade Nehru openly to support Kripalani's candidature but Nehru had been unwilling to come out into public conflict with Patel. After Tandon's election and his treatment of Kidwai, Nehru encouraged Kidwai and Kripalani to form, late in September 1950, a Congress Democratic Front. The Front's aim was to 'energize the organization of Congress and rid it of the corrupting influence of power politics and make it more democratic and serviceable'. The Government, the Front maintained, had failed to fulfil the minimum expectations of the people and implied that the reason was that Congress was threatened by 'irresponsible authoritarian forces'. Kidwai's main purpose, though not Kripalani's, was to rally pro-Nehru factions in order to defend their leader.

Early in December the Congress Working Committee met to decide whether disciplinary action should be taken against the Front. There was some danger that if action was taken the Front might break away from Congress in the same way as a number of dissidents in West Bengal had done the month before. The Committee therefore decided to take no action. The right-wing elements in Congress were unwilling to create a final breach with Nehru, whose support in the country was greater than anyone else's in Congress, because their leader, Patel, was seriously ill. Without their principal tactician they were not quite sure how to act. Patel had not wanted to replace Nehru as Prime Minister. The only possible candidate was himself and Patel knew that not only was he old and sick but he did not have Nehru's popular following. Patel's aim was always to influence Government policy, to cage Nehru not to dispose of him. While he was alive therefore, Patel was a restraining influence on the extremists. On 15 December however that restraint was removed. Early in the morning Patel suffered a severe stroke and died.

Patel's death inspired Nehru to a private pettiness and public eulogy. Patel had died in Bombay and the funeral was to be held there. Nehru tried to prevent Prasad from attending the obsequies on the grounds, he said, that it was a bad precedent for the head of state to attend the funeral of a minister. Prasad took this as an attempt to blacken Patel's reputation and refused Nehru's advice. The two men shared the same plane to Bombay. In parliament Nehru ended his eulogy of the late Deputy Prime Minister: 'We shall remember him as a friend, and a colleague and comrade above all, and I, who have sat here on this bench side by side with him, feel rather forlorn and a certain emptiness will steal upon me when I look to his empty seat.' To see that the seat remained permanently empty at least in terms of power, Nehru refused afterwards to appoint another Deputy Prime Minister.

The death of Patel ended the principal challenge to Nehru but it did not reconcile him with the right-wing leaders who still dominated the party organization. The right wing became more and more vocal in its criticism while the left was openly considering leaving Congress to form a new party. Yet the habit of putting unity above everything else, ingrained by the Mahatma, was hard to abandon. The prize was still not the replacement of Nehru but the authority of Congress over the Prime Minister and the cabinet. At a meeting of the AICC in January both sides called for unity, though Nehru referred to the rot which he said had entered the soul of the party. No major issues were agreed upon but the door was left invitingly ajar for mediation. Nehru took the first initiative by persuading the Congress Democratic Front to disband. Kripalani however preferred to leave Congress and he was followed by a number of others. Attempts were made to get them to return but Kripalani went ahead with a meeting at Patna in June at which a new party, the Kisan Mazdoor Praja Party (Workers and Peasants People's Party), was formed.

Kidwai, though present at Patna and selected to the central council of the new party, did not speak at the meeting nor, more significantly, did he resign immediately from Congress. The excuse given was that he would have to give up his position in the Government as well and he wanted to give Nehru time to find a substitute. The real reason however, was that Kidwai expected Nehru to intervene and force changes on the Congress Working Committee which would allow Kidwai to remain. This implies that there was some consultation between the two, a not unreasonable assumption as Nehru and Kidwai were very close. What followed certainly seemed to have been prearranged though there is no reliable evidence that it was. But Nehru's tactics were uncharacteristically decisive. It seems likely that the action was devised by Kidwai.

At a meeting of the AICC in Bangalore in July 1951 Nehru made an attempt to bring the dissidents back into Congress. In order to forestall any plan of Nehru's to try and reconstitute the Working Committee, the AICC gave him a free hand to draft the manifesto for the forthcoming elections under the new constitution. This bribe was ineffective for Nehru did ask the Congress president to reorganize the Working Committee and the Central Election Committee to include Kidwai and some of his supporters. Tandon insisted that it was the exclusive right of the Congress president to choose his own Working Committee. It was now obvious that there must either be a showdown or a capitulation.

Events moved very rapidly after the AICC session. A few days later, on 17 July, Kidwai submitted his resignation from the cabinet. Nehru refused to accept it and received a curt note from Tandon maintaining that it was wrong for a man openly opposed to Congress policies to remain in ministerial office and reminded the Prime Minister that he too only held office at the pleasure of Congress. Kidwai now resubmitted his resignation and this time it was accepted. On 3 August Kidwai announced that he was leaving Congress and joining the KMPP. The next step was for Nehru to take. On 10 August after an exchange of letters with Tandon he resigned from the Working Committee and the Central Election Committee. His resignation was followed by that of Maulana Azad.

Nehru's resignation caused a sensation throughout India. The thought of Congress without Nehru was inconceivable to those millions who saw him only as the successor of Gandhi. Inside Congress the thought of the party entering the general election without Nehru was unacceptable. The first to react was the Congress parliamentary party which gave Nehru an overwhelming vote of confidence. The pressure put upon Tandon and the right wing by all those interests who expected to benefit from the elections was now so strong that Tandon had no alternative but to resign. On 9 September the AICC elected Nehru to succeed him. Three weeks later Kidwai rejoined Congress. The campaign, so reminiscent of that which had ended in the resignation of Subhas Bose twelve years before, was over. Nehru was now both Prime Minister and Congress president. For over ten years his dominance was to be virtually unchallenged.

Chapter 18
Unchallenged Caesar

In November 1937 there appeared in a Calcutta journal a sharp profile of Nehru: '. . . he has all the makings of a dictator in him – vast popularity, a strong will, energy, pride . . . and with all his love of the crowd, an intolerance of others and a certain contempt for the weak and inefficient.' The writer went on. 'In normal times he would just be an efficient and successful executive, but in this revolutionary epoch Caesarism is always at the door, and is it not possible that Jawaharlal might fancy himself a Caesar? Therein lies the danger for Jawaharlal and India.' The author of this apparently candid though essentially misleading portrait was Nehru himself though he never officially admitted it.

In 1951 on the edge of a great democratic experiment and with complete control of Congress within his grasp some thought that Nehru would now become the unchallenged Caesar. They were right but the Caesarism of the next decade was to be the Caesarism of Nehru's weaknesses. The arrogance and the pride were to have full rein and were tolerated because those who really held the levers of power needed his vast popularity to preserve their positions. Democracy, the shackle Nehru placed upon his own anti-democratic tendencies, turned out to be an admirable preservative for the status quo. Caesarism implies a concentration of power, a single fountainhead of decision, but Nehru was an inefficient executive and an incompetent administrator who could not delegate even if he had wanted to. The alliance between Nehru and Congress was an alliance of weaknesses. Congress had created Nehru and Nehru could have led only a party like Congress. This is why he only once challenged Congress openly and then only under the influence of a more dynamic personality. Congress needed Nehru and *all he stood for* because only a leader like Nehru could sustain them in the minds of the voters.

After the trauma of the Tandon affair it was soon made clear to the right wing that it had nothing to fear. The old Nehru reasserted himself at the first meeting of the All-India Congress Committee – he retained almost all of the members of the Working Committee and made no attempt to infuse new ideals into the party. At the AICC meeting Nehru indicated that he needed more than a show of hands to prove that they wanted him as Congress president. For a moment the delegates expected the worst. When one of the members asked Nehru what proof they could give him, the new president called on the whole Committee to shout 'Jai Hind' (Hail India) with him. This was done twice. No effort was made to purge the Committee of right-wing communalists, no new doctrines were propounded and no new allegiances required. There is little doubt that Nehru could have had anything he asked for. The election was at hand and only Nehru could win it.

The anxiety of Congress members to fight the election with the weapon of Nehru's personality, with his *charisma* rather than policies, was well founded. Previous elections had been held in an atmosphere of struggle against the British and with the mystic presence of the Mahatma to give them the aura of a religious rite. The electorate now had been vastly increased by the introduction of universal suffrage – 173 million were to vote this time as against 30 million in the election of 1937. The whole scale of the election was immense. More than 3,800 seats were to be filled, 489 in the central parliament and the rest in the state assemblies. Contesting the elections were 59 different political parties and many thousands of independents – 17,000 candidates in all. The gamut of appeals to special interests was almost comprehensive. No one knew quite how the voter would react. Universal suffrage in an extremely poor and harshly inegalitarian society was something new. The dangers were there to be feared but were not satisfactorily defined.

Congress's national campaign, therefore, centred on Nehru to the exclusion of practically everything else. There was a party manifesto – written by Nehru and containing all his well-known views on foreign policy, secularism, social reform and economic development. The emphasis of the campaign was placed on service, the brahminical ideal – selfless, all embracing, emotional

– of Nehru's mentor, Vivekananda. For Nehru the elections seemed to be a special form of catharsis, an emotional release after the drama of independence. But he also seemed to think that it was an almost Gandhian exercise in spiritual renewal – primarily for Congress. It did not matter, he told Congress leaders, whether the party won the election at all. 'It is better,' he had told them while the leadership crisis was still upon Congress, 'to keep our soul and to lose an election than to win that election in the wrong way and with the wrong methods.' Now at the apogee of his power he called for a new cleansing. Congress candidates must be men of integrity, non-communal, progressive. The right-wing leadership ignored him and got on with the task of selecting the sort of men who would never endanger their tenure of power.

Three years of independence had produced a sea-change in Congress. It no longer had to fight for freedom only to divide up the perquisites of freedom achieved. Self-sacrifice, austerity, idealism were the propaganda of the dispossessed. The contrast between the asceticism of the freedom-fighter and the luxury of the imperialist was a weapon in the fight itself. The figure of Gandhi and others in their homespun clothes looked very well against the bright uniforms and the glistening orders of the British rulers. Gandhi had wanted to turn the grandiose palace of the Viceroy into a hospital for the poor. Instead it became the residence of the president of independent India with all the trappings of viceregal display untarnished. Nehru moved into the luxurious house of the former commanders-in-chief, surrounding himself with guards. Large cars, bodyguards on prancing horses, pomp and protocol all contributed in some measure to national stability by emphasizing the continuity of government but they also formed a sure base for the expansion of privilege and status seeking.

The competition for such privilege was high. New types of politicians had emerged responsive both to patronage and the pressures of special-interest groups and with few, if any, ideological inhibitions about working for them. It was these men who were the choice of the Congress organization dominated, as always, by the conservatives. Nehru expressed his disappointment at the lists of candidates presented to him but endorsed them just the same with the power of his name.

Nehru's election tour in 1951 was a repetition of that of 1937. He talked of broad and mostly incomprehensible issues and almost never of the local candidate. It was always Congress the liberator from British rule, Congress the hope of the future, never the Congress of the present. The campaign was an immense and rather pathetic confidence trick played on those who knew only too well the corruption of local Congress officials. Nehru continually made a plea for faith and despite their experience the masses gave it to him. Perhaps it was his utter sincerity in the midst of a crowd which was so effective. Like some great actor Nehru responded to his audience. 'I am particularly sensitive to public reactions, to mass reactions,' he was to write; 'the functioning of democracy is very largely the sensation you create in the public mind.' No politician in modern times received so much uncritical love from so many millions. 'Whenever I feel stale and tired, I go among the people and I come back refreshed.'

The whole election was essentially a travesty of democracy. The air was heavy with political statements but the only real issue was – Congress, for or against. The other main parties – the Kisan Majdoor Praja Party, the Socialists, the Communists, the newly formed communalist party of S. P. Mookerjee, the Jan Sangh – all attacked Congress on its record and there was much to attack. None of them expected to replace Congress in the seat of power but to erode its following, and in terms of votes they succeeded. Congress certainly swept back into Government, but with a minority of the votes cast. Though Congress won everywhere, more than half the voters expressed their dissatisfaction with it. The results made Nehru even more important to Congress than he had been before.

Organizationally, the election was a triumph. Over $2\frac{1}{2}$ million ballot boxes and 600 million ballot papers opened a front for corruption. There was some but very little, and only at 109 places was a re-vote necessary. There was very little violence or impersonation. Some votes were certainly bought but more were gained by promises. Some people, not all of them anti-democratic, queried whether it had been worth over 50 million rupees for such a desperately poor country to demonstrate that it was the world's largest democracy. Nehru too expressed some doubts, though not about the cost. Before the election he had not been sure whether adult franchise would succeed in India. 'The voter reacts to sound and din,' he said, 'he reacts to repetition, and he produces either a dictator or a politician that is insensitive.' A few days later he was reported as saying that 'there should be some sort of indirect elections in the higher stages and direct elections in the lower'. Indeed, Nehru's 'attachment' to western-style parliamentary democracy for which he acquired in his lifetime so much prestige in the democratic west was not quite as deep as his admirers made out. Nehru would have liked to experiment with differing systems. The real attachment to democracy was to be found in those who benefited from it. And not only in the plutocracy which dominated Congress but also in the Communists who having unsuccessfully tried revolution in the Telengana district of Hyderabad between 1948 and 1951 turned to the democratic process instead. In the elections of 1957 the Communists were to poll 12 million votes to become the largest opposition party in the central parliament.

Though Nehru was fully aware that Congress had not won the election on its merits – and his exhortations on the subject increased after the results were known – it made very little difference to the party leaders. Over the next decade special-interest groups entrenched themselves in the party system at all levels building up what was virtually a parallel administration in the states where the real profits were to be made. The identification of more and more Congress members with the practical issues of everyday life led to further corruption and nepotism. As the state party bosses took over control of the political machine the high principles frequently laid down by Nehru became more and more divorced from reality. Indian politics which during the struggle for freedom had been largely a genuine expression of sacrifice became instead an avenue for profit. There is nothing particularly surprising in this. Even genuine revolutions inevitably give way to bourgeois values but India was and still is to some extent unique. The range of radical social and economic policies continually endorsed by the dominant party and ignored in principle is unequalled elsewhere.

The gap between radical policy and conservative practice, a legacy both of the years of struggle against the British and of the need for stability during the trials of the first years of independence, was institutionalized after the 1951 elections by a shift in the basis of political power in Indian society. This shift was from the predominantly upper-class Congress leadership of pre-independence vintage to the rural élite. Dominant social groups making up that élite had remained aloof from the freedom movement. After independence, however, they were anxious to participate in the spoils of power and political patronage.

The ambitions of the rural élite – landowners and middlemen – lay behind the demand for the creation of linguistic states and the controversy over a national language. The boundaries created by integration of the princely states with the old provinces of British India were generally assumed to be temporary. The essential criterion had been speedy integration not rationalization. But even during the years 1948–9 the demand for reorganization along linguistic lines was already becoming vocal. A commission of inquiry was set up and delivered its opinions at the end of 1948. The commission's view was that things should be left as they were. The provinces of British India had the sanction of the years. It was recognized that the old boundaries contained dominant linguistic groups but also many minorities. No new boundaries could remedy this. The commission most strongly criticized the creation of linguistic states on the grounds that they would inspire linguistic and therefore local patriotisms which would inhibit the growth of a national consciousness and the acceptance of a national language which was fundamental to such growth.

Though there was some support within Congress for states reorganization, a Committee set up by the party to consider the commission's report also came out for the preservation of things as they were. The committee of three, Nehru, Patel and Pattabhai

Sitaramayya, obviously considered the need for national unity more important at the time than the demands of what was then only a small number of Congressmen. Nevertheless, on the Congress principle that there should always be a loophole in any decision, the committee agreed that should there be a continuing demand for states reorganization the matter would receive more detailed study.

The local structure of Congress itself insured that such a demand would be forthcoming. From 1921 the organization had been centred on linguistic areas and pledges were constantly renewed that on independence these would be formed into states. The problem of national stability had eroded Congress attachment to these pledges in the first years of freedom, but after the elections of 1951-2 national stability seemed to have been achieved. Nevertheless the fear that administrative reorganization might imperil that stability remained uppermost in the minds of the national Congress leadership. The election however had shown that national issues were not those on which the election had been fought and won. On an all-India level, Nehru's personality had been the most important factor, but on the local level the appeal had been to particularist desires, to caste sensitivities and strictly local interests. The candidates of opposition parties, having no Nehru to help them, had competed for the support of those who could influence the voters. Congress candidates had been forced to follow suit. As the majority of constituencies were in rural areas it was the dominant social groups – landlords, merchants and money-lenders – who received the most attention. It was at this stage that these groups realized their potential political power. They also saw that new outlets must be created for them to express it. They were not interested in participating in the central political process which was dominated by nationalist modernizers like Nehru but in suitable media for the satisfaction of purely parochial ambitions.

The first high-level demand for a new linguistic state had been in 1949. Some member of the Congress Working Committee suggested the creation of a separate state for the Telugu speakers of what was then Madras. The Government resisted and the request was not pressed at such a level again. After the elections the scene moved to Madras. There a Congress government under the former governor-general, C. Rajagopalachari, was divided amongst itself. The chief minister's differences with T. Prakasam popularly known as the Lion of Andhra, intensified the clash between the Tamil and Telugu speakers. The demand for the partition of the state on a linguistic basis was based on the antagonism between the two men who represented the two linguistically based Congress Committees making up the unified state of Madras. The Congress election manifesto for 1951 had contained the statement that on the matter of states reorganization the democratic right of the people to express their opinion would be taken into consideration. But the central government did not want to go through the cumbersome process of a plebiscite. The decision therefore rested with the contending Congress organizations.

The Andhra Provincial Congress Committee representing the Telugu-speaking areas of the Madras state passed a resolution demanding the division of the state on linguistic lines. The Tamilnad PCC felt obliged to concede that on the basis of the election manifesto such a division must be made. The central government however was unwilling to agree. Nehru told his colleagues that he would not be intimidated by such tactics and there seems to have been complete agreement. The matter was then taken on to an emotional level when a highly respected Telugu leader, Potti Srimarulu, announced that he would take no food until the central government agreed to take steps to establish a Telugu-speaking Andhra state. Again Nehru assured cabinet members that he would not yield to blackmail but when the Telugu leader's fast to the death actually ended in death – a consummation then unique in the history of fasting as a modern political weapon – Nehru gave in and even referred to Srimarulu's 'sacrifice' with admiration during a debate in parliament. His speech was an open invitation to extra-democratic pressure.

In order it seemed to underline his capitulation to violence – Srimarulu's death had been followed by widespread rioting – Nehru personally attended the inauguration of the new state of Andhra in October 1953. The message was immediately read

by other special-interest groups – the Government was susceptible to mass agitation. Nehru appealed for rational behaviour.
He tried to pretend that the Government had yielded only
because partition made administrative sense. To demand
states on a linguistic basis, he said, was giving way to tribalism.
But nobody listened. Pressure built up so rapidly that less than
three months after parliament had agreed to the formation of
Andhra, the Government announced the appointment of a
States Reorganization Commission.

Nehru's change of attitude was not merely another example
of his protean political style. On a visit to the town of Belgaum
then in Bombay state he was greeted by hostile demonstrators
carrying black flags demanding a Kannada-speaking state
comprising Mysore and parts of Bombay and Hyderabad.
Nehru, always abnormally sensitive to the mood of crowds,
came back convinced that if something was not done to satisfy
what he took to be popular feelings he would lose his own
popularity in the country. The result was the Commission,
though Nehru did his best to try to delay any decision it might
recommend. The Commission was warned not to overlook the
essential need to preserve Indian unity but its members seemed
more concerned with the validity of regionalism. During its
inquiry there was considerable agitation and the Commission
seems to have been influenced by it.

The 1948 Commission had stressed the viability of multi-
lingual states and had made its principal argument the point
that people speaking different languages living in one political
unit constituted a guarantee against narrow nationalism. The
new Commission rejected that argument. 'In states having more
than one developed language,' ran its report,'there has been
no marked tendency in the past to develop a sense of loyalty to
the state. There was never any noticeable Madrasi sentiment
when that state was a composite one. On the other hand, such
loyalties as did develop within the area were based on languages.'
The Commission's conclusion was that 'the idea that multi-
lingual states will weaken the loyalty to language groups does
not seem to be justified'. The members supported their opinion
with a great deal of evidence from European experience.

The Commission's report was delivered in October 1955. It suggested that the number of states should be reduced to sixteen with three Union, or centrally administered, territories. The moment the report was made public, discontent was openly expressed and was succeeded by agitation. Though there was trouble in Orissa, Bengal and Bihar the real centre of violent dissent was in Bombay and the Punjab. Bombay was a bilingual state made up of Marathi and Gujarati speakers with some small minorities. In January 1956 there was serious rioting in Bombay city where the population was mainly Marathi-speaking but in which the upper classes were preponderantly Gujarati. The state government was also overwhelmingly Gujarati in character. The city police indulged in irresponsible firing and eighty people were killed and over 400 wounded in clashes.

The central government acted with fatal indecision. It changed its mind frequently – the state would be divided but the city of Bombay would become a separate state. Then it announced that Bombay would become a Union territory. When this was badly received the Government suggested a plebiscite in five years' time. Finally it was decided in 1960 that Bombay should go to the new Marathi-speaking state of Maharashtra. At this there was rioting in Ahmadabad, the proposed capital of the new state of Gujarat, primarily with the aim of ensuring that the Government would not change its mind once again. The Government took the hint.

In the Punjab the Sikhs demonstrated for a state of their own and for a time it seemed as if the terrors of the partition riots of 1947 were about to return. The Sikhs' anger was aroused by the decision to merge into a greater Punjab the state of Himachal Pradesh, an area Hindu in population and Hindi-speaking. Both sides, Hindu and Sikh, organized demonstrations overtly communal in character but which turned out, surprisingly enough, to be peaceful. In the end a compromise was arrived at. The Hindu area became centrally administered and both Punjabi and Hindi were made the official languages of the Punjab state. The decision did not end agitation but the formation of a Punjabi-speaking state was delayed until after Nehru's death.

There were more changes before the States Reorganization Bill was finally passed through parliament in November 1956. The original suggestion for sixteen states and three Union territories became fourteen states and seven territories. There is no doubt that much of the blame for the Government's fumbling and indecision must be placed on Nehru. When he received the report of the Commission he was shocked by its recommendations. A number of leading Congress figures advised him to shelve the report, one for as long as twenty-five years. The chief ministers of Bengal and Bihar even went so far as to suggest a merger between their two states in order to check 'linguistic madness'. Nehru, however, encouraged the linguistic-minded by referring in a broadcast in October 1955 to his opinion that 'no decision is irrevocable in a democracy'. Once again there was an open invitation to any linguistic group to exert the maximum political pressure with a guarantee of success. Such pressure was continually exerted after the broadcast.

Nehru's willingness to hear all sides and to give the impression that he always saw clearly their separate virtues has been taken by most commentators to reflect his unwillingness to impose any solution not democratically arrived at. Nehru undoubtedly rationalized his inability to give clear-cut guidance as abhorrence of dictatorship. But his public utterances on vital issues were more those of a schoolmaster balancing rival arguments than a practical politician, even in an ideal democracy. His refusal to make a decision – even in support of a deeply held ideological conviction – had by the mid-1950s become almost a technique. While his father and Gandhi were alive Nehru could leave decisions to these dominating personalities. After Gandhi's death there was no one for him to go to. Without any single person to leave the decisions to, Nehru was compelled to allow events to take their course, or to be directed on course by others more purposeful, until there was only one choice left to him to make. He would then accede – often with dire warnings about the consequences – to what had become irresistible.

The price of indecision was high. States reorganization

brought into power reactionary elements who would successfully frustrate the modernizing ideals of those who hoped for
great social and economic change. This in turn eroded Congress
support among the masses who were continually promised
revolutionary reforms only to observe that the institutions
created to put them into effect became a source of profit to the
old élite. The competition for political power in the states
facilitated the growth of factionalism inside the Congress party.
Competing factions could only be held together by a policy of
continuing compromise which, though it gave some stability
to both the party and the country, inevitably encouraged stag-
nation.

The most dramatic display of hostility between factions came
almost immediately after the settlement of the states reorganization issue. Not unnaturally, as the states were linguistically
based, the cause was the old controversy over a national
language. The constitutional compromise of 1950 by which
India's fourteen major languages had been given equal status
and English guaranteed its position as an official language for
fifteen years had calmed the fears of non-Hindi speakers. However in 1955 an Official Language Commission was appointed
to recommend a timetable for the change over to Hindi in ten
years' time. The Commission's report appeared in 1957 and
revealed that only two of its twenty members had felt any
misgivings about the replacement of English by Hindi. This
revived the fears of non-Hindi speakers and in particular those
in the south.

Opposition in south India centred upon the claim that the
imposition of Hindi would endanger national unity and dis-
criminate against non-Hindi speakers in the public services.
Opposition was translated into demonstrations in which Hindi
signs were defaced. Southern feeling was so intense that it
seemed that the ruling party would split. That it did not do so
is at least partly explained by the performance of the party in
the second general election held in the spring of 1957.

Superficially Congress once again won a resounding victory.
In the central parliament the party had 75 per cent of the seats
and 65 per cent of all those in the state assemblies. It had even

increased the size of its popular vote. This had been largely due to the party's political machine organized by S. K. Patil, a right-wing Congress leader from Bombay. The opposition parties suffered from lack of funds, and their unwillingness to unite against Congress. Nehru's name was still a talisman – Congress posters always bore his portrait and the adjuration to 'Vote Nehru. Vote Congress'. Nehru did not make a countrywide tour as he had done in the first election and concentrated on areas where his presence was thought to be necessary.

But there were losses just the same. In five of the states the Congress majority and share of the vote was reduced and in one, Kerala, the party was defeated by the Communists. Even the presence of Nehru there could not bring victory for Congress. The Kerala result and the emergence of the Communist Party as the major opposition demonstrated the fact that Congress could no longer bank on its prestige as the bringer of Indian freedom to sustain it in power. The appearance of non-Congress regional parties with strong linguistic bases suggested that a national language controversy could lead to the loss to Congress of other states. Even the most fanatical Congress supporters of Hindi accepted this argument against precipitate action on such a delicate subject. When Congress met at its annual session in 1958 Nehru's appeal for compromise was listened to. Though 1965 must still be the date for the formal adoption of Hindi it was recognized that there could be no dictation to non-Hindi areas and that English might continue in use after that date.

Apart from the language issue, the 1958 meeting was dull and dispiriting. Congress had all the appearance of a party in decline. In the years between the elections Congress membership had fallen by a half and the party was suffering in Nehru's words from 'a deep malaise'. He exhorted delegates in ten lengthy speeches but seemed to make no appreciable impact on the general apathy. The performance of the party in states where the scramble for the fruits of office among factions was both blatant and vicious had been poor. This and the failure, on practically every front, of Government policies combined to force Nehru into taking some sort of action. The real determinant was probably physical exhaustion. But whatever the proximate cause, Nehru shocked everybody a few months after the 1958 Congress session by indicating his wish to resign.

Warnings had been there for all to hear in many of his speeches. He was feeling 'flat and stale' he said, but he had said that before. In 1951, before the Tandon clash, he had talked about retirement. In 1954 he had also said that he was tired. But Congressmen had judged him as they did themselves. Their motives for hanging on to power were certainly different but no less compelling. Some gestures were made. In 1953 he had been relieved of the Congress presidency, but in his place was elected a hand-picked successor. In 1957 Nehru had also expressed a desire to give up office. Everyone then took it for what it was, a fit of pique at not being able to get his own choice as the second president of India.

Nehru's relations with Prasad, whom he had not wanted as first president, were never easy. Prasad had tried to make the presidency much more than the constitutional office it had been intended it should be. As early as September 1951 Prasad had sent a note to Nehru in which he expressed his wish to act solely on his own judgement and without the advice of ministers, when giving assent to Bills, when sending messages to parliament, and when returning Bills to parliament for consideration. Prasad's action had been dictated by his hope of preventing the Hindu Code Bill from becoming law. Under the pressure of legal opinion, Prasad had given way but his relations with Nehru had not improved, even though when the Bill finally came up before parliament Prasad made no attempt to delay it.

In 1956 the question was raised of a second term for Prasad. Nehru was anxious for the vice-president, S. Rahdakrishnan, a distinguished scholar from Madras, to succeed. Despite Nehru's appeal to the Congress chief ministers of states they supported Prasad who was re-elected. It was alleged at the time that Nehru believed Prasad was planning a coup with the Hindu communalist parties, a story that is still being perpetuated by some Indian journalists. There are no grounds for believing that Nehru's dislike of Prasad was any more than personal antipathy.

There was no reason why anyone should take Nehru's wish to resign in 1958 as any different in quality from previous occasions. The Congress parliamentary party – which in the course of one of the Prime Minister's rambling talks heard him say: 'I feel now that I must have a period when I can free myself from this burden and can think of myself as an individual citizen of India and not as Prime Minister' – reacted predictably. After making this remark Nehru had characteristically put the burden of decision on other people, it was up to them, of course, to decide for him. Naturally, the Congress M.P.s responded by beseeching him not to leave them 'as orphans'. For the next four days the whole party went through a dramatic series of appeals to which Nehru replied after another talk with the words; 'I shall not proceed to take the step I had suggested.'

In a conversation (with the present author) some years later Nehru insisted that on this occasion he really had wanted to be relieved of office. His sincerity was undeniable. Why then did he give in? His answer was that India needed him, that his constituency was the Indian people. Why then did he not leave Congress and form a new party more in tune with his own ideas? The answer was that it would take too long and that at sixty-nine he had not known how long he would have to live.

Nehru's disillusion had sound bases in fact. The trend of events abroad was anything but reassuring, and nothing seemed to have gone right on the domestic front. Only a few days before he had indicated his desire to retire from office Nehru had had to make drastic cuts in the second Five-Year Plan.

The concept of national planning had been fundamental to Nehru's hopes for social and economic revolution. Congress had allowed itself to be committed to a modernizing ideology in pre-independence times and had arrived in power with a definite policy programme to implement. The programme was essentially radical in intent and had played a significant role in attracting that smallest of Indian minorities, the westernized intelligentsia, to the support of Congress. After independence this minority expected a Congress Government to realize its radical programme. The need for stability, however, overrode the desire for reform.

This was exemplified in April 1948 when Nehru announced his Government's industrial policy. There was neither socialism nor revolution. Public ownership was to be restricted to railways – already a state monopoly – munitions and atomic energy. As for the rest, the Government would only establish new ventures and leave existing ones untouched. For those who had expected wholesale nationalization Nehru explained his position. 'After all that has happened in the course of the last seven or eight months,' he told the constituent assembly, 'one has to be very careful of the steps one takes so as not to injure the existing structure too much. There has been destruction and injury enough, and certainly I confess to this House that I am not brave or gallant enough to go about destroying any more.' Government economic activity, it was made clear on this and subsequent occasions, would be confined to those areas in which private enterprise was not already active.

Nehru's approach to planned development was almost entirely emotional. He had neither knowledge nor understanding of the functioning of an economy, whether capitalist or socialist. He was indeed convinced that private enterprise sustained a system which accepted poverty and even flourished upon it. Nevertheless private enterprise in a poor country must have its place, though only in a regulated economy. In Nehru's mind there was quite rightly no separation of social and economic development – both were essential parts of the modernizing process. The ideals he held were embodied at his insistence in the Directive Principles contained in Article 39 of Part IV of the Indian Constitution.

These principles included the obligation to ensure:

(a) that the citizens, men and women equally, have the right to adequate means of livelihood;
(b) that the ownership and control of the material resources of the community are so distributed as best to subserve the common good; and
(c) that the operation of the economic system does not result

in the concentration of wealth and means of production to the common detriment.

The Directive Principles were not enforceable in law but were intended as a guide to government action. That action Nehru saw as the enactment of progressive social legislation allied with economic planning. The instrument of Nehru's hopes for reform was the Five-Year Plan and its animateur, the Planning Commission.

A National Planning Commission was set up in 1950. Its primary function was to draw up a programme for planned development. At its head was Nehru and the whole philosophy of planning in India bears the marks of both his ideals and his weaknesses. Though it was established that the widest range of discussion would be encouraged before decisions were made, at the centre of the decision-making process was the Prime Minister, the chairman of the Planning Commission and later the chairman of the National Development Council, offices all held simultaneously by Nehru.

India's First Five-Year Plan which ran from 1951 to 1956 was not so much a plan as a programme of public works. Special attention was paid to agriculture and particularly to irrigation and flood control. Transportation, too, received a considerable amount of the funds allocated. Industrial development was given the least attention on the assumption that having created a satisfactory agricultural base and ensured a rise in food production, the Second Plan could concentrate on industry. The aims of the Plan were achieved. Food production increased though this was almost entirely due to exceptionally good monsoons in the years 1953-4 and 1954-5. In fact the Plan targets were passed to the extent of five million tons of food grains more than had been estimated. There were substantial rises in national income and in the production of capital and consumer goods.

Though the plan was judged a success by the planners, it was clearly unambitious. In the preamble to the published outline of the Plan basic social and economic objectives were formulated but the machinery for implementing them did not exist. It was also clear that though the Plan had achieved its stated aims and even surpassed them, the quality of Indian poverty was virtually untouched, unemployment had increased and there was a fall in agricultural prices. Nehru decided that planning must have a bolder ideological framework. In November 1954, announcing the creation of a National Development Council, Nehru declared that what he wanted was a 'socialistic picture of society', though he added, 'not in a dogmatic sense at all'. A few weeks later with the revision of the 1946 Industrial Policy Resolution, the phrase became 'a socialistic *pattern* of society'.

In January 1955 Congress endorsed Nehru's views by what came to be known, after the session's meeting place, as the Avadi Resolution. The 'socialistic pattern of society' was set down as the objective of planning so that 'the principal means of production are under social ownership or control, production is progressively speeded up, and there is equitable distribution in the national wealth'. Nationalization was hardly mentioned. Private business would continue to have 'a definite place in our economy at present' but only if it functioned within a national plan. The overall aim was to create an economic system in which the State would 'play a vital part in planning and development', would 'initiate and operate large-scale schemes', and 'have overall control of resources, social purposes and trends and essential balances in the economy'. Among the ways in which the State would operate would be through the 'maintenance of strategic controls, prevention of private trusts and cartels and maintenance of standards of labour and production'.

Under the influence of the Avadi Resolution India's Second Five-Year Plan was inaugurated in 1956.[1] It was considerably more ambitious than the first, doubling the outlay but with only 25 per cent of necessary finance guaranteed from revenue. The

1. Any detailed analysis of the Five-Year Plans is outside the scope of this book. For a study of the Plans during Nehru's lifetime see: A. H. Hanson, *The Process of Planning: A Study of India's Five-Year Plans 1950–1964*, Oxford University Press for the Royal Institute of International Affairs, 1966.

rest was to come from loans, deficit financing and the remainder, a quarter of the whole, was to depend on foreign aid and unstated domestic resources. Private foreign investment was not to be encouraged for obvious ideological reasons though it is doubtful whether at that time India could have raised loans from private capital abroad. The only sources both acceptable and available would be international institutions such as the World Bank and aid from friendly countries. With the Second Plan, Indian development became closely linked with India's foreign policy.

The Plan's first setback came from the Indian weather. The good monsoons during the First Plan had inspired over-confidence in the planners. Within a year of the inauguration of the Second the weather had almost destroyed it. There were widespread floods, hail storms followed by drought. Harvests were seriously cut and food reserves almost wiped out. The food crisis coincided with a serious shortage of foreign exchange, much of the reserves having been used for the purchase of capital equipment abroad. In order to save the Plan drastic action was taken. Imports requiring foreign exchange were banned unless the sellers were willing to accept a delay in payment. Communist countries in Europe including the Soviet Union immediately agreed and their example was quickly followed by others. New taxes were imposed raising the cost of consumer goods and the level of income at which income tax started was lowered. Both these actions pressed most heavily on the poor and the lower middle class, though there were also new taxes for the rich.

The performance of the Second Five-Year Plan revealed the essential weakness of planning in India – the profound influence of Nehru. His own views on the overriding importance of industrial expansion were supported not only by the Indian intelligentsia but by foreign advisers and became almost articles of faith. Even though the planners tried to rectify their' neglect of agriculture when they outlined the Third Plan which began in 1961 the importation of larger and larger quantities of grain to feed the population had become established policy. The failure to reach Plan targets in other areas increased dependence on foreign grants and loans. To some extent the shortcomings of planning criteria have been rectified since Nehru's death but the gap between policy and implementation has not.

The gap was created by Congress precedent and sustained by the political élite in the states who not only diverted economic programmes intended primarily to benefit the poor to their own advantage but also successfully prevented the implementation of social legislation designed to create a democratic and egalitarian society. Nehru considered that social inequalities were the result of economic forces and could be changed by new ones. In one sense it was true. In a rigidly inegalitarian society economic status and social, i.e. caste, status are correlated. Unfortunately the democratic system tended to assist those of the highest economic and social status to maintain their position.

Against this Nehru would only exhort. Failing to insist on the implementation of social reforms he hammered away instead on the *need* for social revolution. He continually attacked 'casteism, communalism, provincialism and linguism'. 'We say,' he told Congress leaders after the 1957 election, 'we are against . . . all that. And yet you know well enough how poisoned we are to the very core.' Year after year Congress accepted with acclaim ideals which became more radical as Congress became more reactionary in practice. The gap between ideal and reality constantly underlined by Nehru encouraged cynicism and gave to modernizing ideals an air of unreality and make-believe. It also tended to diminish Nehru's own integrity and that of the Government and democratic system with which he was associated. The growth of scepticism intensified Nehru's own frustration and loneliness and drove him more and more into the inspiring and dramatic area of international affairs where his policies and decisions were virtually unquestioned and his growing authority as a world statesman could disguise the inadequacies of the domestic politician.

In December 1947, in a speech to the Constituent Assembly in Delhi, Nehru tried to inform his listeners on the fundamentals of foreign policy. 'Whatever policy we may lay down,' he said, 'the art of conducting the foreign affairs of a country lies in finding out what is most advantageous to the country. We may talk about international goodwill and mean what we say. We may talk about peace and freedom and earnestly mean what we say. But in the ultimate analysis, a Government functions for the good of the country it governs.'

Two years later, in an address at Columbia University in New York, Nehru gave his definition of the foreign policy that would best serve the good of India. The objectives, he said, were 'the pursuit of peace, not through alignment with any major power or group of powers, but through an independent approach to each controversial or disputed issue; the liberation of subject peoples; the maintenance of freedom both national and individual; the elimination of racial discrimination; and the elimination of want, disease and ignorance which afflict the greater part of the world's population'.

To this fairly comprehensive statement later Nehru added a more positive content with the concept of *Panchsheel* or five principles of peaceful coexistence: mutual respect for territorial integrity and sovereignty; non-aggression; non-interference in internal affairs; equality and mutual benefit; and peaceful coexistence. The two statements together with *Panchsheel* sum up the three essential elements in Nehru's approach to foreign affairs: an apparent awareness of the purpose of foreign policy; a high moral tone; and a general air of unreality.

The five principles were first enunciated in the preamble to the Sino-Indian Agreement on Tibet of April 1954. This agreement was concerned with the movement of traders, pilgrims, porters and mule-drivers through the Himalayan passes – a somewhat incongruous setting. The principles were first put forward as a panacea for peace in a joint statement by Nehru and the Chinese Prime Minister Chou En-lai in New Delhi in June 1954: 'If these principles are applied not only between various countries but also in international affairs generally, they would form a solid foundation for peace and security and the fears and apprehensions that exist today would give place to a feeling of confidence.' From that time on the propaganda in support of non-alignment and *Panchsheel* came from China as well as India. Under its influence the countries of Asia and Africa emerging into independence adopted non-alignment as the basis of their foreign policies or at least claimed it as the basis.

Nehru's thinking on foreign policy was properly founded on India's own circumstances. The determinants of geography, history and poverty were inescapable. India's central position in the Asian mainland, its clearly defined frontiers and great size, was one factor. The imperial experience which naturally inspired anti-colonialism and anti-racialism was another. It was not only in Nehru's mind that there remained the permanent fear of an imperial return disguised behind military alliances and treaties of mutual aid. Above all, any solution to the problem of India's poverty demanded freedom from external wars and the fear of wars. Long-term development would not be possible unless most of the country's revenue could be used for constructive purposes and not diverted to spending on armed forces. There was also the need to keep every source of foreign financial aid as uninhibited as possible. For these reasons world peace was vital to India. In a situation in which the two superpowers, America and Russia, and their satellites were contesting for supremacy in a Cold War, that peace was particularly fragile. War between the super-powers would put an end to the ambitions of India's Five-Year Plans. It was therefore necessary for India to avoid foreign entanglements and to work actively for the preservation of peace.

These elements frequently enunciated by Nehru were hardly unique either in sentiment or application but foreign policies are always more then their basic premises. Many factors affect a country's foreign relations but in none has the personality of the foreign minister played so dominant a role as in those of India. Nehru had prepared himself throughout the years of the freedom struggle for India's entry upon the world stage. His experience was centred upon his reaction to colonialism, above all to its arrogant assumption that the white man's judgement was better than the coloured. Nehru made it quite clear that he would not yield his right of individual judgement to leaders of other countries, however powerful. 'I am not prepared even as

an individual, much less as the Foreign Minister of this country,'
he told members of India's parliament in 1958, 'to give up my
right to individual judgement to anybody else in other countries.
That is the essence of our policy.'

This was all very well, but Nehru insisted – with as much
arrogance as any western imperialist – that his judgement,
India's judgement, was superior to anyone else's. His foreign
policy statements often became lectures, suffused with a high
moral tone, to the statesmen of other countries. Most of these
lectures were directed to leaders in the west. Even criticisms of
the Cold War though ostensibly impartial were primarily
addressed to the United States. This bias too emerged out of
Nehru's past. Next to colonialism the strongest influence on
Nehru's thinking was the events that had taken place in Europe
in the 1920s and 1930s and the analysis of them by intellectuals
of the British left especially those grouped around the political
scientist Harold Laski and the socialist journal the *New Statesman*. From them he acquired a superior attitude to the United
States, too rich, too powerful and essentially 'immature', and a
tendency to give the Soviet Union the maximum benefit of any
doubt. Nehru never lost his view of the Russia of the inter-war
years, embattled and revolutionary, and its post-war imperialism
was always somehow less offensive to him than the pre-
war imperialism of the west. This was particularly obvious
in 1956 when the Anglo-French invasion of Egypt was immediately and indignantly condemned while the Soviet suppression
of the Hungarian rising of the same year was only mildly de-
precated.

So far, Nehru's view of the world, however susceptible to
criticism, was reasonably pragmatic and secular. Above all, it
had resulted in success; non-alignment could be seen to work
to India's, and possibly to the rest of the world's, advantage.
But well could not be left alone. Non-alignment had to be
elevated into an act of faith embodying the Good and the True.
The initiative did not come exclusively from Nehru but his
growing need for identification with the India he ostensibly
ruled was an invitation to courtiers and flatterers. Nehru
encouraged, and participated in, a deliberate attempt to

clothe political non-alignment – contemporary and modern in its conception – with the sanction of an exclusively Indian past.

The attempt took two forms. The first was to allege that India's foreign policy was non-violent and Gandhian. The other was to claim that it was pacifist and Buddhist. Nehru both supported and denied the Gandhian thesis. On Gandhian non-violence as a source he said, non-alignment 'is a policy inherent in the past thinking of India, inherent in the conditioning of the Indian mind during our struggle for freedom' and 'basically our outlook is derived from that old outlook which Gandhi gave us and which made us powerfully in favour of peace and peaceful methods'. But against that he stated: 'I am not saying that a military approach can be completely given up in this world. I am not speaking as a pacifist.' 'We may not in this world as it is constituted today, even rule out war absolutely.' 'I am not a pacifist. Unhappily the world of today finds that it cannot do without force.' At least Nehru's opposition to Gandhi's views had some element of consistency. Gandhi had envisaged an independent India as the first state to practise non-violence. India, he alleged quite incorrectly (and he knew it) had 'an unbroken tradition of non-violence from time immemorial . . . her destiny is to deliver the message of non-violence to mankind'. Of this Nehru had written in *The Discovery of India* that such a view was 'far-fetched and many Indian thinkers and historians did not agree with it'. And neither did he. Nevertheless Nehru did not discourage others, some of them quite near to him, from continuing to emphasize the non-existent Gandhian roots of his foreign policy.

For the Buddhist interpretation Nehru had much more sympathy. It was more venerable, for one thing, and could be associated with an Indian ruler whom Nehru admired – the 'Buddhist' emperor Asoka who ruled in the third century B.C. It also permitted him to push aside the essentially violent, realistic and cynical outlook of Hindu political thought. Nehru made continuous references to the Buddha and encouraged others to do so. His sister, Mrs Pandit, in 1956 still a mouthpiece for Nehru's beliefs, wrote that the Indian approach to peace was 'not new to India. It is her traditional outlook both philosophical and historical' – philosophically in the Buddha and historically in Asoka.

Asoka was invoked to give character and depth to the commonplaces of *Panchsheel*. 'Peaceful coexistence,' Nehru told members of the Indian parliament in September 1955, 'is not a new idea for us in India. It has been our way of life and is as old as our thought and culture. About 2,200 years ago, a great son of India, Asoka, proclaimed it on rock and stone which exist today and give us his message. Asoka told us that we should respect the faith of others, and that a person who extols his own faith and decries another faith injures his own faith. This is the lesson of tolerance and peaceful coexistence and cooperation which India has believed in through the ages. In the old days we talked of religion and philosophy; now we talk more of the economic and social system. But the approach is the same now as before.'

Apart from Nehru's anxiety to set himself and his ideas in the mainstream of Indian history, even through a perversion of it, it is difficult to see what purpose there could be in surrounding the trivialities of *Panchsheel* with such moralistic claptrap. There was nothing new about the principles. Even an official Indian Government publication admitted that *Panchsheel* was only a restatement of the principles of the United Nations Charter and those were not particularly new either. The Five Principles were platitudes and dangerous ones at that, because with their clothing of magic culled from India's past they became substitutes for creative thinking. Nehru himself admitted that the third principle (non-interference in the internal affairs of other countries) tended to support the status quo: 'You will see that the only way to avoid conflicts is to accept things more or less as they are.' Some commentators have seen in this statement a clue to the real, though obscured, purpose of *Panchsheel*: the preservation of the status quo between India and China. In this it certainly failed.[1] But perhaps the most serious criticism that can be made of *Panchsheel* is not that it turned out to be useless in the local defence of India's security

1. See Chapter 19.

but that it raised hopes among ordinary people thoughout the world which it could not possibly fulfil.

The foundation of non-alignment, what was in effect a doctrine of defence by friendship, did not apply to Pakistan. Throughout the years of their independence India and Pakistan were engaged in conflicts which displayed all the profound hatreds of a civil war. Minor disputes between the two countries were often solved primarily because the attempt was made to solve them but there always remained the problem of Kashmir. In spite of Nehru's desire to limit defence expenditure, the level of spending constantly increased because of the fear of an attack by Pakistan. That fear compounded when Pakistan itself, fearing an attack by India, joined western treaty organizations directed ostensibly against the Soviet Union. Membership gave Pakistan American weapons on a scale that it could not have afforded otherwise. Constant tension on the frontiers, tension which finally exploded into war the year after Nehru's death, allowed Pakistan to dominate strategic thinking. The borders with Pakistan were heavily patrolled. Military training, weapons systems, intelligence, were all responsive to a possible Indo-Pakistan clash to the detriment of other sensitive areas. The emotional furnace of Kashmir seemed to burn up reason and common sense among Indian decision-makers.

After the tribal invasion of Kashmir in 1947 had been stopped only to be followed by further fighting, Nehru agreed in effect to hold a 'fair and impartial plebiscite' to decide the future of the state. The Indian delegate at the United Nations told the Security Council in 1948 that the accession of Kashmir to India was not irrevocable and that after the emergency was over the people of Kashmir would be free to ratify the accession, or accede to Pakistan or even to go independent if they so wished. After making this promise India refused to go ahead with the holding of a plebiscite, using legalistic and other excuses. As time went by there piled up a vast monolith of lawyers' argument the only purpose of which appeared to be to hide the fear that if a plebiscite was held it would go against India.

Nehru's motives in the Kashmir affair remain opaque. Why

did he promise a plebiscite? Why was the issue taken to the United Nations and the offer repeated? What changed his mind about the advisability of holding a plebiscite at all? It seems clear that the initiative both for the holding of a plebiscite and referring Kashmir to the United Nations came from Mountbatten – an example of his influence at the time. After Mountbatten's departure Nehru's attitude changed. The private conclusion of the first U.N. Commission for Kashmir that a plebiscite would favour Pakistan was known to Nehru and supported by intelligence reports. Had the offer to hold a plebiscite been conditional on the result favouring India? It would seem that the commitment was made without adequate thought and regretted afterwards.

To the legalistic arguments others were added. India was a secular state. One loss of territory, now Pakistan, had been accepted – on religious grounds – in order to achieve independence. But if India gave up its claim to Kashmir it would suggest that citizenship was a matter of religion and leave the way open to Hindu communalists to reinforce their claim that Indian Muslims were really Pakistanis in disguise. This rationale seems to express Nehru's dominant feeling over Kashmir. There is no other adequate explanation for his refusal until a few weeks before his death to take any meaningful initiative in relations with Pakistan. It permitted him to accept a state government in Indian-held Kashmir which was virtually a dictatorship of the corrupt. It permitted him to give credence to those who insisted that Pakistan was India's only real enemy. Kashmir also became something of a touchstone in India's relations with other countries.

Kashmir did not affect Nehru's startling decision to allow India to remain in the Commonwealth after becoming a republic in 1950. In staying in the Commonwealth and by doing so changing its nature, Nehru denied his past attitude but confirmed his present belief that India would lose by leaving. Keeping the connexion did no harm; on the contrary it made both political and economic sense. Most of India's equipment and machinery was British; India's sterling balances were in London and the country's economy was geared to sterling. The

Commonwealth also offered a world stage for Nehru himself. For all this India need give little or nothing in return.

Nehru's decision was not greeted with overwhelming enthusiasm in India but was accepted when it became clear there were no obligations, no restriction on Indian actions and no threat to Indian interests. Criticism of Britain and other members of the Commonwealth was often virulent and there were frequent calls for India to leave the Commonwealth. These were particularly strong after the Suez affair of 1956 but Nehru firmly resisted any step that might lead to a break. Because of his obvious attachment to the Commonwealth connexion, Nehru's defence of it was always endorsed by both the parliamentary party and Congress. There was never any deep commitment among articulate Indians to the Commonwealth as such but there was recognition of the fact that it somehow amplified India's voice in the world. That Britain's apparently pro-Pakistan stance was not allowed to alter India's position in the Commonwealth was also an indication that Nehru understood Britain's declining authority in the world. The same criteria could hardly be applied to the United States. American military aid to Pakistan and a generally critical attitude on Kashmir reinforced Nehru's feeling about the United States. Nehru's freedom of action in foreign policy was at its height during the years 1952 to 1958, years which coincided with the McCarthy era in domestic American politics and the domination in external relations of John Foster Dulles. This combination of hysteria at home and neo-imperialism abroad led to considerable friction between the two countries. In addition there was a complete lack of sympathy between Nehru and Dulles. In part this was due to their similarities. Both took a darkly moralistic view of the world, though Nehru pretended to conceal it while Dulles did not. Where Nehru saw Pakistan as the embodiment of evil, Dulles saw the Soviet Union. American support of Pakistan could only be anti-Indian to Nehru. Nehru's frequent apologies for Russia, in Dulles's view made Nehru at least a crypto-communist.

Nehru attacked the United States for having a blinkered view of the world but his own attitude to Kashmir would not permit him to accept that it was totally blinkered. Dulles both in private and in public tried to assure Nehru that the United State was not anti-Indian on the question of Kashmir. In 1956 he said that the position the United States had taken on Kashmir was that 'it wanted to see a peaceful settlement'. Further Dulles assured Nehru that on the matter of military aid to Pakistan, 'there can be every confidence on the part of India that there will be no use of these armaments in any aggressive way against India. Pakistan knows that if that should happen, there will be a quick ending of its good relations with the United States, and that under the United Nations Charter the U.S.A. would support India if she became a victim of armed aggression.' Unfortunately Dulles followed up a short time later with what appeared to be an endorsement of Portugal's right to its Indian colonial territory of Goa.

The inconsistency Nehru saw in Dulles's statements, sometimes assuring, sometimes reactionary, sometimes attacking colonialism, sometimes apparently supporting it, undermined faith even when the two countries agreed, as they did over the Suez affair of 1956. But from Nehru's point of view, and that was the one that fundamentally counted, two factors dominated his attitude towards the United States: the Cold War which threatened the peace Nehru was convinced was necessary to the social and economic revolution he hoped for in India and the United States' initial unwillingness to contribute financial aid. There was also the not unimportant factor of personal pique. Nehru's first visit to America in 1949 had not been a success. He believed he had been patronized and did not like it.

Nehru did very little to soothe American fears. Though on the outbreak of the Korean war in 1950 Nehru condemned North Korean aggression, after the United States had ignored his advice not to cross the Yalu River he refused to name China as an aggressor. This unwillingness to condemn communism tended, for the Americans, to diminish Nehru's very real contribution to the bringing about of peace. Nehru also appeared to encourage his representatives at the United Nations, and in particular, Krishna Menon, to take a distinctly anti-American line on many issues. The need for American aid, did, however, modify Nehru's own statements. At the end of 1956 and after the Suez affair in which India and the United States had found themselves on the same side, Nehru visited America again. His speeches were more than conciliatory. He reminded an American audience that India could 'never forget that in the days of our struggle for freedom we received from [the U.S.A.] a full measure of sympathy and support'. India and America were alike, he said, in their dedication to democracy. 'We wish to learn from you and we plead for your friendship, cooperation and sympathy in the great task we have undertaken in our country.'

Even though relations between India and the United States improved after the Americans began to think that India might be built up into a countervailing force to communist China, Nehru's belief remained fixed. In part this was still due to Kashmir. The Soviet Union was publicly and vocally on India's side, the U.S.A. was not. But essentially the rigidity of Nehru's foreign policy reflected the lack of flexibility in Nehru's own mind. The more he became aware of the failures of his domestic policies the more he clung to the principles which he believed had created his position as a world statesman. It was only after these were also proved a failure by the Chinese invasion of the north-east frontier areas in 1962 that he was compelled to admit that he had been living 'in an artificial atmosphere of our own creating'.

One contribution to that 'artificial atmosphere' was the belief fostered by Nehru and welcomed by many that India was the leader of that 'third world' which came into being as more and more of the former colonial dependencies of Britain and other European countries achieved freedom. Though Nehru frequently denied any desire for leadership he consciously worked for it. The Asian Relations Conference held in Delhi on the eve of independence was the first move. Two years later an emergency conference was called to bring pressure upon the Dutch and the U.N. in order to ease Indonesian independence. After this conference Nehru's enthusiasm for conferences declined partly because he believed that the western empires were breaking up of their own accord but also because he did not wish to frighten the west by the formation of an overtly anti-western bloc.

Though India was continually active in the anti-colonial lobbies of the U.N. where rhetoric was a substitute for action, Nehru remained comparatively quiet until after the enunciation of the famous principles of *Panchsheel* in April 1954. A conference of India's immediate neighbours met in Colombo in the same month but the initiative did not come from Nehru. Nevertheless Nehru was naturally the most significant figure and out of the Colombo meeting emerged the seeds of another conference, that held at Bandung in Indonesia in April 1955.

The meeting of twenty-nine 'Afro-Asian' nations at Bandung produced no organization and nothing of practical value. Nehru saw it primarily as a gesture, a thumbing of the nose, almost, to the western world. 'Bandung,' he said in the Indian parliament after the conference, 'proclaimed the political emergence in world affairs of over half the world's population. . . . It would be a misreading of history to regard Bandung as though it was an isolated occurrence and not part of a great movement of human history.'[1]

Nehru had hoped to make the conference a stage for the principles of *Panchsheel*. In this with the aid of the Chinese Prime Minister Chou En-lai, he succeeded. During the six years that separated the 'first Bandung' from the 'second Bandung' held at Belgrade in 1961, non-alignment and peaceful coexistence became the publicly stated policies of twenty-four countries and had received the accolade of the Soviet Union and of the western powers.

With the universal acceptance of his ideas, Nehru consciously attempted to assert leadership. He was constantly exhorting new nations. His representatives at the U.N. were inclined to treat new Afro-Asian members as children in need of a strong hand. Nehru's growing acceptance by the great powers and his positive ant-colonialist stand won him the respect of the newly independent countries of Asia and Africa, gratified that one of themselves could speak on terms of equality with the

1. For a realistic account of Bandung, and of non-alignment, see G. H. Jansen, *Afro-Asia and Non-Alignment*, Faber, 1966.

super-powers. Unfortunately Nehru took this respect to mean the acceptance of Indian leadership and Indian tutelage. He believed that the interests of former colonial territories were identical when in fact they were, not infrequently, competitive. He convinced himself that out of the anti-colonial struggle had emerged a community of suffering which transcended national divisions. This was a major error.

Nehru did not realize that India had come to occupy a special place in the world which defied definition. The role Nehru was so successfully playing in world affairs was in fact moving India into isolation. This isolation ironically enough was increased by the changing attitude of the United States and the Soviet Union towards non-alignment. Nehru consciously claimed for India – and himself played – a special role in international affairs. Acceptence of this by the two super-powers eroded any implied Indian claim to represent the revolutionary mood of newly emerging nations. The leaders of these nations, resenting Nehru's often hectoring tone of superiority, began to challenge his leadership, though they did not do so strongly. Some, like President Sukarno of Indonesia, privately, though not too privately, expressed the hope that one day Nehru would suffer a setback. When it came at the end of 1962, and Nehru in the face of Chinese aggression asked for the first time for support and sympathy for India, the non-aligned rallied reluctantly, conditionally or not at all.

Chapter 19
The Tarnishing Image

The prospects facing Nehru and Congress as India moved towards its third general election due to be held in January 1962 were not particularly reassuring. The failures of the Second Five-Year Plan were about to be reflected in the more limited aims of the Third. Foreign exchange crises, food shortages, a serious underestimate of population growth had contributed to the erosion of hope and expectation. So too had the inability of the central government to enforce progressive social legislation. The threat to Congress as the dominant party lay partly in general dissatisfaction but also more directly in what Indians were now calling 'fissiparous tendencies'. Agitation for the creation of more linguistic states continued. There was serious trouble in the south once again over the matter of the national language. All this had encouraged the opposition parties, most of all those of the right, to become more vocal in their criticism of Congress.

In August 1959 a nationwide conservative party, the Swatantra or Freedom Party, was formed. It pledged itself to private enterprise, as its statement of objects made clear: 'We are of the opinion that social justice and welfare can be reached more certainly and properly in other ways than through techniques of so-called socialism . . .' The sponsors of the party were a mixed lot. At their head was C. Rajagopalachari, still intellectually vigorous in his eighties, some distinguished businessmen, and Professor N. G. Range, whose entire political life had been associated with peasant movements and agrarian reform. The rest of the leading party members included maharajas, dispossessed landowners, retired civil servants and disgruntled politicians from other parties.

Nehru was openly scornful but the significance of the new party lay in the fact that it was the first *non-communal* party of the right and its appeal was not to religion or community but to a reasonably defined economic group – the small capitalist, the peasant proprietor and the professional man. The main effect of the formation of the Swatantra Party was upon the right wing of Congress which became more critical of Congress policies and, therefore, of Nehru, though their disapproval remained muted, until the border dispute with China gave critics of Nehru the courage to attack him directly. In fact the failure of Nehru's policy towards China opened the door to opponents of his domestic policies. Where previously critics inside Congress had been content to try to pervert those policies to their own advantage – and had done so with some success – they now felt strong enough to question the policies themselves. Under the guise of patriotism they felt sure of widespread support in parliament and among the articulate political class which in India makes up 'public opinion'. All the dislike of Nehru, of his charisma, his claim to superiority, his indispensability, his concept of social and economic revolution, which had remained latent inside Congress, was slowly released as the border dispute moved to its culmination in the disasters of November 1962.

Though Nehru's executive authority was constantly resisted, except in the area of foreign affairs, his *moral* authority had never been seriously challenged. From the middle of 1959, however, the foundations of that authority were steadily undermined. The dispute with China over the Himalayan frontiers came to dominate Indian political life and the behaviour of both Nehru and Congress was almost exclusively responsive to its impact. That impact was compounded by the fact that the growth of conflict between India and China had been deliberately concealed by Nehru behind the pretence of *Panchsheel*. Three events in 1959 combined to rip aside the pretence and to propel India and China along a collision course which was to end in the humiliation of India and of Nehru.[1] In March the Dalai Lama fled from Tibet to political asylum in India. In

1. Only the most significant incidents in the history of Sino-Indian relations up to and including the Chinese invasion of the North East Frontier Agency in October 1962 are detailed in the following pages. For an exhaustive and revealing study see Neville Maxwell, *India's China War*, Cape, 1970.

August there was a clash between Indian and Chinese patrols at Longju on the north-east frontier and in October a more serious incident at the other end of the border at the Kongka Pass.

With independence India inherited not only the imperial borders left untouched by partition but their ambiguities as well. The British had been constantly preoccupied with a possible Russian threat to the northern frontier and built what was in effect a chain of protectorates, Nepal, Sikkim, Bhutan, and had encouraged Tibet in its claim to independence from China, as a buffer against an invasion. There had been many disputes over the exact position of the frontier at various places and times but lines had been drawn on maps and as far as the British were concerned those marked the frontiers even if there had been no agreement among the parties nor any demarcation on the ground. This attitude was reasonable when India, as part of the British empire, had been strong and China weak. By 1950, however, the situation had been reversed. Independent India was weak while China, revitalized by the communist success over Chiang Kai-shek, was strong. India, which had continued British policy on the northern frontiers now found itself with competition in what for many years had been an area of Indian influence.

The continuance of British policy in Tibet by independent India had been condemned by the Chinese communists before they achieved power. Nehru had been personally accused of harbouring 'imperialist designs for the annexation of Tibet'. Within a few weeks of the establishment of the People's Republic of China in October 1949, the new Government announced that the People's Liberation Army would shortly march into Tibet. India protested and received a sharp reply; but there was very little that India could do. Military intervention to protect Tibet was out of the question. By far the most sensible policy was to give up the imperial legacy, now outmoded, in favour of friendship between India and China. In pursuit of this, India discouraged the Dalai Lama from fleeing to India and blocked his appeal to the United Nations in November 1950, a month after the 'liberation'.

The Chinese presence in Tibet was not welcomed in India, particularly by right-wing elements both inside and outside Congress. For Congress opinion Patel was, as always, the spokesman. In November 1950 he wrote Nehru a long letter criticizing the Prime Minister's policy on Tibet and warning him that the Chinese were a potential enemy. Patel called for a total reappraisal of policy, including 'if necessary, reconsideration of our retrenchment plans for the army'. What reply, if any, was made to this letter has not been made public, but just over a month later Patel was dead. Without him there was no effective anti-Nehru voice. Nehru continued his policy of friendship towards China but he did order that the frontier areas in the north-east which, under the British, had never been fully administered now should be. This move, which included the ejection of Tibetan officials from Tawang, meant that the Indian Government now claimed actually to rule up to a frontier inherited from the British which had never been accepted by China. In fact the convention which had arrived at this frontier (known as the McMahon Line) in 1913 had been repudiated by the Chinese Government a year later. Nehru made it quite clear in parliament that the Government considered the frontier clearly fixed by the convention. As for the western end of the frontier in Ladakh that was 'defined by long usage and custom'.

This having been said, it seems that Nehru decided that the boundary question would never be first raised by India. Nor indeed was it brought up by China except for a statement in September 1951 that there was no dispute over territory between the two countries. When it came to negotiating away the Indian Government's treaty rights in Tibet no mention was made of the borders. The 1954 agreement, which was prefaced by the statement of *Panchsheel*, led to the withdrawal of Indian garrisons from Tibet, reduced the Indian mission at Lhasa to a consulate-general and symbolized the acceptance by India that Tibet was irrevocably a part of China. In exchange India got China's endorsement of *Panchsheel*. If that seemed an extremely unfair exchange, two factors correct the balance. The sustenance of India's quasi-imperial position in Tibet was quite out of the question and it was best to give it up quickly and quietly. The other factor, it has been suggested, lies in the first of the *Panchsheel* principles: mutual respect for each other's territorial integrity and sovereignty. If India could occupy territory up to the claimed frontiers *before* China raised the subject, then China would be bound by *Panchsheel* to accept those frontiers as non-negotiable. This view is supported by a memorandum from Nehru circulated to the ministers concerned in July 1954, two months after the completion of the agreement with China. In it Nehru described the agreement as a new starting-point in India's relations with China and that as a consequence the northern frontier should be considered firm and definite and not open to discussion. Nehru then directed that check posts should be set up along the entire frontier and in particular at such places over which there might be a dispute.

This rigid instruction must have seemed reasonable at the time. There had been no objection from Peking over the McMahon Line or the Indian occupation of Tawang and it was not unreasonable to assume that the Line was acceptable to the Chinese. At least the Line itself was drawn on a map, but at the western end of the frontier no such line existed. The area had never been properly surveyed and even the British had been unable to agree among themselves exactly where the frontier actually lay. It was unfortunate that India chose those lines which rendered some future dispute with China unavoidable especially as once having published them on new maps these lines *were* the frontier and following Nehru's directive could not be negotiated with anybody.

As the frontier posts were set up there were complaints from China that India was violating Chinese territory in the central sector of the border. India claimed that the areas were Indian. Diplomatic exchanges on the subject went on throughout the late 1950s but India was totally rigid – what had been decided in Delhi was the frontier and China must accept it. The circumstances were now assembled for a genuine clash. All that was needed was some Chinese move which could be claimed by India to be a flagrant violation of its territorial rights. It was to come in a bleak and desolate area on the western end of the border, known as the Aksai Chin. This was considered to be part of India – though on rather doubtful premises – but because of the difficulty of access frontier posts had not been set up there by 1958. Access from the Chinese side, on the other hand, was comparatively easy and in 1950 Chinese troops from Sinkiang had entered western Tibet by that route. In 1956 the Chinese began to construct a road across the Aksai Chin which on their maps was shown as part of China. From their point of view there was no dispute over the territory. British maps had never shown more than a boundary marked 'un-determined' and though the Indian Government had publicly claimed the McMahon Line as the boundary in the north-east as early as 1951 it had made no such precise claim in the western sector, except on a map published late in 1954 which was either overlooked or ignored by the Chinese. No *formal* Indian claim was made until 1958. In fact the Indian Government was not aware of Chinese activity in the Aksai Chin until it became suspicious in 1957 after it was announced in Peking that a road between Sinkiang and western Tibet had been finished. As the location of the road had been left extremely vague by the Chinese it was decided that Indian patrols should penetrate the Aksai Chin in order to determine whether the road violated territory claimed by India.

News of the border incidents and of Nehru's suspicions about the Aksai Chin road had been concealed not only from the public but from members of the Indian cabinet. After Patel's death, Nehru became highly secretive particularly over foreign affairs and other members of the cabinet exercising secrecy over their own responsibilities did not press Nehru for information. Foreign policy was exclusively the concern of Nehru and a few top officials of the Ministry of External Affairs. Even they were often kept in the dark when ambassadors and others reported to Nehru directly through the Prime Minister's secretariat.

Nehru visited China in 1954 and came back impressed by the communist achievement there. The visit to India of the Chinese Prime Minister Chou En-lai in 1956 was used to reiterate Sino-Indian friendship and the principles of *Panchsheel* and wherever Chou went he was greeted by cheering crowds. It seems highly probable that if the question of the frontiers had been discussed between the two Prime Ministers at this time, a settlement could have been arrived at. Though Chou mentioned the McMahon Line during talks he did not clearly indicate what China wanted – a renegotiation not of the line itself but of the imperialist treaty which had established it. The western sector was not mentioned by either party.

This reticence lasted until the discovery by India of the road through the Aksai Chin. India protested to Peking in October 1958. From the diplomatic exchanges which followed it is clear that though in most sectors the Chinese were prepared to accept existing boundaries they insisted on doing so through new treaties free from 'imperialist' overtones. This was understood in Delhi to mask a desire to alter the actual boundaries and an indication of China's aggressive intentions. The euphoria of Sino-Indian friendship began to evaporate. In public the smile of *Panchsheel*, like that of the Cheshire Cat, remained after the substance had disappeared, but not for long. Nehru, in correspondence with Chou, claimed that as the boundaries were clearly set there was nothing to negotiate about. In accepting a suggestion from Chou that until agreement was reached the status quo should be maintained, Nehru in highly ambiguous language actually demanded that China should vacate any territory that it had occupied recently. After this correspondence Nehru was committed to the line that before any discussions took place the position as India said it was must be not only accepted but actually recreated on the spot. When this commitment was made public Nehru was to be left without any room for manoeuvre.

In March 1959 a tribal rebellion which had begun in the south-eastern regions of Tibet three years earlier spread to the central and southern areas and the Dalai Lama came out in support of the rebels, proclaiming Tibet independent. The Chinese however moved so quickly that the Dalai Lama was forced to flee from Lhasa arriving on Indian territory on

31 March. This sensational event could not have been concealed by the Indian Government even if it had wanted to. There were anti-Chinese demonstrations in many Indian cities, including one in Bombay in April during which a portrait of the Chinese leader Mao Tse-tung was pelted with eggs and tomatoes. The arrival of the Dalai Lama in India revived the old criticisms of the Government's policy. Nehru tried to quiet public opinion in India while behaving diplomatically towards the Chinese. This satisfied no one. The Chinese were offended by India's reception of the Dalai Lama. Indian critics of the Government accused Nehru of appeasing the Chinese. While the Indian Government publicity media released provocative statements by the Dalai Lama, the Chinese attacked Nehru for what they described as 'walking in the footsteps of the British imperialists and harbouring expansionist ambitions towards Tibet'. In this atmosphere of mutual suspicion, any border incident was liable to cause trouble.

What was probably an accidental clash between border patrols at Longju on the McMahon Line on 25 August 1959 was not concealed by the Government and was condemned in parliament and in the press as an act of aggression. The Indian protest to Peking used the words 'deliberate aggression'. By the time a second clash took place in October in the western sector at the Kongka Pass, Indian public opinion was ready to be roused to the point of bellicosity. Ever since the Longju incident Indian newspapers had carried rumours of Chinese troop concentrations on the McMahon Line and many questions were asked in parliament. Three days after the Longju clash Nehru was attacked for misleading members about the border situation. News of the existence of the Aksai Chin road had also leaked out and members demanded a statement from the Prime Minister. Nehru admitted that such a road did exist. Under further pressure he revealed his thinking on the border question. Much of what he said was vague and misleading but he did make clear that though there was no doubt about the actual boundary in the north-east, that in Ladakh and particularly the Aksai Chin was not so certain. There was, Nehru said, genuine confusion about which country owned the territory the road passed through. This was very different to what was then being said to Peking: the Aksai Chin was and always had been part of India. But this discrepancy was eliminated after investigations made in London in November 1959 by the then head of the historical division of the Ministry of External Affairs, Dr Gopal, convinced Nehru that India's claim to the Aksai Chin was better than China's.

Nehru was now sharing information with members of the cabinet foreign affairs committee and there appears to have been some uneasiness among them about the validity of Nehru's view, though this was not expressed to the Prime Minister. It was unlikely that Nehru would have changed his opinion if it had been, for his pride had been sharpened by what he took to be Chinese arrogance and a desire to bully him. His public statements became a mixture of almost jingoistic nationalism – the Chinese were claiming the Himalayas, 'the crown of India' and a part of her 'culture and her veins' – and reminders that India must remember the Gandhian way of peace and tolerance. It is impossible to avoid the impression from these speeches that Nehru felt that his prestige was at stake and that Chinese actions were part of a deliberate attempt to reduce his status in the world. This attitude was to blind him to any reasonableness in the Chinese case and to take any suggestion from Peking that the frontiers should be the subject of discussion as a prelude to sweeping Chinese claims to Indian territory.

As the Sino-Indian dispute was now public knowledge not only in India but also outside, and was being given the widest publicity in newspapers throughout the world, Nehru decided to publish official correspondence with Peking almost as soon as it was delivered. In effect these communications became primarily propaganda directed at public opinion in India and at the international political community. For the latter there was a mass of historical and quasi-historical argument; for the former, there was in addition an appeal to the doubtful but emotive sources of Hindu literature and in particular to the *Mahabharata*, the *Ramayana* and the *Upanishads*. The myths and legends of Hinduism were mobilized to justify the alignment of the Himalayan frontiers, a device which appealed to

Indians but naturally irritated the Chinese. Nehru in his public utterances continually referred to the mystic significance of the Himalayas in Indian thought as if it was a legal argument. The religious overtones of his speeches were either demagogic in intent – if true a sad decline in Nehru's standards – or they reflected genuinely held feelings. In that case they represent another stage in the shift of Nehru the secularist towards a Hindu view of the world.

Despite the somewhat aggressive tone of Indian diplomatic communications, the Government was much less so in practice. After the incident on the Kongka Pass in which there were a number of Indian (and Chinese) casualties, Nehru's speeches were full of appeals for calm and caution. These merely inflamed public opinion. There were attacks on Nehru's leadership and calls for the abandonment of non-alignment, for rearmament and for the joining of military pacts. In reply Nehru claimed that the Indian armed forces were in excellent condition and perfectly capable of defending the northern borders. This was in fact untrue but Nehru appears to have believed it. After the Kongka Pass incident he was already considering the probability that India would have to use armed force to expel the Chinese. Proof of this was contained in a memorandum sent to Indian ambassadors in key capitals and leaked by one of them to the *New York Times*, which published a summary on 12 November 1959. Though Nehru continued to deplore the use of force, he conveyed the impression that its use was probable and that India was capable of using it decisively. Coupled with the publication in the form of White Papers of the story of past humiliations and the instant disclosure of diplomatic correspondence Nehru's commitment amounted to a surrender of that flexibility which a potentially explosive situation demanded. Nehru became the captive not only of parliament but of the articulate political élite. Any apparent concession to China, however sensible, would inevitably be condemned as appeasement, if not as treason.

This crippling restriction on the Government's freedom of action was not clear at the time. For the Indian and the international audience Nehru appeared to be highly flexible. Against opposition he repeated again and again that he was prepared to negotiate, to meet anybody for talks. At the same time he confused the issue by maintaining that India's borders were not negotiable. The contradiction, though recognized, was almost entirely ignored, especially outside India where opinion gradually hardened in favour of Nehru and the Indian case. Because much of the world was prepared – and even anxious – to think the worst of China, the ambiguity of Nehru's words was pushed aside so that Indians came to believe that not only was right and justice on their side but the mass of international opinion as well.

By the end of 1959 the diplomatic front was exhausted. Suggestions by Chou En-lai that he should visit Delhi for talks had been rebuffed. The frontiers themselves were quiet but Indian public opinion was not and there were demands that the Indian army should expel the Chinese from the Aksai Chin before lack of action was taken to mean that the Indian Government acquiesced to Chinese aggression. This was resisted by Nehru but unless he could take some *diplomatic* initiative there would be no alternative to ejecting the Chinese by force. Nehru still preferred to talk even if talking did not mean negotiating. That force should never be preferred to the reasonable discussion of outstanding problems between nations was the basis of Nehru's theology of foreign affairs.

That theology, after years in which it had been assumed by both the United States and the Soviet Union to be essentially heretical, had by the end of 1959 become respectable. The Cold War seemed to be ending with the visit of the Soviet Prime Minister Khrushchev to the United States. For the melting of the ice Nehru publicly claimed some of the credit and quoted it as a proof that his foreign policy was correct and that India had become an example for others to follow. The claim was just and had been reinforced through visits to India by the President and Prime Minister of the Soviet Union and the President of the United States. Praise of India by the leaders of the two countries had gone considerably further than the requirements of politeness. As for India's dispute with China – details of which had been made known to both the Soviet and American Governments by Nehru – that too had done nothing to harm India's image. On the contrary – at least in the case of the United States. There the fact that India had dropped its uncritical friendliness for China was taken as a sign that Nehru was not after all a communist. Recognition of this was to lead to an immense increase in American aid. As for the Soviet attitude, India had some cause for apprehension. The Soviet Union and China were two great fraternal communist countries. In fact, though it was not then known to the outside world, the quarrel between China and the Soviet Union which later became open and virulent had reached a serious stage. This accounts for the apparently neutral but actually pro-Indian stance initially taken by the Soviet Union on the border dispute. The Soviet attitude was very welcome to Nehru who still believed that the Russians were in a position to exert influence in Peking. Under these circumstances the advice given to Nehru by the Russians to negotiate with Peking became almost mandatory. It was also essential, to Nehru at least, that India must not appear to reject the course constantly advocated to other countries, that they should try and settle disputes by negotiation. A decision was therefore made to invite Chou to Delhi. The invitation was received in Peking on 12 February 1960.

For some reason this letter was kept secret for four days after its delivery and Nehru even gave the impression that such a meeting would not be worthwhile. Naturally when the invitation was revealed there was an outcry in India but some of it was stilled when Nehru insisted that India's frontiers were not negotiable. Many politicians believed that Nehru might actually negotiate a settlement with Chou but they had really nothing to fear. The Chinese were still ready for a reasonable settlement which would give them the Aksai Chin but Nehru was not. Even though the frontier was not delimited, as far as Nehru was concerned the Chinese had crossed it and were in illegal possession of Indian territory. The general reasonableness of Chou's approach and the desire of the Chinese to defuse a potentially dangerous situation were concealed behind a smokescreen of emotive phrases from Nehru after the Chinese Prime Minister had departed empty-handed. The problem then facing the Indian Government was – what next?

Unfortunately Nehru and his advisers came to the conclusion that there was only one course open to them – to press forward an Indian military presence in the western sector. It was assumed, despite Chinese warnings to the contrary, that such a forward movement would not be resisted by the Chinese. The possibility of war was constantly in the mouths of politicians, both Congress and opposition, some of whom even took up Nehru's theme of the early 1940s that India would be renewed by suffering. Nehru himself did not repeat this callous hope. He condemned war as terrible and warned the bellicose that conflict between India and China would set off a third world war. But now caught by the rising tide of patriotic emotion Nehru was compelled to balance these remarks with the shibboleths of national pride.

Having decided on a forward movement, the Government seemed to think that it could be left to the army to carry out, with all the attendant but discounted dangers of a border clash with a distinctly more powerful neighbour. The army however was not, in spite of Nehru's assurance to parliament, in good fighting condition. The defence budget had for years been kept as low as possible, non-alignment had inhibited the acceptance of military aid from abroad, and Indian military thinking had been predicated on the belief that the only enemy facing India was Pakistan. The army had been stretched to supply troops against the Naga tribal rising in the north-east which had begun in 1956. The frontier incidents of 1959 had resulted in the movement of troops into the border areas though this was extremely slow partly because the army was ill-equipped for expansion but also because of the absence of roads. The army leaders were fully aware of the deficiencies and were constantly pressing the Defence Minister, at this time Krishna Menon, for more equipment and money. This was resisted on one set of political grounds – ingrained Gandhian dislike for the military and the need to conserve funds for economic development – while on another – the forward movement on the borders – the

army was being called on to take ever widening security responsibilities.

This state of affairs caused considerable dissatisfaction in the
army. Just after the Longju incident in August 1959 the then
Chief of the Army Staff, General Thimayya had submitted his
resignation. Fearing that it might be used further to criticize
the Government and in particular the Defence Minister, who
were already under heavy attack for neglecting border defence,
Nehru persuaded Thimayya to withdraw his resignation, but
news of it leaked out. Nehru pretended that the issue had been
trivial and implied that it had been a question of conflict with
the civil power. Thimayya was publicly humiliated while Nehru
took the opportunity to praise Menon's work at the Defence
Ministry, so in effect defending himself. This episode was
important because it proved to the army that it was unwise to
go against Menon and his favourites among the senior officers,
one of whom, Lieutenant-General B. M. Kaul, was not only
on extremely good terms with Nehru, a distant relative, but was
being groomed by Krishna Menon for the highest army command. Kaul was to play a disastrous role in the débâcle of
1962. In fact by the beginning of 1960 the formula for catas-
trophe was established. First there was Nehru's commitment
to the non-negotiability of frontiers made immutable by the
nationalist pride of the articulate political class. Second, the
belief that China would not attack India. Third, that if it did
the Indian army was capable of victory and, fourth, the penetration of the higher echelons of military command by officers
politically orientated and militarily inefficient. By the middle
of 1961 the civilian belief that the forward movement of troops
was merely an extension of a diplomatic ploy was unquestioned
by army leaders and *military* criticism of the Government's
policy had dissolved in sycophancy.

The question of the northern borders and relations with
China had by the end of 1961 come to dominate the political
scene to such an extent that it seemed to Congress leaders that
the Government's handling of border affairs might become the
central issue in the coming elections. Criticism of the Govern-

ment's domestic policies would undoubtedly be linked with its failure to settle the border question by ejecting the Chinese from the sacred soil of India. Patriotic ardour allied with the genuine grievances of the majority of the people might make an irresistible combination. It seemed therefore to certain Congress leaders that some sort of a diversion was required. An ideal subject was available and one which would satisfy a variety of emotions. That subject was the Portuguese colonial enclave of Goa.

When the British left the sub-continent in 1947 two other colonial powers remained on Indian soil: the French at Pondicherry near Madras and the Portuguese at Goa, some 200 miles south of Bombay. The French departed in 1954 but the Portuguese stayed on. Some four centuries of Portuguese rule had given Goa a character very different from the India which adjoined it. Over half the population was of the Catholic faith. The standard of living was higher than that in India and though there was no self-government the administration was both mild and more efficient than that of India. There was little discontent with Portuguese rule except among political exiles in Bombay. Though they had been given Indian Government support they had been unable to arouse any substantial demand among Goans for union with India. In 1955 an attempt was made to occupy Goa by the sort of non-violent methods which some Indians still believed had disposed of the British. The numbers crossing the frontier were too large for the small Portuguese police force to arrest so they opened fire. A number of the demonstrators were killed and many wounded. Naturally there was considerable reaction in India and especially in Bombay but the Indian Government did no more than break off diplomatic relations with Portugal and the anger died down. On the whole, although there was some resentment over the continuing Portuguese presence in Goa, it was only there when people were reminded of it.

Autumn 1961 seemed the right time for such a reminder. A settlement of the Goa problem, especially a *military* settlement, offered a chance for the Government to disprove opposition allegations that either the Government was frightened to back up its bellicosity against the Chinese with force or the Indian army was not in a fit state to eject the Chinese – or both. Further, the ending of an 'imperialist affront' like Goa would quieten criticism abroad that India was not really committed to the cause of anti-colonialism. Doubts about that commitment were forcibly expressed by delegates to an Afro-Asian seminar on Portuguese colonialism held in Delhi in August 1961. A reminder that India was also committed to the settlement of disputes by peaceful means was not well received. Nehru took the hint and told a public meeting in Bombay that 'the time has come for us to consider afresh what method should be adopted to free Goa from Portuguese rule'.

While Nehru was away on a trip which included visits to Washington – where he failed to impress President Kennedy – the U.N., Belgrade and Moscow, the Government began a propaganda campaign against the Portuguese in Goa. Ironically enough, while at the U.N. Nehru had proposed a year devoted to peaceful cooperation. Back in India certain persons – among them the Defence Minister, Krishna Menon, General Kaul and senior members of the Intelligence Bureau – were planning an operation against Goa. Goan freedom fighters who had risen in rebellion, it was alleged, were being massacred by the Portuguese. An Indian passenger ship had been fired on by Portuguese shore batteries. Portuguese troops were massing on the border with India, armed with the very latest weapons supplied by Portugal's allies in the North Atlantic Treaty Organization. All these pieces of 'news' were given banner headlines in the Indian press. Obviously inspired articles on the terrors of the Inquisition in Goa in the sixteenth and seventeenth centuries also appeared and the rumour was put about that the Portuguese were intriguing with Pakistan. All these stories except some of the historical information on the Inquisition were either totally untrue or deliberately exaggerated. The 'passenger ship' was actually a small country craft sailing boat which had ignored warnings that it was in Portuguese territorial waters. Goa was as sleepy and peaceful as usual, though All-India Radio horrified its listeners with tales of blood running in the streets. As for Portuguese troops 'massing', there were only 2,500 in the whole colony. As for NATO arms which were alleged to include a cruiser there may have been some hand weapons but the 'cruiser' was an ancient frigate almost too rusted to take to sea.

On his return to India Nehru seems to have accepted, as did most Indians, the propaganda as fact. His first speeches were so ambiguous as to defy definition but it was at least clear that he admitted that there was a crisis and that if Portugal did not give up Goa, then a peaceful solution was not possible. Diplomatic pressure from abroad and offers of mediation were refused. A suggestion that U.N. observers be sent to the borders was rejected. At the beginning of December large numbers of Indian troops were moved to the frontier with Goa. With a full Indian division 'massing' on the frontier there were naturally incidents. In an attempt to avoid them, the Portuguese pulled back their guards from the border. While all this was going on, Nehru, though retailing atrocity stories to foreign diplomats, continued to emphasize that India was still committed to peaceful solutions. But the situation was out of his control. Others had set up a pattern of events, now he was enmeshed in it. However much he might wriggle he had allowed himself to be taken to a position where there was only one choice to be made. However he was not prepared to make the final decision himself. On 17 December the American ambassador who had been trying to persuade the Prime Minister not to invade Goa was so eloquent that Nehru called Krishna Menon at 10 p.m. and told him that orders for the movement of troops into Goa should be countermanded. Menon informed the Prime Minister that they were already on their way. According to General Kaul in his published apologia, the invasion had been twice postponed and finally fixed for midnight on that day. However the troops were not across the border when Menon assured Nehru that they were.

A few hours later at 2 a.m. on 18 December Indian forces did cross the Goa border and were met with no opposition. The Indian air force bombed the only airfield on which there were no military aircraft. The Indian navy shelled the Portuguese 'cruiser'. The air force and navy action was totally unnecessary and seems to have been authorized only on the principle that the invasion should not be left, for prestige reasons, to the army alone. The publicity media of the Government of India played up the invasion into an heroic affair and Indian journalists were kept away from Goa for several weeks so that they could not reveal the truth. Fortunately there were foreign newspapermen inside Goa at the time. Their stories, however, were discounted; in some cases they were not published for fear of antagonizing the Indian Government. Only a few Indians of standing questioned the Government's version of the affair but their voices were drowned in another outburst of jingoism. Nehru argued that the invasion was not against India's declared policy of non-violence, entirely on the basis that the invasion had not been resisted by the Portuguese! When criticism grew abroad he became more casuistical. He even went so far as to suggest that the criticism was racial in origin. The Portuguese were white and so were the critics. But the gravamen of the charge made by the United States and other countries was that Nehru after lecturing the world on the righteousness of the non-violent approach to disputes had used that same force which he had so frequently declared could never be justified. Though the Soviet Union and many non-aligned countries supported Nehru, his image in the rest of the world was suddenly tarnished. Nehru felt the criticism deeply but apparently without understanding the justice of it. 'Why is it,' he wrote to President Kennedy, 'that something which thrills our people should be condemned in the strongest language?'

The Goa affair was significant on several levels – both overt and concealed. The propaganda screen which hid reality created the impression that the Government was not only willing but also able to settle disputes by force. The implication for the dispute with China was explicit. Nehru confirmed this himself at a press conference just after Goa when he was asked whether India would now use force against China. 'The use of force,' he replied, 'is of course open to us and should be used according to suitability and opportunity.' In the election campaign Government spokesmen were more open. 'If the Chinese will not vacate the areas occupied by her,' said Lal Bahadur Shastri, Home Minister in the central government, 'India will have to repeat what she did in Goa.' The election campaign made much play with the successful invasion of Goa, the readiness of the army to take on any enemy and the general toughness of the Government.

No information was allowed to reach the public that the army's capabilities had been untested. Nor was there any hint that the army had been short of equipment, and not only of weapons and wireless sets but also of such essential things as boots. Concealed, too, was the weakness of the decision-making process in the Government of India. Cabinet ministers could create situations without informing the Prime Minister what was going on and that once presented with a situation in which public opinion had been aroused, Nehru would give in, even when his own instincts were against it.

Congress entered the elections of 1962 in an atmosphere of euphoria. In Bombay, where the Defence Minister Krishna Menon was under attack from the opposition candidate, the one-time Congress president Kripalani, Nehru personally defended his protégé. At an election meeting there in January 1962 Nehru declared that Menon was responsible for creating in the army a strong and efficient fighting force and claimed that he said so 'with intimate knowledge'. His speeches during the campaign constantly reiterated India's military preparedness and implied that his China policy was based on strength and not on weakness. As Nehru was not given to the occupational mendacity of politicians it can only be assumed that he actually believed what he was saying. Certainly the majority of the political class, even the most outspoken of opposition critics, did.

The election was yet another victory for Congress. How much of that success might be assigned to Goa and how much to the continuing charisma of Nehru is impossible to assess. Congress lost twenty-three seats in the central parliament. The Communist Party increased its representation and so did the right-wing parties, especially Swatantra. But the Congress majority at the centre and in the states was still overwhelming.

Soon after the election was over Nehru was taken ill. Officially he was merely suffering from overwork and needed a rest. In fact it was discovered that he had a debilitating kidney disease, pyelonephritis. Despite a thorough medical examination in London and a widely publicized report that he was in excellent health, it was obvious to most people that now in his seventy-second year Nehru had indeed been seriously ill. He had acquired a slight stoop and was known to have been put on a rigid diet and advised to cut down on his work. Though the question of the succession had been raised in the middle 1950s, in the spring of 1962, the problem of 'after Nehru, who?' now became the subject of open discussion.

There was certainly no obvious successor and Congress was well aware of it. Among all the factions there was no one with anything approaching Nehru's status. He towered so high above everyone else that it was difficult to see who lurked in his shadow. Not all the ministers in his cabinet were mediocrities though most were. They had been chosen partly because of their ability as courtiers, partly to satisfy the factions inside Congress, but wholly because they did not pose any personal threat to Nehru's dominance. The more competent of the ministers paid Nehru back in the coin of his own secretiveness and got on with the affairs of their own ministries without keeping him informed and in doing so constantly thwarted the policies he laid down. But this was merely a technique of government not a claim to succession. Nehru had few personal friends. His substitute for friendship was often a respect for someone's intellect. He had respected Maulana Azad but there had been a certain coldness in their relations for two years before Azad's death in 1958.

Closest to Nehru inside the Government was Krishna Menon, who had become Defence Minister in 1957. Menon had been outside the mainstream of Indian nationalist activity, having spent many years in London as a secretary of the India League. He had, however, returned to India at the moment of independence and had caught Nehru's ear. He had been given the appointment of first Indian High Commissioner in London

(1947–52) but there had been considerable criticism of his administrative laxity which had permitted a heavy financial loss to the Government. Menon had returned to India as a sort of unofficial adviser to Nehru, who had wanted to bring him into the cabinet. This was achieved in 1956 when he joined as Minister without Portfolio. Menon articulated Nehru's foreign policy at the United Nations and did so with intelligence, wit and not infrequent sarcasm. His arrogance mirrored Nehru's own and had antagonized many. He was assumed, because of leftist leanings, to be a communist sympathizer. His closeness to Nehru and his undisguised contempt for his cabinet colleagues made him heartily disliked inside Congress. Menon had no power base in the party and his influence lay only in his friendship with the Prime Minister. As long as Nehru protected him, he was safe. For critics of Nehru outside Congress Menon had become a surrogate. As for succeeding Nehru it was loudly whispered that he was building up a cabal of officers inside the army in order to have a base for a bid for power after Nehru's death. This seems highly improbable and there is no reason to doubt Menon's commitment to the democratic system. The rumours were an index of the almost universal dislike for Menon rather than any belief in the possibility of a military coup.

Among the names mentioned after Nehru's illness was that of General Kaul but few took the suggestion particularly seriously. A more significant name was that of Nehru's own daughter, Indira Gandhi. There were signs for some to see that Nehru had already begun grooming Mrs Gandhi for the succession. In 1955 she became a member of the Congress Working Committee and began to appear more and more in the public gaze as Nehru's official hostess, accompanying him on his official visits abroad and on his tours inside India. In 1958, to the surprise of many, she was elected president of Congress for the following year and began to take an increasingly influential position in the Indian political process though Nehru was stung by critics into denying that he had any intention of founding a dynasty.

As Nehru came to look something of his old fit self again

public speculation about a possible successor died down but inside Congress, leaders began to make preparation for when the time must come to choose. None of this was overt; Nehru was still the great indispensable but there were discussions among leaders who for the first time began to think seriously about what might happen should Nehru die or be incapacitated for office.

Speculation over the succession did not damp criticism of the Government's policy towards China nor did it effect India's march towards an unavoidable clash with the Chinese. Troops were moving into the wastes of the western sector supplied only by air. Winter clothing was in short supply and the heights, ranging between 14,000 and 16,000 feet, put great physical strain on the soldiers. On the diplomatic front the original *Panchsheel* statement was symbolically buried by the refusal of the Indian Government to renew the Tibet agreement of 1954 until China had evacuated territory claimed by India. As the patrols moved closer to Chinese posts in the Aksai Chin Nehru assured parliament that there was nothing to fear from repeated Chinese warnings because India's position was now much more favourable. In fact by the middle of 1962 a few hundred Indian soldiers at some sixty scattered posts armed almost entirely with obsolescent weapons faced more than five times their number of Chinese troops possessing automatic rifles and modern artillery.

Chinese warnings that these posts were a provocation were dismissed as bluff and when it seemed in July that the Chinese would overrun one of them and then actually withdrew the event was taken in India as a triumph for Indian arms. Chinese caution seemed to confirm the generally held opinion that once faced by a resolute Indian army the Chinese would see the error of their ways and move aside. A consequence of this particular episode was that the army, which in the past had been ordered to fire only if fired upon, was now told to fire if the Chinese came too close to its positions. The Government publicity media and journalists close to the Prime Minister and the Defence Ministry continued to put out stories of Indian preparedness on the frontier. In fact the feebly armed posts scattered about difficult terrain had to be supplied by air. The Chinese, on the other hand, were backed by roads and short lines of communication. Little of this was mentioned in Indian newspapers and when it was, was usually discounted.

The assurances of military preparedness were accepted as truth by the opposition but did not diminish their cries for action. On the contrary, they intensified them. If there was adequate strength on the frontiers then why was it not used to throw the Chinese out of Indian territory? There were racial overtones in some of the bellicose claims of the politicians. Every Indian soldier, one trumpeted without denial, was worth ten Chinese. The Government was under almost constant attack for not defending the country's honour, for truckling to the Chinese by implying that negotiations were still possible. To these attacks Nehru responded with shock that anyone should suggest that his Government would bring dishonour to India. In fact the Government's position on the non-negoti-ability of the frontiers was unchanged though Nehru had once again indicated to Peking that he was prepared to talk – on the understanding, of course, that China accepted the validity of India's claims and withdrew from those territories it had ille-gally occupied. The Chinese, though unwilling to accept pre-conditions, were still anxious to negotiate. Nehru's problem was how to present his actual rigidity as willingness to be reasonable. Though India was being uncritically backed by the United States and Britain, opinion among the Afro-Asian countries was divided. Many favoured negotiations, partly because they were not convinced of India's case, and partly because they were secretly pleased to see India in trouble. It was necessary therefore for India to convince as many people as possible that it was actually *China* that was unwilling to negotiate. This Nehru succeeded in doing by constantly point-ing to the Chinese rejection of preconditions. Those who feared and hated the Chinese were ready to believe him anyway. Others, who might have queried India's claims, were kept away from the truth by the complexity of the historical evidence and the inaccessibility of archives.

Uncritical support from abroad only intensified the Indian opposition's attack on the immobility of the Government. The border affair became a vehicle for a wider questioning of the Government's policies. Clashes took place on the western sector, with Chinese casualties, and protests from Peking became menacing. They were dismissed as bluster. The Indian Government, however, had got itself into a position of extreme danger. By pretending that it was the Chinese who were actually penetrating Indian territory when in fact it was Indian troops who were pressing forward into areas already occupied by the Chinese, the Government was left without a satisfactory reply to criticism that it was not expelling the Chinese. As the public had also been misled into believing that the Indian army had the strength to eject the Chinese, Nehru was left without choice.

So far, all attention was directed towards the western sector. In NEFA, though the area had been quiet, the Indian army had continued setting up forward posts. In September 1962 one of these, in fact *north* of the claim line, was invested by the Chinese using much the same tactics as those in the western sector. The post was not attacked but it meant, at least to Delhi, that Chinese troops had deliberately crossed the McMahon Line which up till then they had respected though not accepted as the *legal* frontier. The Indian Government's policy of revealing every event as soon as it was known meant that there was an immediate reaction among the political class. Why was the Government not doing something about it? As in the case of the western sector, the Government, though admitting the difficulties imposed by the terrain in NEFA, insisted that the Indian army was well placed to resist Chinese aggression. The reverse was actually the truth.

From the Chinese side of the north-eastern frontier, communications were fairly easy and a number of all-weather roads had been constructed up to the McMahon Line. On the Indian side the area between the McMahon Line and the valley of the Brahmaputra to the south was heavily jungled and mountainous. Such valleys as there were lay from north to south and transverse communication was extremely difficult.

The rivers ran through deep gorges and were crossed only by primitive wooden bridges. The heaviest rain and snow fall was on the Indian side. High altitudes made slow acclimatization essential for Indian troops arriving from the plains. The Chinese, on the other hand, were accustomed to operating at great heights because their troops had been stationed in Tibet and the border areas for many years. All this was known to the Indian army and to the Intelligence Bureau. How was it, then, that as late as October 1962 Nehru was still maintaining that the advantage in NEFA lay with India? The answer is inescapable: he was not informed of the actual situation and made no attempt to find out for himself.

On 7 September 1962 Nehru left for a meeting of Commonwealth Prime Ministers in London. As usual he left no minister officially in charge of the Government – if he had done so it would have indicated Nehru's preference in the succession and he had become particularly sensitive to the question 'After Nehru, who?' Two days later there was a meeting at the Defence Ministry. At that meeting Krishna Menon presided. The chief of the army staff, General Thapar, was present and probably the head of the Intelligence Bureau, but no cabinet minister other than Menon. At that meeting a decision was made to use force if necessary to evict the Chinese from NEFA. No one else in the cabinet was informed of this decision except Nehru, then in London. The army officers present seem to have made no protest. As a result Indian troops neither properly equipped nor acclimatized began to move forward in NEFA. At the same time pressure was growing in India for some sort of speedy and decisive move against the Chinese.

A conflict now arose between the army commanders on the spot and the politically orientated senior officers at Army headquarters in Delhi. Protests that the state of the Indian army and the difficulty of the terrain made the essentially political decision to move forward impossible to carry out were ignored. The fears of local commanders that there would be massive Chinese retaliation were rejected on the premise that China would not risk a major war. This assumption, assiduously fostered by the Intelligence Bureau on no basis whatsoever except the fantasies of its director, was accepted as an immutable truth. It was therefore necessary to remove from their command those officers who persisted in raising objections. This was done and more pliable men appointed. The most pliable of all was the man who was already convinced of the righteousness of the Government's policy – General Kaul. Kaul's appointment to active command was unprecedented. Not only was Kaul without actual combat command experience, he was also the chief of the general staff. The decision to move a senior officer from an important staff appointment to an active command for which he was known to be unfitted by experience can only be rationalized through the generally accepted belief that the Chinese would not react to Indian provocation. When General Thapar raised the possibility that the Chinese might indeed counter-attack, Nehru is reported, by Kaul, to have replied that he had 'good reason to believe that the Chinese would not take strong action against us'.

By 3 October Nehru seems to have convinced himself that there was no option but to expel the Chinese from NEFA. The alternative was to lose public confidence altogether. According to Kaul, who is not altogether untrustworthy, Nehru qualified his opinion that the army must expel the Chinese with the phrase 'or at least try to do so to the best of its ability'. This gives the impression that he was aware that the policy he was following might lead to disaster but that he could not afford to go against public opinion. He was in fact admitting that he was no longer in a position to control events.

This indeed was true, for as General Kaul left for his new command the newspapers headlined the appointment in such a way that it left no doubt that Kaul was going to NEFA to oust the Chinese. The newspapers that carried these headlines had been privately briefed by Kaul's staff without the knowledge of the Defence Ministry or of Nehru. On his arrival in NEFA, Kaul was insistent that operations must be got under way immediately despite the fact that there were inadequate supplies and most of the troops were without winter clothing. The protests of officers more knowledgeable than he were disregarded. The Indian push forward resulted in a Chinese reply. On 10 October in the presence of Kaul the Chinese reacted by opening fire on an Indian unit and destroyed it. For Kaul this was a revelation. He decided to return to Delhi to inform the Government that it was not possible to evict the Chinese.

Kaul reached Delhi in the evening of 11 October. At the meeting which took place immediately after his arrival were Nehru, Menon, officials of the External Affairs and Defence Ministries, General Thapar, Kaul and other staff officers. No other member of the cabinet was invited. After describing the situation Kaul advocated a request for military aid to the United States. This was rejected by Nehru. Kaul then suggested that the eviction operation should be postponed. This seems to have been agreed, though no precise instructions were issued to the troops on the spot. The assumption that the Chinese would not attack *on any large scale* was maintained.

The next day Nehru left for an official visit to Ceylon. At Delhi airport he was questioned by newsmen about the fighting in NEFA. In reply he claimed that the army had instructions to 'free our territory'. As for when, 'that is entirely up to the army'. He was categoric that there could be no negotiations as long as China occupied Indian soil. Nehru did mention the difficulties facing Indian troops in NEFA but this was ignored and the headlines reporting him centred on the statement about freeing Indian territory. The press in India and abroad took his words as a declaration of war. So did China. India was warned once again of the consequences. The Chinese, in fact, were being extremely tolerant under a barrage of adverse propaganda. The local Chinese commanders had informed Peking of the state of Indian troops on the border – ill-clothed, ill-armed and small in number. China had nothing whatsoever to *fear* from India, yet it made every attempt to avoid a major conflict. But what was China to do in the face of Indian in-transigence? As a major power it could not retreat in the face of a footling Indian threat, yet all its attempts to get meaningful negotiations had been balked. The current situation could not be allowed to go on for ever. For one thing it tied up men and material. For another the growing propaganda barrage against

China, originating in India but expanded by the United States and tacitly supported by the Soviet Union, could only weaken China's international status. There was also the possibility that the Indian army might get military aid from abroad and actually *become* a threat to China's security. Undoubtedly there were other factors – the Sino-Soviet rift for example – which influenced Peking. The decision to teach India a lesson seems to have been taken sometime between 6 and 17 October.

Decision in Peking but hesitation in Delhi. Commanders on the spot in NEFA were advising a withdrawal from the lightly held forward posts during the winter. The Government – or at least Nehru and Menon – were still talking of throwing the Chinese out. Kaul, suffering from pulmonary trouble brought on by the altitude in NEFA, was back in Delhi on 18 October, not in hospital although his condition had been diagnosed as too serious to be treated by the first-rate military hospital at Tezpur in the plains below NEFA. From his bed Kaul maintained his command over a thousand miles away by long-distance telephone. On the night of 19–20 October Chinese troops on the Thag-la ridge deployed for assault. In the morning of the 20th their artillery opened fire. Simultaneously there was a Chinese attack in the western sector.

The Indian public was caught by surprise. Though the border problem occupied many people's thoughts it did so without any overtone of apprehension. When the news that the Chinese had pushed aside Indian troops and were on the move into NEFA became known the shock was profound. Krishna Menon produced instant excuses. Nehru was not available for comment. Perhaps for the first time in his life he was not prepared to talk. Blame, and it was swiftly assigned, was not placed at Nehru's door but at Krishna Menon's and within three days of the opening of the Chinese offensive a move to bring about his resignation was under way in Congress. It is an indication of the peculiar status of Nehru both in Congress and in the country that the reaction of the political class was to allege that both he and parliament had been misled by Krishna Menon.

The move to oust Menon quickly acquired momentum. The opposition in the Congress parliamentary party was supported by the Congress chief ministers of the states and behind them was the influence of the president, Dr Radhakrishnan. Nehru's response was characteristic – he gave way to pressure but not all the way at once. On 31 October Menon was relieved of the defence portfolio but given another, newly created, that of defence production. This, in fact, meant no change for though Nehru officially took over the defence portfolio himself Menon remained where he was in executive charge. Menon was foolish enough to say so in public. Nehru, however, was no longer in a position to flout opinion inside Congress. When he met the parliamentary party on 7 November and tried to defend Menon by claiming that the whole responsibility rested on the Government and not on any individual minister he was faced for the first time with revolt. On his suggesting that the whole Government should resign including himself – a threat that before had always produced consternation followed by contrition – he was told in no uncertain manner that if he insisted on keeping Menon and following the policies associated with his name then the party would have to do without Nehru. The next day Menon's resignation from the cabinet was announced. His place was taken – with considerable reluctance – by the then chief minister of Maharashtra, Y. B. Chavan.

Meanwhile the débâcle in NEFA was plain to everyone. In excuse Nehru claimed somewhat pathetically: 'We were getting out of touch with reality in the modern world and living in an artificial atmosphere of our own creating.' There was positive sympathy for India in the United States and in Britain, but the non-aligned countries were unwilling to commit themselves, Ethiopa and Cyprus being the only two to come out in unequivocal support. Nehru was quick to express his resentment. The Soviet Union's attitude was at first in favour of negotiations and there was an unstated bias towards China. This was a product of another crisis taking place at the same time – that of the Soviet missiles in Cuba and the need, in face of the United States' decision to blockade Cuba, to mend fences with China in case of a conflict.

While the Chinese were advancing in NEFA against a demoralized Indian army, Peking was still offering to negotiate but all overtures were rejected. The apparent hope of the Chinese to shock India into negotiating had not been achieved. Indians were convinced that China planned an invasion of the plains and that though the Indian army had suffered a reverse in the high hills it would still be able to win a victory. Nehru certainly shared this belief. It would, he was sure, be a long war and a long war meant that India must have aid from outside. Gone was non-alignment; military aid would be accepted from anywhere. As the Soviet Union was unwilling it left only the 'imperialist' west, the United States and Britain. Both countries offered aid and it was accepted. The Chinese quickly pointed out to the non-aligned that 'the Nehru Government has finally shed its cloak of non-alignment . . .'

After the first Chinese move they paused in the hope of opening a diplomatic front. The lull in military activity was taken in India to mean that the Chinese were hesitating in the face of a roused India. A wave of patriotic enthusiasm hit the political class and to a minor extent the masses. Politicians began to talk of the unity of India pointing out that all the fears of 'fissiparous tendencies' had been unfounded. Nehru, not to be outdone, thanked China for taking action which 'had suddenly lifted a veil from the face of India, giving a glimpse of the serene face of India, strong and yet calm and determined, an ancient face which is ever young and vibrant'. He nevertheless went on to invoke India's essential pacifism, reminding his listeners of Gandhi and conveniently overlooking the fact that the Mahatma had been fully aware that Hindus 'had always been warlike'.

The lull on the frontier brought back a feeling of confidence. All-India Radio began to call for sacrifices in pursuit of a just war. The Hindu past was resurrected to remind Indians not only of the sacred nature of the Himalayan border but also of battles in which right had been on the side of the defeated. The Hindu scriptures were interpreted to apply to the current conflict. The epic of the *Mahabharata* was particularly apposite with its story of the godlike heroes of the battle of

Kurukshetra and the resounding call of one of them: 'Not even as much land as can be covered by the tip of a needle without fighting.'

Any rising criticism of Nehru himself had been stilled by the resignation of Menon and the pause in the fighting. He had also averted any attack on his policy of non-alignment by his acceptance of military aid from Britain and the United States. There was, however, resentment at the lack of support for India among the non-aligned countries even though more of them had come out on India's side.

During the lull Indian forces in NEFA had been reinforced but without any sensible strategic plan. The wisest move would have been to withdraw troops from the difficult NEFA terrain to positions which could be easily supplied and at which lines could be held in force. But the decision was political not military. The premise was still that the Chinese could be defeated and, it was maintained, their initial victories had been due to a lucky fluke. General Kaul had resumed active command on 28 October and was determined to rehabilitate himself. With him went the Government's hopes that he would justify their policies. But this was not to be. On 16 November the Chinese began a new thrust at Walong sweeping the Indians before them. Kaul sent a frantic telegram to Delhi giving his opinion that the army could not hold the Chinese and suggesting that foreign countries should be asked to provide troops.

The news of the fall of Walong reached Delhi on 18 November. The effect was more shattering than that of the defeat of the Thag-la ridge. When parliament met on 20 November angry members attacked the Prime Minister and for the first time he remained silent. His old dominance of parliament was at an end. The same night Nehru broadcast to the nation. It was the speech of a tired and dispirited man. He seemed to imply that there was nothing the Government could do to stop the invasion of the plains of Assam by the Chinese. There was panic in the state and near panic in Delhi. There were rumours of expected air attacks on Calcutta and the capital. Late that night Nehru requested American intervention in the form of aircraft to attack the Chinese invaders. The request was granted and an aircraft-carrier left its Pacific base for the Bay of Bengal. Since fifth column activity by members of the Indian Communist Party was feared, orders went out for the arrest of its leaders even though many of them had come out in open support of the Government. Those arrested who were known to be pro-Moscow were later discreetly released one at a time so that it would not look as if the Government had made a mistake.

Meanwhile the Indian army in NEFA was totally demoralized. At Tezpur in the plains refugees were streaming from the town and preparations were being made to blow up buildings and power stations not only in Tezpur but elsewhere in Assam. Fortunately the army was so disorganized that there were not enough engineers for scorching the earth. In Delhi General Thapar submitted his resignation. Nehru's first thought was that he should be succeeded by Kaul but President Radhakrishnan pointed out the foolishness of such a thing, suggesting Lieutenant-General J. N. Chaudhuri, a soldier of proved capabilities, instead. Nehru accepted this advice but the appointment was announced as only 'officiating', as Thapar had been granted long leave because of ill health. General Chaudhuri's first order to the troops was to stand where they thought they could make a stand. Kaul was removed from his command and a new officer, General Manekshaw, who had suffered from Krishna Menon's dislike, took over in his place.

Still believing that China intended a full-scale invasion of the plains, Nehru decided to send the Home Minister, Lal Bahadur Shastri, to Assam to stiffen civilian morale which had been considerably lowered by Nehru's broadcast. Early in the morning of 21 November the Minister's party gathered at Delhi airport. One of his staff, noticing a crowd around a newspaper stand, went to buy a paper and discovered that the Chinese had announced a unilateral cease-fire and that they would then withdraw from NEFA. When the Home Minister arrived and was shown the paper he left at once for the Prime Minister's house. Nehru gave the impression that he had not heard the news but admitted that he had expected it. If he had, the possibility had been kept a closely guarded secret.

The Chinese action caught the opposition off balance, though it was quick to see in it only a trick. Nehru was asked for assurances that the cease-fire would be ignored. Officially it was, for no instruction was ever given to the army to observe it. General Chaudhuri, who made it quite clear to the Prime Minister that the army was in no position to do anything except stand still, ordered his troops not to fire unless fired upon. The Chinese action was, indeed, startling. What had been seen as a full-scale invasion of India now turned out to be a punitive expedition. The Chinese decision to withdraw was not to result in any settlement of the border dispute but it did succeed in tarnishing the image of India – and of its Prime Minister.

Chapter 20
Twilight in Teen Murti

Nehru's public reaction to China's unilateral decision to withdraw in NEFA was cautious, unlike his previous responses to Chinese moves. In parliament on 21 November he declined to comment as no official communication from the Chinese had then reached him, but he maintained that as for negotiations the Government's attitude remained that 'the position as it existed prior to 8 September 1962 shall be restored'. Great pressure had been brought to bear on Nehru by the American ambassador not to reject the Chinese proposals out of hand.

When the Chinese Note arrived it was found to be fairly straightforward: beginning at midnight on 20 November the Chinese would cease fire along the entire Sino-Indian frontier and beginning on 1 December Chinese troops would withdraw to positions twenty kilometres 'behind the line of actual control which existed between China and India' on 7 November 1959. The Note added further clarifications of the Chinese action and what was expected from India in return. Indian troops must also pull back twenty kilometres from the 'line of actual control' and China would 'reserve the right to strike back' if they did not do so. Officials from both sides should meet on the frontiers to discuss the siting of posts and later the two Prime Ministers could get together to discuss an amicable settlement. The Chinese would prefer a meeting in Peking but Chou En-lai was prepared to come to Delhi if the Indians wished. Even if the Indian Government did not respond to the proposals quickly, and China hoped that it would, China would go ahead anyway.

The date '7 November 1959' referred to a letter of Chou En-lai in which he had suggested that a way to defuse the tension on the borders was to accept the Indian and Chinese positions as they were at the time, i.e. the 'line of actual control'. This had been repeated in other communications but had been consistently rejected with the demand that China must vacate territory claimed by India before discussions could take place. The reasonableness of the Chinese in their moment of victory surprised everybody. China made no new demands as might have been expected if it really had the aggressive and irredentist ambitions India alleged. Naturally such generosity was immediately suspect even though it was accompanied by a threat that if it were not taken at its face value by the Indians, the Chinese reserved 'the right to strike back'. The suspicion of Chinese motives was based entirely on the fact that the Indian Government's version of the dispute had been widely accepted.

The Indian Government's response after the proposals had been officially received was to ask for clarifications but it did not change its attitude on the validity of the frontiers nor of India's case. In fact the Chinese hope that a salutary slap in the face would produce meaningful negotiations was not fulfilled. On 8 December the Chinese Government demanded that India stop procrastinating and say whether it accepted the cease-fire or not. In public Nehru took the attitude that the struggle continued. In practice, as the Indian army was totally incapable of action, the cease-fire was observed. Nehru could therefore appear to be intransigent for the sake of domestic and international effect while not antagonizing the Chinese on the frontiers. Nehru's border policy was dead but the slogan of 'no negotiations' had to be repeated in the interest of his own political future. Rumours were put about that the Chinese had withdrawn for reasons quite different from the real ones. The Russians had sent an ultimatum to Peking, ran one rumour. With the Cuban crisis settled, the United States was about to intervene on India's side, was another. The explanation preferred in India was that the Chinese had withdrawn because their lines of communication had been stretched to breaking point and they feared they would be open to Indian attack if they penetrated the plains.

If there had been any doubt that the Chinese meant what they said it had vanished by the end of November when it was observed that the Chinese were preparing to withdraw. Promptly on 1 December their troops began to pull back. In some places the exact requirements of the cease-fire were not observed by the Indians but the Chinese made no response. The Indians were, however, very careful to avoid any provocation. But there was no move towards negotiations. The attempted mediation by some of the non-aligned countries broke down on the unwillingness of the Indian Government to talk directly to the Chinese. Nehru told parliament yet again that no talks were possible unless 'the position of 8 September was restored'. But he insisted as he had done before that he was *prepared* to talk as long as the condition was accepted. So confused did the situation remain that India was still able to sustain the impression that it was the Chinese who were obstructing the opening of talks. That impression lives on today and no negotiations have as yet taken place.

When Indians, or at least that tiny minority, the politically conscious class, came to take stock after the end of the border war they could temper bitterness with some satisfactions. On the debit side was the revelation that the special position claimed for India by Nehru was lost forever. Non-alignment was no longer a magical phrase and India's pretence of Afro-Asian leadership completely discredited. The Afro-Asian countries by not supporting the Indian case but pressing instead for an end to the fighting had, in the Indian view, been guilty of betrayal. Fortunately for India, even if its international standing had changed so had the international climate that had made it possible. The Cold War was over. After the settlement of the Cuban missile affair there appeared the makings of a détente between the two super-powers. Though there was some criticism in India of the Soviet Union the fact that the Soviet Government had made no protest over the flow of American arms into India was significant. As the Sino-Soviet dispute came into the open, the Russians increased their military and economic aid to India. Under these circumstances non-alignment changed into bi-alignment – to India's profit.

This process took some time and immediately after the end of the border war there was criticism in India that the Government had virtually given up its neutralism for alignment with the United States. This was strongly denied by Nehru but he was profoundly grateful for American aid. When the news of the cease-fire was received the American aircraft-carrier, on its way to the Bay of Bengal in reply to Nehru's cry for help, turned back, thereby concealing Nehru's panic at the time (it was kept concealed until a year after his death). But American transport planes could be seen ferrying supplies to the frontiers and high-level delegations from both the United States and Britain arrived after the cease-fire to arrange assistance for the modernizing of the Indian army. Though Nehru always denied it and the two Governments have remained silent on the subject, some commitment was made by the Americans to supply immediate air cover to India in the case of another Chinese attack.

The essence of non-alignment had been the unwillingness of India to accept any form of dependence on another country because such dependence implied the possibility of interference in India's internal affairs. India's new dependence on Britain and the United States certainly brought demands. Both Britain and America made it clear very soon that in return for their immediate and unstinting military aid they required from India a settlement of the dispute with Pakistan over Kashmir. Though the initial suggestion was couched in polite and diplomatic terms, Nehru's reluctance soon sparked heavy and unequivocal pressure, particularly from Britain. At the end of November 1962 when the suspicions of China's motives in declaring a cease-fire were at their height it was announced in Delhi that Nehru and the Pakistan President, Ayub Khan, would meet to discuss a solution to the Kashmir problem.

If Britain and the United States expected that even in an hour of crisis Nehru would actually be willing to reverse Indian policy on Kashmir they were soon disillusioned. The day after the meeting between the Indian and Pakistani leaders was announced Nehru declared in the Indian parliament that he would never be willing to 'upset the present arrangement in Kashmir'. Again it was clear that Nehru applied to Kashmir the same proviso which was still inhibiting settlement of the Sino-Indian border dispute: there could be *talks* but no negotiations. After a fruitless series of meetings at ministerial level, the

Kashmir problem was allowed to settle back into its customary intransigence. So powerful, however, was the American commitment to India that it made no difference to the supply of arms, though this in turn so frightened Pakistan that it made that country even more unwilling than it had been before to make any concession over Kashmir.

This permitted Nehru to appear as immovable as most patriotic critics demanded he should be without endangering American aid in building up the Indian army's strength. While satisfying the most jingoistic demands for a powerful army, the Government proceeded to whitewash the military. Though an inquiry into the army's performance was authorized, the results of that inquiry were only partially released. General Kaul, after being removed from his command, retired from the army with an affectionate letter from Nehru and a request to a financier, who was later alleged to have used his influence with the Prime Minister to defraud the Government of huge sums of money, to give him employment. The commission of inquiry though its terms of reference had been closely confined by the Government, could not avoid the finding that senior officers in charge of the general direction of the border campaign had been willing to accept political directives which were militarily impractical. The blame however was not specifically placed and in any case the report was labelled 'top secret'. Such bits of it that were released by the Government appeared not unexpectedly to whitewash both the military and the civilian command.

It is a tribute to Nehru's towering position both in Congress and in the country that he neither suggested that he should resign nor was his resignation ever called for – even by the opposition. It is difficult to believe that in any other democratic state he and his cabinet could have survived. In part his survival was due to the fact that the Sino-Indian imbroglio had left the mass of the Indian people untouched and those inside Congress who might have wished to topple Nehru and were in a position to do so were unwilling to lose their greatest electoral asset. Indeed the Congress Party rallied behind him in order to combat opposition attacks on the party itself. Nevertheless Congress leaders were soon aware that Nehru no longer dominated the political scene. The immense powers which the Government had assumed in time of war might have been used by Nehru to destroy those who had thwarted his policies but there was no indication that he was prepared to do so. The Congress parliamentary party had got its own way over the matter of Krishna Menon and it had been shown that Nehru's threat to resign had no longer the same effect as heretofore. The balance of power in Delhi had undoubtedly shifted. As some of those closest to Nehru admitted later, he appeared crushed by the border war and was withdrawing more and more into a deliberate isolation. It seems likely that he began to feel menaced by those who might try to take his place. The army, now receiving the weapons it had always been asking for and conscious that the civilians realized their major contribution to the débâcle, was making it clear that it would not welcome such interference again. Fears of a military coup revived and the Government took secret measures to protect itself. Under the direction of the Intelligence Bureau senior army officers were the subject of physical and electronic surveillance and a para-military force, the Central Police Reserve, stationed some of its battalions near the capital. Plans were made to whisk Nehru away to a secret location should the need arise.

The Government had in fact nothing to fear from the highly professional officers who now commanded the army. They were so pleased at having the war material they wanted that apart from requiring non-interference in purely technical matters their interest in the political process was almost nonexistent. The danger to the Government and the ruling party lay in the parliamentary system, not in any possibility of extra-constitutional action. That danger was demonstrated in the spring of 1963 by the results of three by-elections for seats in the lower house of the Indian parliament. Three important political figures once members of Congress but now estranged from it in three different and differing political postures defeated Congress candidates (two ministers in the central government

and a former party president) in prestige seats against a powerful Congress machine. The victors were J. B. Kripalani, now
an isolated but much respected Independent, Dr Ram Manohar
Lohia, the Socialist Party leader and Minoo Masani of the
Swatantra Party. All three had been defeated in the 1962 elections. All three disliked Nehru, Lohia almost pathologically so,
though his attacks on the Prime Minister were frequently justified. Masani, who had once been a socialist, was now among
the most articulate of right wingers. All three men on their
return to parliament kept up a constant personal attack on
Nehru. Kripalani went so far as to give notice of his intention
to move a no-confidence motion against the Prime Minister in
the monsoon session of parliament which was due to open on
16 August 1963, the first time a challenge to Nehru's leadership
had been given formal parliamentary expression.

The shock of the by-election defeats released fears on several
levels of the Congress Party. India's growing domestic troubles
had been intensified by the border war. Many Congress leaders
had deluded themselves into thinking that the patriotic ardour
aroused by the war had in fact reflected a new unity, a new
sense of solidarity among the groups and factions competing
for profit and power. But any appearance of solidarity was
purely temporary and when the immediate dangers receded so
did displays of national unity. Criticism of Congress emerged
once again and was now sharpened by open insinuations that
the central government had not adequately defended India's
national interest.

The first open demand for some sort of action inside Congress appears to have come in June 1963 – from eighty members
of the All-India Congress Committee who presented a petition
asking for a special session of the AICC to discuss shortcomings in the party organization. Though this demand was
resisted by the party president and other leaders, pressure was
such that it was finally agreed to call a special meeting for
9 and 10 August. In the meantime on 5 July the Working
Committee, perhaps in the hope of forestalling criticism at an
open session of the AICC, appointed its own seven-man body
under the Labour Minister, G. L. Nanda, to investigate the

causes of the recent electoral reverses. The general impression both inside and outside Congress was of internal dissension and a weakening of the grip of the Working Committee on party discipline. Factions in many of the Congress state governments had become so hostile to each other that it seemed in some that a head-on collision was inevitable and instructions from the party executive to reconcile differences were constantly ignored.

With factional fighting threatening completely to demoralize the party the growing menace of parties in opposition to Congress became much more serious. In Madras, for example, a regional party with openly seccessionist beliefs, the Dravida Munnetra Kazagham (D M K), which had won only fifteen seats in the state assembly in 1957 had gained fifty in 1962. Its platform was based on dislike of the north and opposition to the attempt to force a northern language, Hindi, on the south. The local Congress Party leader and then chief minister of Madras, K. Kamaraj, was convinced that in order to sustain Congress majorities not only in Madras but also in the other states it was necessary for there to be a complete shake-up of the organization, with leaders paying much more attention to the party's grass-roots than they had done before. Kamaraj devised a plan which he believed would not only serve an organizational purpose but would also have a dramatic effect on the sagging spirits of party workers. The plan on the surface was extremely simple – and sensational: some senior and well-known Congress members holding Government office should resign their posts and take up full-time organizational work. Kamaraj was prepared to leave office himself for that purpose.

The plan was not quite as simple in its intention as it looked. It was not just means of revitalizing Congress at the roots, it might also be used to create those alignments of power which could be exploited when the time came to appoint a successor to Nehru. The Prime Minister was obviously tired and feeling his age, and though medical reports were reassuring it seemed highly likely that his days were numbered. First, then, it would be necessary to sell the plan to Nehru and then manipulate it to the best advantage. It seems improbable that Kamaraj had thought out his plan in all its implications but certain Congress chief ministers had been meeting unofficially to discuss, among other things, the succession to Nehru since the middle of 1962 and there appears to have been agreement among them that preparations had to be made for that eventuality though there was no agreement on who might be the successor. The chief ministers meeting together were Kamaraj himself, S. Nijaling-appa of Mysore, Sanjiva Reddy of Andhra, and Biju Patnaik of Orissa. According to Patnaik, Kamaraj told him of his plan, Patnaik put it to Nehru during a holiday in Kashmir, and Nehru took up the idea with Kamaraj in Hyderabad early in August.

The plan was then put to the Working Committee who adopted it in principle on 8 August. Next day Nehru offered to resign as his contribution but was naturally refused. Apart from everything else it would have opened the problem of succession before anyone was ready. The Committee also turned down Nehru's suggestion that a small group be given the task of implementing the plan and instead asked the Prime Minister to take over the sole responsibility himself. On 10 August the AICC accepted the Working Committee's recommendation with acclaim and a few hours later most of the members of the central cabinet and the state chief ministers submitted their resignations. The gesture was made with the maximum of publicity but no one expected that there would be any wholesale acceptance of the resignation offers. Nehru, however, had quickly realized what a powerful weapon Kamaraj had put into his hands. After the NEFA débâcle his authority in the cabinet had been openly flouted by a number of ministers particularly those with right-wing leanings. These men, he believed, had been at the bottom of the movement against Krishna Menon and had also forced him to get rid of another leftist minister, K. D. Malaviya, under suspicion of corruption, only seven days after the AICC had accepted the Kamaraj plan.

Nehru appears to have discussed his use of the hatchet so unanimously put in his grasp only with his daughter, Indira, and Lal Bahadur Shastri, who, though disliked by Mrs Gandhi, had after Menon's departure become very close to her father. Nehru wanted to retain Shastri in the cabinet but Shastri advised him that he must accept the resignations of some of his own supporters in the central government and in the states in order to avoid allegations of bias. On 21 August Kamaraj was urgently called to Delhi to decide with the Prime Minister who should be axed. An operation on the scale Nehru had decided upon needed careful consideration. There had to be a balance. For one thing no particular region should be given any cause to allege favouritism. Factions had to be satisfied. Nehru was primarily concerned with disposing of two right-wing central cabinet ministers, Morarji Desai, at Finance and a strong candidate for the succession, and S. K. Patil, who held the portfolio of Food and Agriculture. A lesser contender for the succession, Jagjivan Ram, an Untouchable who was Minister of Transport and Communications, was also to be disposed of.

On 24 August Nehru announced his list at a meeting of the Working Committee. Apart from Desai, Patil, Jagjivan Ram and Shastri, there was Gopala Reddy, a nonentity who was sacrificed on the grounds that he had accepted an American offer to build a high-power radio transmitter in return for airtime for American anti-communist propaganda (in fact it had been Nehru's responsibility), and K. L. Shrimali, Minister of Education. The chief ministers of states to go were Kamaraj, Patnaik, Bakshi Ghulam Muhammad (Kashmir), B. Jha (Bihar), C. B. Gupta (U.P.) and B. A. Mandloi (Madhya Pradesh). Just in case there might be any complacency among those who had not been axed Nehru added: 'It is possible that some other suggestions might have to be made by me at a somewhat later date.' None were.

Nehru's choice was recognized in certain circles for what it actually was – a paying off of scores and a clearing away of candidates for the succession. Only one of the fallen ministers actually said so. S. K. Patil declared on two occasions that Nehru had used the Kamaraj plan to get rid of people he disliked. Considering that Patil had seconded the Kamaraj resolution in the Working Committee, his remarks could be taken as an admittance that he had been outmanoeuvred. Others remained silent until after Nehru's death. Then Desai revealed that he had not at the time considered Nehru's action as inspired in any way by undisclosed motives but that he now (October 1964) believed that it had been really designed to clear the way to the succession for Indira Gandhi.

When Nehru reconstituted his cabinet after the purge he felt it necessary to defend his motives. He put the onus for the decision which ministers would be axed on Kamaraj and it was not denied at the time. Whatever the motives and there was certainly more than one, it was absolutely clear that Nehru had by one stroke reasserted his dominance in the Congress Party. His action had indeed disposed of claimants to the succession but it had not shown anybody to be the chosen. Nehru was not willing to name a successor. It was therefore open to others to arrange that the choice should fall upon someone who had their approval. The hint was quickly taken by those leaders who had already discussed possible names and had come to the conclusion that the most suitable was Lal Bahadur Shastri.

Early in October 1963, with what turned out to be a vain hope of secrecy, five men met in a secluded bungalow in the town of Tirupati in Andhra. Two were chief ministers of states, S. Nijalingappa of Mysore, and Sanjiva Reddy of Andhra. The other three were Kamaraj, Atulya Ghosh, the Congress Party boss in Bengal, and Srinivas Mallayya, a senior member of the Congress parliamentary party. The problem they had come to discuss was who should be appointed Congress president for the following year. Whoever was picked, it was thought, would be the most natural choice for the succession to Nehru. The general consensus of opinion was that Lal Bahadur Shastri was the obvious candidate. Morarji Desai's name was mentioned but all agreed that he should be kept out of the line of succession if that was at all possible. It was certain that Nehru would not welcome Desai as party president. Would he welcome Shastri? There had been rumours that Nehru would like to combine the offices of party president and Prime Minister once again. If this was so then there could be no resistance.

But what if Nehru neither wanted the office for himself nor Shastri as a substitute? The meeting decided that should that be the case Kamaraj must be the candidate. This was not altogether to Kamaraj's taste but he accepted the majority opinion because he did not think that Nehru would be against Shastri. In any case Kamaraj agreed that there must be no question of a contest for the office of president. It was known that Desai badly wanted the post in order to consolidate his bid for the succession when the time came. The Syndicate, as the caucus of leaders came to be called later, was determined that whatever happened Desai must not be allowed to win. In this the Syndicate had the support not only of Patnaik but of Patil, who had once been thought to be a partisan of Desai.

The opening shot in the campaign to get Shastri for party president was fired by Atulya Ghosh who issued a statement proposing Shastri's name. Desai then announced that he would like the appointment himself but would be prepared to accept Ghosh as president instead. The issue was further confused by Patil who revealed that he too would be happy to see Ghosh as president because there had not been a Bengali in that office since Subhas Bose. Ghosh, however, stated publicly that he was not a contestant. Nehru, who did not want Desai, was also cool towards Shastri though in a conversation with Kamaraj he did not reject the proposition. Instead Nehru asked Kamaraj why he should not take on the job himself. The hint was taken and when Desai raised no objections Kamaraj accepted. He knew that he stood no chance of the succession himself but felt that the office of party president might be used to forward Shastri's claim. On 20 November the unanimous selection of Kamaraj by the Working Committee was announced at a meeting at Jaipur of the AICC.

The position inside Congress at the end of 1963 had the air of change without any definition of how that change might effect the succession. Only one thing was sure – *all* the contenders were out in the wilderness. After the cabinet reshuffle which had followed the fall of the 'Kamaraj axe', Desai, Patil and Shastri were appointed to the Congress parliamentary board which selected candidates for seats but none of the three had been given any positive role in the revitalization programme. Into Desai's place as unofficial number two in the cabinet went Gulzarilal Nanda, who took over the Home Ministry vacated by Shastri. Back into the cabinet as number three came T. T. Krishnamachari, who had left the post of Finance Minister in 1958 under something of a cloud. Neither were considered contenders for the throne. The very uncertainty inspired criticism inside the party especially among those ministers who had been dropped. Shastri, however, made no display of his views, contenting himself with defending the Kamaraj plan or saying nothing at all. Nevertheless the belief that he was Nehru's favourite for the succession began to grow despite attempts by Mrs Gandhi and others to discredit it.

How long this situation would have continued is open to speculation but suddenly and without warning a catalyst was added. On 8 January 1964 as Congress met in annual session at Bhubaneswar in Orissa, Nehru suffered a severe stroke which paralysed his left side. When the seriousness of the attack was recognized, the Syndicate met and decided to advise Nehru to take Shastri back into the cabinet in order to relieve him of some of the burden. This was supported by some of the state chief ministers. According to a reliable witness, Nehru called Shastri to his bedside and told him: 'You will have to help me now.' In actual fact nothing happened for a fortnight. During that time the Government was in the hands of Nanda and Krishnamachari, the former taking over those responsibilities exercised by Nehru as Prime Minister and Krishnamachari those of Minister of External Affairs. The delay in the recall of Shastri was caused by an attempt to exert pressure on the still badly shaken Nehru. Nanda is known to have advised against it. Jagjivan Ram strongly opposed Shastri's return and said so in public. Others, including Morarji Desai, were more subtle in their approach. The Syndicate, however, wanted Shastri back in the cabinet as soon as possible.

On 14 January Shastri met President Radhakrishnan and received his support. Kamaraj arrived in Delhi on 20 January and in a conversation with Nehru pressed strongly for Shastri's return. The following day the President backed up the proposal.

On 22 January it was announced that Shastri would rejoin the cabinet as Minister without Portfolio and would 'perform such functions in relation to the Ministry of External Affairs, the department of atomic energy and the cabinet secretariat as may be assigned to him by the Prime Minister from time to time'. It was obvious to all that Shastri was to be a sort of assistant to the Prime Minister but in order to show no open prejudice in his favour as a possible successor he was carefully ranked number four in the cabinet. No one took this ranking seriously but the unwillingness of Nehru officially to name a Deputy Prime Minister still left doubt and uncertainty. Shastri modestly made no claims, leaving others to make them for him. The struggle for the succession was under way.

After being flown back to Delhi from Bhubaneswar, Nehru remained in bed inside his residence, the mansion known as Teen Murti House, surrounded as usual by the ubiquitous black-clothed security men and a new atmosphere of intrigue and conspiracy. The Government of India was now a some-what uneasy alliance of Nanda, Krishnamachari and Shastri. The rest of the cabinet carried on with their respective minis-tries taking as little initiative as possible. The triumvirate kept in constant touch with Kamaraj, now emerging in public as a man of power. For the first time in India's independence, party and Government were functioning closely together. Inside Teen Murti Mrs Gandhi played a special role. She controlled access to Nehru – even for the triumvirate. Shastri was reported to have complained that he had to wait to get an appointment with Nehru and that he was being discriminated against by Mrs Gandhi. The opposition – and some members of Con-gress – spread the rumour that Mrs Gandhi was acting like the wife of the President of the United States, Woodrow Wilson, who concealed her husband's inability to function as head of state by making the decisions herself. This was something of an exaggeration but Mrs Gandhi had undoubtedly become an essential element in the structure of power. Perhaps the most blatant characteristic of this period of Nehru's twilight was that of Government inertia. Mrs Gandhi may have been in a position to influence decisions but no decisions of consequence were being taken.

The general atmosphere in Delhi was one of gloom. Most people were convinced that in Teen Murti lay a stricken Caesar. Some suggested that the best thing Nehru could now do for India was to end the uncertainty by resigning but Nehru was not prepared to give up office. At the end of January 1964 it was announced that he had completely recovered but on his first visit to parliament on 10 February it was quite obvious that he had not. His left side was still paralysed and he dragged his foot. He was forced to speak sitting down and his articulation was difficult. His mind seemed as sharp as ever though there were signs after an hour or so that it was becoming blunted. Those present seemed to recognize – perhaps for the first time – that Nehru was an old and weary man. This recognition only tended to intensify the barely concealed war of succession. Although aware of this, Nehru would not indicate a successor. At the end of March he explained that he would not appoint a Deputy Prime Minister, though he paid compliments to Shastri. In April he said he would not name a successor because 'if I nominated somebody that is the surest way of his not becoming Prime Minister'. He also denied that he was grooming Mrs Gandhi 'for anything'.

Those close to him at this time recalled after his death that Nehru was withdrawn, speaking seldom to anyone and radiating an aura of sadness. He seemed also to be moving even further away from the agnosticism of his middle age. During the years in which he had sought to identify himself more and more with Indian India, he had moved closer to religion. His hatred of religious communalism had kept him from formal faith but had not prevented him from trying to create a personal syncretism that would satisfy both his desire for traditional roots in the Hindu world and his belief in progressive socialism. Intellectual rationalization he had found in Vivekananda's brahminical ideal of selfless service. With it he had tried to articulate socialism with an Indian voice. Yet it was clear that something had gone wrong. *Panchsheel* had been traced to a unique Indianness, the Buddhist past. That too had failed.

During the Sino-Indian dispute reason had slipped further towards faith in the use of India's myths and legends to support claims to the Himalayan frontiers. From the late 1950s Nehru had talked often in private conversations about Hindu ideals and ideas, though his uncompromising dislike of formal religious expression tended to conceal his growing religiosity.

One Hindu characteristic – the belief in astrology – had marked Nehru's Government for many years. Most ministers kept their own astrological advisers, some of whom acquired considerable influence over their clients. Nehru had constantly ridiculed the dependence of his ministers on the occult but made no effort to discourage it. Though he had been told of a number of accurate predictions his attitude remained one of scepticism until his illness of 1962. According to a former minister in his Government, Nehru agreed to have his horoscope cast by Nanda's astrologer. When the man reported that Nehru would be betrayed by his best friend and that India would be involved in a war with China, Nehru was said to have exploded with derision. After the Chinese invasion, however, Nehru seems to have modified his opinion and allowed Nanda to reintroduce the astrologer. His forecast was sinister: the Prime Minister would die very shortly unless some action was taken to prolong his life. Fifty priests were engaged by Nehru's courtiers to perform the necessary rites at a temple in a suburb of Delhi. According to one source when the priests went to get Nehru's permission for the ceremony – it could not be totally effective without the consent of the person for whom the rite was being performed – he angrily refused. Another source denies this but the ceremony took place just the same. All sources, however, agree about a similar ceremony late in January 1964. Nehru did not refuse this time.

The ceremony which took place in the same temple in Delhi comprised the repetition of a 'death conquering' mantra 425,000 times accompanied by fire-sacrifices. The ceremony began in considerable secrecy on 26 January and was completed on 2 April. While this ceremony was going on it was reported that a magical rite to encompass Nehru's death had been performed at a temple in the U.P. The name of a minister in the central government was mentioned. This was however officially denied in the U.P. by the chief minister, who insisted that the ceremony far from being to bring about Nehru's death was, on the contrary, a rite for his recovery. Whatever effect this acceptance of the occult might have been expected to have, Nehru also allowed himself to be treated by practitioners of Ayurveda, the ancient Hindu homeopathy. His father Motilal had been cured of asthma by this system of treatment after the failure of western medicine to relieve the complaint and had become a wholehearted devotee of Ayurveda. When Nehru first allowed himself to be treated by the same method is not clear, but it seems to have been soon after his 1962 illness.

The astrologer who had warned Nehru that his days were numbered also forecast a serious illness in January 1964 – presumably the first series of magical rites had only been partly successful – and that he would not survive beyond 27 May. Whether this was known to the Prime Minister or not, Nehru seems to have been conscious that he had not long to live. After seventeen years of his rule India appeared to be in a worse state than ever. The Third Five-Year Plan was in considerable difficulties, food was short and communal tensions inflamed. The latter had been exacerbated by a mysterious incident in Kashmir in December 1963. An important and holy relic – allegedly one of the hairs from the beard of the prophet Muhammad – disappeared from a mosque in the Kashmir capital, Srinagar. It was assumed that it had been stolen on the instigation of the former chief minister, Bakshi Ghulam Muhammad, who had been displaced by the Kamaraj axe. On 26 December there were huge and violent demonstrations in Srinagar which lasted for over a week. On 3 January the relic reappeared. Agitation continued and was this time directed towards bringing pressure to bear upon the state government for the release of the Kashmir leader Sheikh Abdullah who had then been detained for eleven years.

The agitation in Kashmir inspired the Pakistan Government to raise the matter once again at the United Nations. The British delegate called upon India and Pakistan to open constructive talks and was bitterly attacked for it in India. A visit to Pakistan by the Chinese Prime Minister Chou En-lai in February and his support for a plebiscite only raised the temperature in India. A proposal in the U.N., put forward by the United States, that Kashmir become independent with its frontiers jointly guaranteed by India and Pakistan was defeated but the excitement that had been aroused by the theft of the prophet's hair had serious repercussions in east Pakistan where there was serious communal rioting. This spread across the border to India where there was bloody retaliation against Muslims in the steel towns of Jamshedpur and Rourkela. In east Pakistan the rioting developed into what looked like an organized campaign against Hindus and there was another tragic exodus of non-Muslims across the border into India. With communal feelings running so high that the chances of war with Pakistan were once again being openly considered, Nehru decided to risk taking constructive action over Kashmir. In April he had Sheikh Abdullah released as a prelude to a meeting between himself and President Ayub Khan of Pakistan. Ironically, news that this meeting would take place hit the headlines on the morning of Nehru's death.

After making this courageous but belated decision Nehru seems to have recovered some of his zest for life. In many conversations with Sheikh Abdullah he was mentally alert and obviously anxious for a solution. He defended his action with vigour and at his last political appearance at the meeting of the AICC in Bombay on 16–17 May it was remarked that he seemed in much better health. Congress leaders went back to their home bases without any fear of a sudden relapse even though some of them had been told of the astrologer's prediction. Nehru returned to Delhi on 17 May and the following evening while walking in the gardens of the presidential palace he suddenly felt unwell. The doctors found no damage and diagnosed extreme tiredness following the meeting at Bombay. Their prescription was rest. Nehru agreed to the extent of postponing a press conference fixed for 20 May to two days later.

Nehru's performance at the press conference did not support

the opinion that his health had improved. He was extremely slow to answer questions. One correspondent asked him if it would not be in the interest of the country 'that you solve this problem of succession in your life time?'. 'That is a leading question', replied Nehru, and received the retort: 'It's on everybody's lips.' 'They may be talking like that,' Nehru answered, and after a long silence: 'My life is not ending so very soon.' The remark was received first with silence and then with a burst of applause. The next day Nehru left for his favourite hill resort of Dehru Dun for a short holiday.

On the evening of 26 May an Indian air force helicopter brought Nehru back to Delhi airport. Among those waiting to meet him was Lal Bahadur Shastri who was told by the Prime Minister that he would be going with him to the Commonwealth Prime Ministers' conference in London in June. On his arrival at Teen Murti House, Nehru went to his study to examine papers and retired at 11 p.m. The doctors and nurses who had been in constant attendance after his stroke had been sent away a month before. A male servant slept in an adjoining room. At about 2 a.m. Nehru awoke and was given a sedative. At 4 a.m. he awoke again in some distress and pain. Two hours later he complained of pain in the lower back and said that he could not get up. Finally the doctors were called. At 6.45 a.m. they discovered that his aorta had ruptured – an occurrence which is inevitably fatal. One doctor is reported to have wanted to operate but no one would take the decision. Without recovering consciousness Nehru died at 1.44 p.m. The machinery that was to move Lal Bahadur Shastri, a very different sort of Indian, into the office of Prime Minister had already been put in gear.

Afterword

The present work, though entirely self-contained, is one of four books covering some seventy years of the political history of modern India. They are the product of an inquiry spreading over twenty-five years and are based on the examination of public and private papers in India and Britain, published and unpublished works in a number of languages, and conversations with most of the principal figures and many other witnesses of the times. In the preparation of this book, I have not been given access to the Nehru papers which are now reserved for his official biographer, but it has benefited from conversations with the late Pandit Nehru and with some of those close to him.

I would like to have listed the names of all who have helped me over the years with reminiscences, appreciations and sometimes 'secret' information, but many of my informants, for the best of reasons, have specifically asked that I should not mention theirs. Though this inevitably means that certain facts and interpretations cannot be substantiated by direct reference to sources, a writer of contemporary history must respect the anonymity of those sources if he is to retain their confidence. I have therefore chosen to thank *all* my informants collectively, and trust that none will feel that I have misinterpreted them or done them any intentional injustice.

Chapters 13 to 16 are largely based on my book, *The Last Years of British India* (Cassell, 1963) and Chapters 17 to 20 owe much to my forthcoming study, *The Successors: Aspects of India and Pakistan since Independence* (Eyre & Spottiswoode). The interpretation of the role of Gandhi will be the subject of full-scale treatment in my biography of the Mahatma to be published in this series of *Political Leaders of the Twentieth Century*. In the section on Sino-Indian relations I am particularly indebted to Neville Maxwell, who generously allowed me to read the typescript of his definitive work, *India's*

China War (Cape, 1970), which strips away the myths that have been manufactured to obscure the truth behind this unsavoury but revealing episode in the twilight of the age of Nehru.

Index

(1946), 166; reaction to Direct Action Day riots in (1946), 174; independence negotiations in (1946–7), 177–82, 199–204; India's sterling balances held in, 271; Dr Gopal's visit to (1959), 285; Commonwealth Prime Ministers' Conference in (1962), 301; Commonwealth Prime Ministers' Conference in (1964), 328; mentioned, 21, 28, 31, 34, 75, 175

Longju, 279, 284, 290

Lucknow, Simon Commission visit to, 73; Motilal Nehru's death in, 89; mentioned, 47, 55, 70

Lucknow Pact, 29, 35

McCarthy, Joseph, 272

MacDonald, Ramsay, 75, 97

McMahon Line, 280–84, 300

Madhya Pradesh, 319

Madras, Annie Besant interned in, 30; communalism in, 55; Congress session in (1927), 65, 71; riots in (1945), 163; mutiny in (1946), 166; newspapers in, 192; partition of, 251–3; Radhakrishnan's activities in, 258; Dravida Munnetra Kazagham activities in, 317; mentioned, 117, 145, 291

Mahabharata, 285, 306–7

Maharashtra, 24, 26, 30, 254, 305

Malaviya, K. D., 318

Malaya, 162

Mallayya, Srinivas, 320

Manchester Guardian, 125, 192

Manchester Guardian Weekly, 107

Manchuria, 101

Mandalay, 28

Mandloi, B. A., 319

Manekshaw, General, 308

Mangrol, 220

mantras, 7, 8, 10, 148, 325

Mao Tse-tung, 284

Maratha, 26

Marathi, 254

Marseilles, 124

martial law, 39

Marx, Karl, 63

Marxism, Nehru's attitude to, 60, 63, 67; influence on C S P of, 114, 183

Masani, Minoo, 316

Mathura, 13

Maxwell, Neville, 278, 329

Menon, Krishna, 124–5, 273, 289–97, 301–8, 315, 318–19

Menon, V. P., 195–7, 199–203, 210, 229

Mexico, 60

Monckton, Sir Walter, 223–5

Montagu, Edwin, 34

Mookerjee, S. P., 238, 239, 248

Moscow, 60, 62, 172, 292, 308

Mountbatten, Admiral Viscount, appointed as Viceroy of India (1947), 184; arrival in Delhi of (1947), 191; and independence negotiations, 194–207; and relationship with Nehru, 194; appointed as Governor-General of India (1947), 209–10; and dealings with princes, 210–12; and communal riots (1947), 216–17, 219; and accession of Hyderabad to India, 223–5; and accession of Kashmir to India, 226–7, 271; and assassination of Gandhi, 234–5; succeeded as Governor-General by Rajagopalachari, 239; mentioned, 231

Mughals, 9, 12, 13, 26

Mughs, 17

Muhammad, Bakshi Ghulam, 319, 326

Muir Central College, 14

Munich agreement, 125

Muslim League, foundation of (1906), 28; and Lucknow Pact, 29, 35; and Nehru Report, 72–3; and elections (1937), 119, 121; regeneration of, 122; opposition

Imperialism, 61; Nehru's trip to (1927), 62–3; constitution of, 236; and India's Second Five-Year Plan, 263; and Cold War, 266, 267, 287; Nehru's attitude to, 267, 272; and Hungarian uprising (1956), 267; and relations with Pakistan, 270; and Kashmir problem, 274; attitude to non-alignment of, 275, 276; and Sino-Indian border dispute, 287–8, 304–6, 311, 312; and Goan crisis, 294; mentioned, 21, 101, 138, 192, 199, 279

Spain, 125

Spanish Civil War, 118, 125

Srimarulu, Potti, 252

Srinagar, 227, 326

States Reorganization Act (1956), 255

States Reorganization Commission, 253–5

strikes, during non-cooperation campaign (1921), 45; in Bengal (1929), 74; in Calcutta (1929), 74; in Bombay (1929), 74; following arrest of Congress leaders (1942), 149; in Bombay (1946), 166; during independence negotiations (1947), 196

The Successors: Aspects of India and Pakistan since Independence (Edwardes), 329

Suez, 124, 272–4

Suhrawardy, H. S., 174, 198–9

Sukarno, 276

Sun Yat-sen, Madame, 60

Surat, 28

Swaraj Party, formation of, 50; elections contested by (1923), 52–3; Gandhi's opposition to, 53–4; recognized as official constitutional arm of Congress, 54–5; abandonment of legislatures by (1926), 61, 65; revival of (1934), 107; mentioned, 56

Swatantra Party, 277–8, 295, 316

Switzerland, 59, 110

Sylhet, 205, 208

Tagore, Rabindranath, 54, 106

Tamil, 252

Tandon, Purushottamdas, 239–41, 243–5, 258

Tawang, 280, 281

taxation, and Bardoli no-tax campaign (1928), 68–9; and campaign against salt tax, 80–81, 86, 87, 91–2; and inheritance tax, 94; and income tax, 94, 263; and United Provinces no-tax campaign (1931), 98, 100; mentioned, 33, 195–6

Telengana, 249

Telugu, 251–2

terrorism, and partition of Bengal (1905), 27; during non-cooperation campaign (1921), 46; in Bengal (1929), 74; in Delhi (1929), 76; and Congress session (1929), 77; in Bengal (1931), 98; and Razakhars, 224; mentioned, 23, 33, 83

Tezpur, 304, 308

Thackeray, W. M., 19

Thag-la, 304, 307

Thailand, 153

Thapar, General, 301–3, 308

Theosophical Society, 19, 26, 30

theosophy, 19

Thimayya, General, 290

Tibet, 265, 278–84, 298, 301

Tilak, Bal Gangadhar, and cultural nationalism, 26–7; mass support for, 26–7; and Home Rule League, 29–30; death of, 44; mentioned, 31

Times of India, 65

Tippera, 176

Tirupati, 320

trade unions, 115; *see also* All-India Trade Union Congress

Trevelyan, G. M., 21